Broadband in Europe:
How Brussels Can Wire the Information Society

Broadband in Europe:
How Brussels Can Wire the Information Society

Dan Maldoom
DotEcon Limited

Richard A D Marsden
DotEcon Limited

J Gregory Sidak
Georgetown University Law Center and American Enterprise Institute

Hal J Singer
Criterion Economics

 Springer

Library of Congress Cataloging-in-Publication Data

A C.I.P. Catalogue record for this book is available from the Library of Congress.

Broadband in Europe : how Brussels can wire the information society / Dan Maldoom.... [et al.].
   p. cm.
  Includes bibliographical references and index.
  ISBN-10: 0-387-25386-6   (alk. paper)   e-ISBN-10: 0-387-25387-4
  ISBN-13: 978-0387-25386-2   e-ISBN-13: 978-0387-25387-9
    1. Telecommunication—Europe.   2. Broadband communication systems—Europe.
  3. Information networks—Europe.   4. Information society—Europe.   I. Maldoom, Dan.

HE8084.B76 2005
384′.094—dc22   2005042643

Printed in the United States of America.

9 8 7 6 5 4 3 2 1   SPIN 11325147

springeronline.com

Contents

Tables and figures

Preface

Broadband is a key enabler of the information society, increasing productivity and competitiveness across all sectors of the economy. Unlike traditional narrowband connections, broadband provides high speed, always-on connections to the Internet and supports innovative content and services. Direct consumer welfare gains from mass-market adoption of broadband across the EU could easily reach 50 billion euros or more per annum. This is quite apart from the more profound societal shifts that ubiquitous broadband could bring. It may allow the individual to distribute content and ideas independent of traditional media and bring together communities of interest without regard to borders.

Public policy for broadband will have a big impact on whether and how quickly these benefits are realised. Getting policy right could bring large benefits for consumers, firms and the economy at large; getting policy wrong risks stifling both the rollout of broadband and new innovative services, and thus the realisation of the EU's e-Europe vision.

In this book, we focus on the residential market for broadband access in EU countries, analysing the current and prospective level of competition and drawing implications for public policy. A key aim is to understand better the relative importance of facilities-based and access-based provision in fostering competition and promoting take-up of broadband services.

To date, regulatory policy in EU countries has tended to carry over the approach of traditional voice telephony regulation, with its emphasis on wholesale access to incumbent networks, rather than encouraging facilities-based competition between providers with their own end-to-end infrastructure. However, broadband provision is not a natural monopoly; effective platform competition is already possible. In many areas of Europe, consumers already have a choice between alternative providers using DSL and cable platforms. New platforms using fibre-to-the-home have been built in Sweden and Italy. Wireless technologies that could dramatically change the marketplace (such as 3G, WiFi and various broadband wireless services) are also being launched.

There are encouraging signs that full facilities-based competition can be a reality for broadband. However, a clear message through this book is that commercial organisations respond to the incentives that regulatory systems place in front of them; every care must be taken to ensure that incentives set by public policy encourage efficient rather than distorted outcomes.

Whilst there have recently been some encouraging noises from regulators about the importance of promoting facilities-based competition, it takes time and patience to achieve such goals. Tough access regulation can always generate competition in the short-run, but this is not the deep and lasting competition over the whole value chain that only infrastructure-based competition can bring. It requires a far-sighted regulator to hold out for these long-terms benefits.

How competitive are European broadband markets? What factors explain the wide variation in broadband take-up across EU member states? What is the relative role of facilities and access-based entry in promoting broadband take-up? Does the availability of regulated access products increase or diminish incentives for infrastructure investment? What policies could the EU and member state governments adopt to further development of broadband over the next decade? These are the questions that we attempt to answer, drawing on evidence and analysis of Western European markets, and lessons from the experiences of other countries, such as the United States and South Korea.

This book was originally conceived as a research project by DotEcon Limited and Criterion Economics, two independent consultancy firms that are specialists in applying economics to telecommunications and other network industries. The authors of this book – Dan Maldoom, Richard Marsden, J. Gregory Sidak and Hal Singer – work for DotEcon and Criterion.

The initial project was funded by the Brussels Round Table, a forum for leading European telecommunication operators and equipment manufacturers. A report was completed in September 2003, and its findings were presented at the Brussels Round Table on the Future of the European Telecommunications Industry with BRT member CEOs and EU Information Society Commissioner Erkki Liikanen. The members of the BRT at the time were: Alcatel, BT, Deutsche Telekom, Ericsson, France Telecom, Siemens, Telefnica de Espaa and Telecom Italia.

This book is based on the report that was released in October 2003. It was updated by the authors in late 2004, taking into account a number of new developments in European markets over the last 12 months.

The authors are grateful for the assistance of colleagues at DotEcon and Criterion for research and helpful comments in finalising both the original report and this draft. In particular, we would like to thank Christian Koboldt, John Gunnigan, Roger Salsas, Tamara Linnhoff, Justyna Majcher, Vesna Milenkovic, Robert Crandall and Brian O'Dea. We would also like to express our gratitude to members of the BRT Working Group in identifying information sources for the original report and providing expert comments on drafts of the original report. However, we wish to emphasise that BRT members have not had any role in commenting on this revised book. Further, this book is the work of the authors, and does not necessarily represent the views of any other party.

Dan Maldoom

Richard Marsden

J. Gregory Sidak

Hal Singer

April 2005

1 Introduction

This book focuses on mass market broadband access and take-up, analysing the current and prospective level of competition and drawing implications for public policy. A distinction is drawn between '*facilities-based competition*', where providers are using all (or some of) their own infrastructure, and '*access-based competition*', where providers depend on access to someone else's network. Amongst EU Member States, there is a general consensus that infrastructure-based competition is desirable in telecommunications and has an important role in delivering innovations such as broadband. However, public statements from national regulatory authorities (NRAs) about the benefits of infrastructure competition have not always been matched by coherent regulatory policy designed to facilitate such competition.

Broadband is a new service. Typically, new services are not subject to specific regulation, owing to the risk that this would discourage investment and stifle innovation. However, from its inception, the development of broadband access has been influenced by intervention from policy makers and regulators. This intervention includes both local and national government initiatives to promote the supply and demand of broadband, and ex-ante obligations on incumbent telecom operators to provide access to their networks.

Broadband penetration is widely portrayed as being disappointingly slow. Although this claim is debateable – penetration is actually quite fast relative to the adoption of comparable technologies – it is often used as a justification for public policy intervention. However, given the prevalence of intervention to date, an equally valid response is to question the effectiveness of existing regulation. Both new entrants and incumbent operators are rational agents who inevitably respond to regulatory incentives; if broadband deployment in the EU has been too slow, regulatory policy is a key area where one should look for an explanation. The current approach of NRAs to broadband is heavily influenced by the existing regulatory framework for traditional telephony services, with its emphasis on access to the local loop. The appropriateness of this approach may be questioned, given that broadband is a new service that requires building new infrastructure (even if existing networks are used) and that it can and is delivered over many different types of platforms, including cable, satellite, fixed wireless and mobile networks.

The introduction of the EU's New Regulatory Framework (NRF) for telecommunications, and its adoption and interpretation by member states provides a critical opportunity to reassess regulatory policies towards broadband. In particular, the EU has a key role in guiding and constraining NRAs in defining new markets for ex-ante regulation and applying remedies that are proportionate to the problems identified.

Against this background, this book has a number of objectives:

☐ to determine the extent of competition in European broadband markets;
☐ to explain the wide variation in broadband take-up across EU member states;
☐ to assess the relative effectiveness of platform competition and access-based entry in propelling growth in broadband take-up and consumer choice;
☐ to assess the impact of existing public policy on incentives to invest in infrastructure; and
☐ to identify policies that the EU and member state governments could adopt to further development of broadband over the next decade.

The book is divided into six main chapters:

☐ Chapter 2 provides background on the broadband market: we review the definition of broadband; discuss the economic benefits of broadband diffusion; and explore the range of technologies that can be used to deliver broadband services.
☐ Chapter 3 describes the extent of competition in broadband markets. Section 3.1 defines facilities-based and access-based competition, and the different types of access products that regulatory systems distinguish. Section 3.2 reviews the extent of platform and access-based competition in broadband provision and assesses their impact on product and pricing innovation. Section 3.3 provides a summary of our findings from case studies of broadband competition in Germany, the Netherlands, Republic of Ireland, South Korea, Sweden, the United Kingdom and the United States. The full case studies are included in Annex I.
☐ Chapter 4 examines the current and potential role of new entrants in broadband service provision, and scenarios for the further development of competition. This section is illustrated with a summary of our findings from case studies of 'new' entrant broadband providers, including Bredbandsbolaget (Sweden), FastWeb (Italy), HanseNet (Germany), Ono (Spain), UPC chello (Netherlands) and selected U.S. CLECs. The full case studies are included in Annex II.
☐ Chapter 5 analyses the appropriate market definition for broadband and assesses the relative merits of facilities and access-based competition, in light of the evidence presented in chapters 3 and 4. This includes the results of empirical analysis testing for a relationship between broadband penetration and one or both of platform competition and access-based competition.
☐ Chapter 6 addresses the strengths and weaknesses of the EU NRF and appropriate policies for broadband going forward.
☐ Chapter 7 provides our conclusions.

2 Broadband and why it matters

2.1 What is broadband?

Broadband provides users with always-on, high-speed connections to access the internet and transfer data. The term 'broadband' has outgrown original narrow definitions based on specific data transmission speeds and is now widely used *"simply as shorthand for high speed Internet access"*[1]. The extensive and growing variety of broadband products available in EU member states – for example, in terms of transmission speeds – demonstrates the need to maintain a flexible definition of broadband in any market analysis. This should be based on the notions of 'high-speed' and 'always on', which differentiate broadband services from narrowband dial-up access to the internet, rather than specific minimum thresholds for transmission speed. Any definition should reflect the fact that it is possible to offer fundamentally identical products from the perspective of the end user over different delivery platforms.

As observed in the Commission's eEurope 2005 Action Plan, there is no universally recognised definition of broadband.[2] The technical term 'broadband' was originally defined by the ITU as transmission capacity that is *faster* than primary rate ISDN (*i.e.* 1.5 or 2 Mbps)[3]. However, it is now widely used by network operators marketing DSL, cable modem and other access services to users starting at speeds of 256 Kbps or even 128 Kbps. OECD governments have attached *"a wide variety of meanings"* to broadband in particular policy discussions.[4] For example, in a 2001 task force report, the Italian government drew a distinction *"between those, such as the FCC in the United States, who have defined broadband exclusively in terms of transmission capacity (number of kbit/s) and those, as in Canada, who have primarily based their definition on the type of services that can be provided."*[5]

For the purposes of benchmarking comparisons, Paltridge (OECD, 2001) defines a minimum threshold for broadband of 256 Kbps for downstream (i.e. data transmissions *to* the user) and 64 Kbps for upstream (*from* the user). This definition has become widely used in statistical exercises and forms the basis for much of the data referenced in this book. Paltridge's downstream threshold is loosely related to an earlier FCC definition, which set a threshold of 200 Kbps, or (in the agency's view) roughly enough to allow users to transmit full-motion video or change web pages as if they were turning the pages of

---

[1] OECD (2001), page 6.
[2] European Commission (2002a), page 7.
[3] ITU-T (1997).
[4] OECD (2001), page 6.
[5] Italian Government (2001), page 10.

a book. The much lower upstream threshold reflects the commercial reality of many residential services supplied by asymmetric digital subscriber line (ADSL). However, as Paltridge points out, defining a "*. . . minimum threshold for 'broadband' only really takes on importance if a government has a specific service in mind that requires a certain level of network performance.*"[6]

There has been significant discussion as to whether there is a distinct market for broadband services that is separate from narrowband internet access. In Box I, we argue that although there is evidence of one-way substitution from narrowband to broadband and some linkages in pricing, there is a distinct market for broadband. This reflects the fact that broadband offers users significant benefits not available via narrowband; in particular: faster access to the Internet; access to high bandwidth applications, such as music, video and games; an always-on connection; and the ability to use the Internet without tying up a voice line. Regulators across OCED countries have adopted similar positions; for example:

☐ In the United States, the Federal Communications Commission (FCC), Federal Trade Commission (FTC) and Department of Justice (DOJ) have all made independent rulings that the provision of residential high-speed Internet access services is a distinct market in its own right.[7]

☐ In its 2002 annual report, Spanish regulator CMT stated: "*la CMT ha considerado la existencia de un mercado de servicios de acceso de banda ancha claramente diferenciado del de la banda estrecha*" ["the CMT considers that there is a market for broadband access clearly different to that of narrowband"].[8]

Since 2002, there has been a significant expansion of broadband product portfolios by operators in most European broadband markets, which is consistent with the maturing of the market and movement along the standard product life cycle. By differentiating products on the basis of transmission speed and/or capacity, pricing and other characteristics, operators are able to serve residential and business customers with differing needs at the low and high-ends of the market. Such differentiation can be expected to stimulate further growth in demand for broadband services; a 2003 report by IDC identified this trend as a "*key driver for the European broadband market*"[9]. Therefore, it is important

---

[6]OECD (2001), page 6.

[7]See for example: FCC – Memorandum Opinion & Order, Applications for Consent to the Transfer of Control of Licenses and Section 214 Authorizations by Time Warner Inc. and America Online, Inc., Transferors, to AOL Time Warner Inc., Transferee, 16 F.C.C. Rcd. 6547, 56 (2001); FTC – Complaint, America Online, Inc. v. Time Warner, Inc., Dkt. No. C-3989 (FTC filed Dec. 14, 2000) 21; DOJ – Competitive Impact Statement at 9, United States v. AT&T Corp., Civil No. 00-CV-1176 (D.D.C. filed May 25, 2000).

[8]CMT Annual Report, 2002, page 50.

[9]IDC (2003).

from a regulatory perspective that any definition of broadband is flexible enough to accommodate the full variety of products available.

Any definition of broadband should also be platform-neutral to the extent that it is possible to offer a variety of broadband products over different delivery platforms that offer users very similar experiences. For example, although the technologies associated with DSL and cable are quite different from one another, both offer comparable bandwidth and always-on connectivity, and are thus largely functionally equivalent from the perspective of users of data services. Although PSTN and cable networks have historically offered quite different services, there is now increasing convergence with similar service bundles being offered over different underlying networks. A platform-neutral approach is consistent with the framework adopted for the *e*Europe 2005 Action Plan, which *"promotes a multi-platform approach to broadband deployment, driven by strong competition between services and networks."*[10]

Box I: Is broadband distinct from narrowband?

The substitutability between narrowband access and broadband access depends on the value that broadband users place on the advantages of broadband access. If enough consumers value broadband's unique advantages sufficiently that they would not switch in large numbers to narrowband access in the face of a small but significant increase in the price of broadband, then the two types of access are not demand substitutes.[11]

Broadband offers three main advantages over narrowband access:

☐ it decreases time costs, as an 'always on' connection provides instant access to the Internet (whereas dial-up requires wait time and lines may occasionally be engaged) and higher bandwidth enables faster download of webpages and files;

☐ it enables access to high bandwidth applications, such as streaming video and real-time radio, home networking, customised Internet video and audio libraries (such as Yahoo's LaunchCast), interactive gaming and high-speed telecommuting; and

☐ unlike narrowband, a broadband connection does not tie up a consumer's phone line, allowing inbound and outbound voice calls.

We consider the value that consumers place on each of these broad attributes in turn:

1. *Time costs*. Consumer surveys suggest that consumers do attach significant benefits to time savings provided by broadband. For example, a survey

---

[10]European Commission (February 2003a), page 6.

[11]See Annex III for a brief introduction to demand substitutability and market definition.

by Enders (2003) found that 41% of UK internet users considered "faster Internet experience" to be the main advantage of broadband. There is little empirical evidence on how much users value this extra speed. A study by Varian (1999) observed a *"very low willingness-to-pay for broadband and very low values for time"* (the average user exhibited a time cost of less than 1 US cent per minute).[12] However, this study is now somewhat out of date and, as Varian acknowledged, the survey sample may have been skewed by the reliance on volunteers (many were students) who may be individuals with a relatively low opportunity cost of time and therefore non-representative of Internet users in general. It is reasonable to expect that those consumers with the highest time cost of money will be among the most likely to purchase broadband services. Roughly 17% of the subjects exhibited a time cost of five US cents per minute ($3 per hour) or greater.[13]

2. *Access to additional content.* Consumer demand for much of the additional content and services available over broadband remains unproven in most OECD countries. In the Enders (2003) survey, just 2% of Internet users cited interactive content to be the main advantage. However, demand for such applications appears to be 'sticky' in that once consumers adopt broadband and begin using advanced functionalities (such as web browsing at speeds equivalent to turning a page of a book), they value broadband more than they did when they first adopted.[14]

3. *Phone line usage.* A consumer who uses narrowband service cannot make or receive telephone calls from her residence while she is connected to the Internet unless she also purchases a second telephone line. A survey by the Yankee Group found that 70% of U.S. households with two or more telephone lines subscribed to a second line to accommodate Internet access.[15] Costs for a second telephone line can be high. For example, in the United States, the cost of a second line in 1999 varied from US$7.70 to US$47.62 per month, plus installation charges.[16] For the United Kingdom, Enders points out that the cost of an additional line plus the cost of dial up access is approximately the same as getting a broadband connection.[17] Of course, not all narrowband customers choose to purchase a second line; many use a mobile telephone for voice communications while connected to the Internet or simply go without telephone services. Nonetheless, the use of narrowband service imposes a cost on consumers by tying up a residential landline phone line. Enders (2003) found that 41% of consumers considered the ability to use the phone and be online at the same time to be the main advantage of broadband.

---

[12] Varian (1999).

[13] Varian notes that his methodology provides only a *"rough-and-ready, nonparametric estimate."*

[14] Office of Technology Policy, U.S. Dept. of Commerce (2002).

[15] Yankee Group (2002).

[16] Hausman, Sidak and Singer (2001).

[17] Enders (2003).

Overall, the benefits to users of broadband relative to narrowband appear substantial, and are likely to increase for many users once they subscribe to broadband. It thus seems unlikely that a hypothetical monopolist of broadband service in a particular local market would need to control narrowband services to benefit from a small but significant and non-transitory price increase above cost. This implies that broadband and narrowband are distinct markets. This conclusion is supported by academic analysis of U.S. internet access prices. For example, Hausman et. al (2001) notes that data on the price variations of narrowband in different U.S. geographical markets demonstrates that narrowband service is a separate relevant market from broadband service: *"[t]he straightforward observation is that narrowband access prices differ by a factor of over 300 percent, while broadband access prices do not vary in any way with these differences."*[18]

This conclusion does not deny that potential substitution from narrowband to broadband exists. There is a vertical relationship between the two markets such that all consumers can be expected to view broadband as superior but vary in the amount that they are willing to pay for the higher quality good; hence, broadband prices act as a constraint on narrowband prices in the sense that many narrowband users might switch to broadband if the price differential between the services were small enough. However, narrowband pricing constrains broadband pricing only to the extent that the size of the price gap acts as an initial constraint on take-up of broadband. Forrester Research argue convincingly that the decline in the broadband premium over dial-up – the European average fell from 178% in 2001 to 101% at end-2002 – has been a key factor spurring take-up in Europe in 2002.[19] Various consultants have talked about threshold prices at which broadband becomes a viable mass-market alternative to dial-up; according to Forrester, this point was reached when the lowest prices available fell to around 30 euros.

Arguably, the distinction between narrowband and broadband is becoming less clear with the emergence of new entry-level broadband products, which feature low-bit-rates or usage restrictions. The objective of these products appears to be *"to tempt consumers away from dial-up, aiming to convert them to pricier, faster products later."*[20] Examples (taken in August 2003) include: KPN's 256 Kbps ADSL product, an ADSL offer from Telecom Italia's tin.it ISP at 27.95 euros per month which has a 20-hour usage cap, and UK cable company ntl's 150 Kbps low-end offer. The presence of these entry level broadband products might increase interaction between the pricing of broadband and narrowband to the extent that this leads to a chain of substitutable products, but this is yet to be seen.

---

[18] Hausman (2001) page 6-7.
[19] Forrester (June 2003a).
[20] Forrester (June 2003a).

Table 1: Broadband forecasts for Western Europe

Forecaster	Year	Broadband subscribers	Broadband revenues per annum
Datamonitor[21]	2006	41 million	US$ 16bn +
IDATE[22]	2007	65-75 million	Euro 22.4bn
IDC[23]	2007	62 million	US$ 27bn
Forrester[24]	2008	49.7 million	na
Strategy Analytics[25]	2008	63 million	na

2.2   The importance of broadband to the EU economy

According to many industry reports, broadband access will be one of the key sectors underpinning productivity and economic growth in the EU over the next five years. The sector is both important in its own right and, as a facilitator of faster and more efficient data transmission and internet access, a key input into other economic sectors.

Independent forecasters project rapid growth for broadband subscribers and revenues over the next five years. In Table 1, we provide a snapshot of forecasts for subscribers and revenues across Western Europe, made in 2003 and 2004. The most conservative, from Forrester and Datamonitor, predict that there will be 38 million and 41 million European households, respectively, using broadband by 2006, up from 10.3 million at end-2002. Forecasts for direct revenues range from at least 14 billion euros in 2006 up to 24 billion euros by 2007. Revenues for direct access and content will be dwarfed by the indirect benefits of faster internet access, for example through greater use of e-commerce and spread of e-government.

Academic research provides strong backing for this assertion that new communication services can lead to very large increases in consumer welfare, through meeting needs that would otherwise go entirely unmet. For example, Hausman (1997) estimated that the consumer welfare gain from voice messaging services introduced in the United States in 1990 would have been 1.27 billion US dollars by 1994 if the FCC had not delayed in authorising such service. He further estimated the gains from the introduction of cellular telephone services at 50 billion dollars a year.[26] Goolsbee (2001) estimates pre-tax consumer surplus

---

[21]Datamonitor (2003), page 5-7.

[22]Idate (2002).

[23]IDC (2003).

[24]Forrester (2003a).

[25]Strategy Analytics (2003).

[26]Hausman (1997), page 2.

from the introduction of broadband in the United States at 700 million dollars per year as of mid-1999, even though penetration at that point was only 2-3% of on-line users. Unfortunately, there are no recent studies estimating the direct contribution of broadband to consumer welfare and none for EU countries. However, inferring from the results of these studies, one would expect a value already in the many billions of euros.

These estimates of the value of broadband services are based on adding together individual consumers' willingness to pay for services. Various external benefits may also arise that are not reflected in end-customers' willingness to pay, particularly if there are network effects, which would not be privately valued. For example, consumers' decisions to use e-commerce to buy goods and services may lead to benefits for suppliers in terms of reduced cost and greater efficiency. The adoption of new technologies and their faster diffusion also benefits equipment manufacturers, via increased demand. Taking all these potential gains into account, Crandall, Jackson and Singer (2003) estimated that the total annual consumer benefit from broadband in the United States would be between 64 and 97 billion US dollars per year if 50% of U.S. households adopted broadband, and could be more than 300 billion US dollars per year if broadband were to achieve universal diffusion in the United States. The authors also found that the ubiquitous adoption of current broadband technology would increase total U.S. GDP by 180 billion US dollars and create 61,000 new jobs per year, and that the ubiquitous adoption of more advanced access technologies (such as FTTH or VDSL) would sustain 140,000 new jobs per year.[27] Given the similar size of the U.S. and EU economies, it is plausible to assume that the benefits to Europe could be of a similar magnitude.

Given the substantial benefits available from broadband development, it also follows that delays in broadband deployment and thus take-up could have significant opportunity costs. In particular, poorly designed regulation can have a detrimental impact on investment and competition, with direct negative implications for consumer welfare and even larger indirect effects for the wider economy. For example, Hausman (1997) estimates the total cost of FCC regulatory delay on the U.S. mobile phone market at around 100 billion US dollars.

The importance of the broadband market has been recognised in numerous documents and speeches made by governments and international bodies in recent years, reflecting not just the utility of services to end-users, but also broader social benefits. For example:

☐ **ITU:** *"Broadband has been referred to as the infrastructure of the knowledge economy. Countries around the world have nominated broadband networks as crucial infrastructure for achieving their social, economic and scientific goals."*[28]

---

[27]Crandall, Jackson and Singer (2003).

[28]ITU (2003), page 3.

☐ **OECD:** *"If, as many believe, new communication tools such as the Internet and wireless networks boosted growth in the latter half of the 1990s, and softened the current cyclical downturn, then the next steps toward broadband access are of critical importance that go beyond the communications sector."*[29]

☐ **European Commission:** *"Distance education (using e-learning), access to government services (e-government), healthcare (e-health), entertainment, videoconferencing, e-commerce, etc. become more practical and often feasible only through the high speed provided by broadband access. . . . The adoption of these services into our daily life, and the opening of new markets, can improve quality of life, increase productivity and stimulate innovation."*[30]

☐ **Ireland, ODTR:** *"[T]he development of a vibrant broadband sector has the potential to not only stimulate growth in a new set of higher-value industries, but to open up new possibilities for all citizens, irrespective of geographic location."*[31]

☐ **UK government:** *"The rapid roll out of high bandwidth technology is clearly a prerequisite to a successful UK e-commerce sector."*[32]

☐ **U.S. FCC:** *"The widespread deployment of broadband infrastructure has become the central communications policy objective today."*[33]

☐ **Canadian Minister of Industry:** *"Broadband can stimulate innovation and improve the quality of life for all Canadians, especially those in First Nations, northern, rural and remote communities. It is applications in areas like distance education, telemedicine and e-business that will touch the everyday lives of communities and advance economic development."*[34]

☐ **South Korea, Ministry of Information and Communication:** *"Broadband Internet, which is 32 times faster than that of the dial-up modem on average, can not only utilize the idle facility of the backbone network, but also promote the related equipment and component industries, nurturing a positive economic cycle in the future. In addition, the high-speed broadband Internet service will pave the way for multimedia contents, application services and e-commerce to prosper."*[35]

At a minimum, EU governments should provide a framework for broadband that does not impede rollout. There may also be a case for more active government promotion of broadband, given the scope for realising positive externalities for the economy at large not reflected in customers' willingness to pay for services. However, the impact of any regulatory intervention on incentives for

[29] OECD (2001), page 4.
[30] European Commission (February 2003a), page 6.
[31] ODTR (2002).
[32] PIU (1999), page 63.
[33] Powell (2001).
[34] Industry Canada (2003).
[35] IT Korea (2002).

both industry players and consumers need to be carefully thought through. Measures that impede or slow the development of broadband services may have very large costs, even if these are not immediately evident.

2.3 Broadband delivery technologies

There are many different technologies currently available that can be used for delivering broadband to both residential customers and businesses. These include DSL, cable, fibre, satellites, fixed wireless access, electrical power lines, mobile communications, wireless LAN and free-space optics. All these technologies have relative strengths and weaknesses, for example, in relation to maximum transmission speeds or vulnerability to interference and capacity constraints. Nevertheless, the types of user experience that they offer – once infrastructure is in place – are sufficiently similar that significant numbers of customers are likely to find services delivered by these different technologies closely substitutable.[36]

In the remainder of this subsection, we describe the various technologies for delivering broadband, highlight their strengths and weaknesses and discuss their potential development over the medium term. Our main observations are as follows:

☐ The current prevalence of **DSL** and **cable** is based on their use of existing infrastructure and first-to-market status, rather than any technological superiority. Actual transmission speeds are often quite low relative to some other platforms, although they may improve as technological advances are implemented.

☐ *Fibre-to-the-home (FTTH)* offers far superior speeds to standard DSL or cable. Although expensive to deploy if new trenches need to be dug, it can be cost effective in urban areas, especially if consumer use of bandwidth-hungry applications takes off. However, the distinction between fibre, and cable and DSL technologies is becoming blurred, as the latter undertake increasing deployment of fibre closer to the end customer and upgrade their distribution capacity.

☐ High deployment costs and problems with upstream connectivity mean that *satellite* is currently not cost effective as a mass market alternative to DSL and cable, except for rural areas, where the cost of building fixed infrastructure is prohibitive.

☐ *Fixed wireless access (FWA)* has now been available for several years in many European countries but as yet has only found a market as a niche solution for businesses. It still has potential to become a mass market technology, particularly if the costs of equipment were to fall. Over such a timescale, it faces being overtaken by more flexible WLAN and mobile technologies.

---

[36] For further discussion of this point, see Section 3.2, which compares broadband offers available in EU markets on different platforms.

☐ Owing to their ubiquity, electric *power lines* have potential as a mass market alternative to DSL or, more likely, a cost-effective way of extending broadband to rural areas. However, some technical and regulatory obstacles apparently need to be overcome. The longer the delay in the mass market deployment in European countries, the less likely that it will gain critical mass.

☐ *WiFi* (wireless LAN) technology currently provides hotspot internet access services, and is starting to be used to provide broad coverage public access networks in both urban and rural areas. This is a mature, cost effective and low risk technology. Many laptop computers are sold with wireless LAN functionality already built in.

☐ *3G mobile* is being deployed by MNOs across Europe. This will ultimately give the mobile telephone customer base an alternative means of broadband access;

☐ *'new mobile'* technologies can provide mobile broadband services, for example, bringing cell structure and cell handover to wireless LANs that currently permit only nomadic use. They can use a variety of different radio spectrum, including unused spectrum that many European 3G licensees hold. Commercial services are already being rolled out (e.g. in Australia) with bandwidth and pricing comparable to DSL services.

Table 2 provides a rough visual summary of the relative strengths and weaknesses of these technologies.

2.3.1   Digital subscriber line (DSL)

DSL technologies make use of existing telephone lines to deliver voice, data, and video traffic simultaneously at high speed. An 'always-on' connection is established between a modem at the user end and a DSL access multiplexer (DSLAM) at the local exchange. Using advanced modulation and signal processing techniques, data is carried over existing twisted pair copper wire at frequencies significantly higher than those used for voice traffic. Both upstream (from the user to the exchange) and downstream transmission is possible. Voice and data signals are separated using a line splitter, allowing simultaneous use of lines for narrowband voice telephony and broadband access for PCs or television set-top boxes.

DSL can be deployed in a number of different ways, for example:

☐ *Asymmetric DSL (ADSL)*. This is the most common form of DSL and is primarily targeted at the residential market. With an ADSL connection, the data channel is split into a number of sub-channels, creating flexibility in the way that data is allocated across the breadth of the connection. Much higher speeds are achievable for downstream (up to 8 Mbps) than for upstream (up to 1 Mbps), which is convenient for most common uses of the Internet, such as web surfing and file downloading.

Table 2: Relative strengths and weaknesses of broadband delivery platforms*

	DSL ADSL	DSL SDSL	DSL VDSL	Cable	FTTH	FWA	Satellite	WLAN/WiFi	Powerline	PPL/FSO	Mobile 3G	Mobile Beyond 3G
Deployment												
Current availability	✓✓✓	✓	✗	✓✓	✓	✓	✓	✓	✗✗	✗✗	✓	✗✗
Suitability for urban areas	✓✓✓	✓✓✓	✓✓	✓✓✓	✓✓	✓✓	✓	✓✓	✓✓	✓✓	✓✓✓	✓✓✓
Suitability for rural areas	✗	✗	✗✗	✗✗	✗✗	✓	✓✓✓	✓	✓✓	✗	✓	✓
Mobility	✗✗	✗✗	✗✗	✗✗	✗✗	✗	✗	✓	✗✗	✗	✓✓✓	✓✓✓
Quality of service												
Transmission speeds	Up to 8 Mbps	Up to 2 Mbps	Up to 52 Mbps	128 Kb - 10 Mbps	2–100 Mbps	2–40 Mbps†	300 Kb – 2 Mbps +	Up to 54 Mbps	Up to 45 Mbps	Up to 1 Gbps	Up to 2 Mbps	Up to 30 Mbps
High-speed service	✓	✓	✓✓✓	✓	✓✓✓	✓	✓	✓	✓✓✓	✓✓✓	✗	✓
Symmetric speeds	NO	YES	NO	YES	YES	YES	YES‡	YES	YES	YES	YES	YES
Degradation due to:												
capacity / shared lines	NO	NO	NO	YES	YES	NO	YES	YES	YES	NO	YES	YES
length of line or link	YES	YES	YES	NO	NO	YES	NO	YES	NO	YES	YES	YES
Costs & development												
Maturity of technology	✓✓✓	✓✓✓	✓	✓✓✓	✓✓✓	✓	✓	✓	✗	✗✗	✓	✗
Costs: equipment	✓✓✓	✓✓	✗	✓✓✓	✗	✓	✓	✓	✓	✗	✗✗	✗✗
Costs: customer installation	✓✓[1]	✓✓[1]	✗	✓✓✓[1]	✗	✓✓	✓	✓	✓	✓	✓✓✓	✓✓✓

Source: DotEcon, September 2003; *This is a rough approximation only, where ✓✓✓ indicates the strongest and ✗✗ the weakest; †At mid-range bandwidths; ‡Two-way satellite only; [1] Assumes that copper or cable connections are already in place; otherwise installation costs would be much higher, as is the case for VDSL or FTTH.

□ *Symmetric DSL (SDSL)*. Standard SDSL systems provide symmetrical upstream and downstream speeds of between 160 Kbps and 2 Mbps. It is generally deployed for small and medium-sized enterprises (SMEs) who require
significant two-way bandwidth. G.SHDSL (single pair high-bit rate DSL),
a new system that allows symmetric speeds of up to 2.3 Mbps, has been
standardised by the ITU and is increasingly being deployed in Europe and
the United States.

□ *Very high-speed DSL (VDSL)*. Even higher bandwidth (up to 52 Mbps downstream and 16 Mbps upstream) can be achieved using VDSL technology.
Unlike ADSL, this system makes use of a fibre optic connection which must
be run to the curb or neighbourhood, such that only the final portion of the
local loop is copper. A VDSL transceiver and gateway are placed at either
end of the copper wire, the latter converting the data for onward transmission
over fibre. Owing to the cost of laying new fibre, VDSL is most suited to
multi-unit sites, such as offices and apartment blocks.

The main advantage of DSL technologies over other broadband delivery platforms are their use of ubiquitous, copper line infrastructure. In theory, the
speeds achievable over DSL rival most other delivery platforms, with the exception of fibre. However, actual bandwidth is highly dependent on line quality
and length of the local loop; the maximum line length for ADSL is about 5,500
metres, while for VDSL it is just 1,200 metres. Consequently, while DSL generally works well in urban areas, it is often not suitable for rural areas, where the
distance from the local exchange is a constraint on providing service to a large
proportion of customers. Additionally, the 'loop' consists of many segments of
copper with different vintages and other characteristics, and the DSL speed is
constrained overall by the weakest link in the chain. Most customers thus enjoy
speeds well below the theoretical maximum.

Relative to other broadband delivery platforms, DSL is already relatively mature, with network operators enjoying the benefits of economies of scale in
equipment manufacturing associated with mass deployment worldwide. Over
the next five years, technological innovation will likely see lower costs, especially in relation to DSLAMs, and some further advances in potential bandwidth
obtainable over copper wires. Where it is cost effective, DSL operators may
also move to upgrade parts of the copper loop with fibre.

2.3.2   Cable

Like ADSL, cable broadband delivers an always-on high-speed internet connection. In a typical cable network, data is transferred between a cable modem
at the user end and cable modem termination system at the local distribution
hub. Line splitters are used to enable simultaneous use of data, television and
(where available) voice, although with some networks (e.g. the United Kingdom
and Spain), there is a separate voice line. The download speeds vary depending
on the quality of the cable infrastructure, but are typically between 2 and 70

times those of a dial-up connection.[37] Typical consumer offerings range from 150 Kbps up to about 3 Mbps, although UPC chello, the leading cable company in the Netherlands, announced in 2003 the capability to offer a 10 Mbps service over some existing infrastructure. For consumers, the data services available are essentially identical to those of DSL, but with the potential advantage that they can be bundled with broadcast as well as voice services.

One potential weakness with cable is that unlike with the copper local loop, users share bandwidth with their neighbours. At peak periods, this sharing may result in a reduced access speeds for some users. However, as demand for bandwidth increases, this can be met by splitting fibre nodes (i.e. the connection from the cable head-end), which has the effect of reducing the number of customers sharing limited bandwidth on coaxial cable. This is a relatively straightforward and cost-effective method of upgrading two-way lines in response to rising demand.

Unlike copper loops, cable roll-out varies widely across European countries, so many potential consumers do not have access to this service. Also, much of the original cable infrastructure in Europe was laid for television and has only a one-way link to the home. Cable needs to be upgraded to two-way links to provide internet access. This requires a change in network topology that is not required for DSL. During the late 1990s, many cable companies pursued aggressive roll-out and upgrade strategies but in recent years this has been checked by financial difficulties. Where cable roll-out and upgrades are extensive – for example in Belgium and the Netherlands, cable companies have generally been very successful in winning broadband market share in competition with DSL, and they are likely to remain so for the foreseeable future. In this regard, they have been helped by economies of scale resulting from the worldwide deployment of the ITU-sponsored DOCSIS standards.

2.3.3   Fibre to the home (FTTH)

FTTH is deployed in a similar way to standard cable, but uses optical fibre all the way to the home rather than only as far as the nearest cable distribution node. FTTH permits exceptionally high bandwidth, typically between 10 Mbps and 10 Gbps, depending on whether the fibre connects all the way to the user or to the curb. This performance is far superior to cable or DSL, notwithstanding the fact that – like cable – shared use of lines can reduce speed for users. It can carry voice, data and video services simultaneously.

The main obstacle to the deployment of fibre is the high cost of some components and of installing new cable, which may require trenching work. However, in many cases, it may be possible to use existing cable ducts into buildings (procedures and regulations for duct sharing are long established and no different for broadband from narrowband). Equipment costs are falling rapidly as

---

[37]IDC (2003), page 10.

deployment increases (although the scale of deployment is modest compared with DSL and cable to date); however, installation costs are mainly due to labour and so cannot be expected to fall significantly. Therefore the economics of fibre deployment can be expected to remain driven by the question of whether returns are sufficient to justify deployment. At present, the much higher bandwidth provided by fibre is not required for most existing applications, although this could change quickly if demand for new bandwidth-hungry services takes off.[38]

Some innovative entrants, notably in Sweden and Italy, are rolling out fibre in selected urban areas, and are winning significant customer bases. There have also been smaller scale FTTH deployments in other countries, notably Denmark and Austria (see section 3.2.1 for a list of examples). Nevertheless, in the immediate future, new fibre build is likely to be focused primarily on new building developments, where there is little reason to deploy copper loops or coaxial cable as the costs of deploying fibre are similar.

2.3.4   Fixed wireless access (FWA)

Fixed wireless access systems employ a point-to-multipoint radio wave link between a base station and multiple antennae. In most circumstances, a line of sight connection is required between the antennae and base station. FWA serves as a wireless replacement for copper local loops or cable drops. It can be used for both voice and data, with transmission speeds in excess of 2 Mbps, depending on the spectrum band being used.

Wireless technology offers a number of advantages over fixed links: there is no need to lay cable into customer sites, so it is much easier to roll out competing infrastructure; customer installation is relatively straightforward; and equipment can be moved and re-used. Therefore, the marginal cost of joining new customers to a network is relatively small. However, the requirement for line-of-sight path means that typically the signal from a base station will only reach about 40% of the people in a given area, potentially necessitating the need for additional base stations.[39] Transmissions are also vulnerable to signal disruption owing to heavy rain or wet foliage. At present, high equipment costs has made FWA largely uneconomic where there is existing copper or cable loop infrastructure. Two notable exceptions are in Mexico City and Hong Kong, where local operators have captured significant market shares in data traffic.

FWA has been heralded as a potential mass-market alternative to cable and DSL. The idea of 'broadband in a box', with consumers able to buy terminating

---

[38]Demand for services requiring high bandwidth and demand for bandwidth to support such services are clearly interlinked. For example, demand for streaming content has increased with greater broadband take-up and is conceivably a driver of take-up.

[39]Strategy Analytics (2003).

equipment off-the-shelf that they then can plug straight into their PCs, remains a potentially attractive proposition. AT&T experimented with this under the name 'Project Angel', but the project has apparently been shelved following the sale of the company's cable units to Comcast. The high cost of equipment (relative to DSL or cable modems and termination equipment) appears to be the key factor preventing operators from penetrating consumer markets at present.

Existing FWA operators in Europe are focused largely on the business data market, usually in second-tier towns and cities with less developed fibre infrastructures. FWA technology has also been flagged as a way of providing broadband to rural communities where the local loop is too long to deploy DSL, but this depends on there being sufficient demand to justify the construction of base stations.

2.3.5 Satellite

Satellites can act as a bridge between users' PCs or TVs and the carrier's point-of-presence (POP) on the fixed internet backbone. They can be employed almost anywhere, and thus are particularly suitable for serving rural areas which cable and DSL cannot reach. Most existing services utilise existing TV satellite receiving dishes combined with digital receivers. However these typically offer only downstream transmission, at speeds of 300 Kbps to 2 Mbps. Upstream connection is completed via a dial-up connection over the phone line. A number of companies in Europe and the United States have begun introducing two-way broadband satellite services. However, take-up has thus far been limited owing to expensive equipment and installation, and problems with capacity and scalability.[40] Certain applications may be frustrated by limited upload speeds and latency.

Two-way satellite offers a potential universal solution to broadband access. However, unless costs can be reduced significantly, it is unlikely to be competitive in urban areas where other technologies are already in place. It has much greater potential in rural areas; reflecting this, many existing service providers, such as BT, Deutsche Telekom, Telefonica and Tiscali have deployed satellite as a complement to their DSL services. All these companies currently price satellite access at levels significantly above DSL services (see section 1.1.1).

2.3.6 Electric power lines

Power line communications (PLC) technology makes use of existing electricity distribution lines to transmit data signals. Users connect their PCs to the electricity network using a protocol translator, which is typically co-located with their electricity meter although some systems utilise buildings' internal

---

[40]Strategy Analytics (2003).

networks. The signal then runs to the local electricity substation where a data concentrator is used to connect it to the communications backbone.

The system offers two main advantages relative to other broadband delivery platforms:

☐ The ubiquity of powerlines means this is a potential universal solution.
☐ It is potentially fast, with theoretical speeds of up to 45 Mbps.[41] Actual systems deployed to date run at about 1 Mbps.

Whether or not this technology can be made to work effectively on a commercial basis remains uncertain. There are a number of significant technical obstacles to carrying data signals over powerlines, such as the risk of radiated energy interfering with radio signals and the swamping of data signals by switching transients (e.g. owing to generators going on and off line). Furthermore, critics argue that since telephone cables are designed to carry far higher frequencies than 50 Hz power cables, data application performance over powerline is doomed to be inferior.[42] The absence of a common position on powerline standards amongst EU member states may also inhibit the development of this technology.

Trials of powerline systems are on-going in both Europe and the United States. For example, in Spain, the three main electricity operators have been carrying out tests and there are now 3,000 users in Extremadura region.[43] Meanwhile, Scottish Hydro-Electric launched trial services in 2003 in three small towns: Crieff, Campbeltown, and Stonehaven.[44] However, Europe's largest commercial trial, involving RWE in Germany, was abandoned.[45] The extent to which these trials have made progress in resolving technical obstacles is unclear. The FCC in 2003 launched an inquiry into broadband over powerlines as part of its ongoing efforts "to encourage multiple platforms for broadband".[46]

If the technical obstacles to implementation can be resolved, then powerlines could play mass-market role. In a 2003 report, IDC commented that it would be "*interesting to see what would happen if a major European provider or equipment manufacturer really began to push the solution.*"[47] However, the focus of trials on rural areas (e.g. Extremadura) which typically lack DSL or cable coverage suggests that the immediate focus is the development of powerlines is as a niche technology for deploying broadband in rural areas.

---

[41] Strategy Analytics (2003).

[42] Cochrane (2003), Silicon.com.

[43] ETNO office notes (2003).

[44] see www.hydro.co.uk/broadband/.

[45] IDC (2003), page 14.

[46] FCC (April 2003).

[47] IDC (2003), page 14.

2.3.7 Point-to-point laser (PPL) / Free space optics (FSO)

This system is comparable to FWA but uses lasers rather than radio spectrum to transmit signals from the customer's premises to a backbone network. The potential bandwidth that can be provided is very large and – as users only require a transceiver mounted against a window – deployment costs are potentially small as the costs of running in cable or fibre (e.g. trenching) would be avoided. However, the technology is still in its infancy. There are potential problems related to line of sight requirements and distortions owing to atmospheric conditions. This may require some form of mesh network architecture for deployment, so that each user has a number of redundant links. In this case, there may be little need for other backhaul infrastructure (apart from to interconnect with other public networks) as the capacity of point-to-point links would be so great. Like FWA, its primary use is most likely to be for SMEs in suburban areas as a cost-effective alternative to running in fibre.

2.3.8 Wireless LANs / WiFi

A further wireless technology which may serve as a substitute to fixed broadband access are wireless local access networks (WLANs). Like FWA, WLANs use radio spectrum to transmit data. They can be used to link communications equipment (usually computers) together for private networking or to provide a public access network. Currently, the dominant standard, operated by the WiFi (Wireless Fidelity) Alliance, is IEEE 802.11b. This system operates at low power outputs, enabling broadband data transfer rates to mobile users of up to 11 Mbps over a distance of 50 metres or so (which means it is possible to have uncoordinated and unlicensed sharing of the spectrum band by many users without the risk of extensive interference problems). By the use of directional antennae, it is possible to link fixed points over much large distances using standard 802.11b equipment. Products using a new standard, IEEE 802.11g, which is capable of speeds up to 54 Mbps, are already available and expected to become widely used in 2003. These various versions of the 802.11 standard allow nomadic users, but do not incorporate any cell structure or handover between cells; therefore, they do not provide full mobility as with a mobile network.

WLANs may act as an adjunct to fixed data networks and data connections over existing mobile networks, enabling users to access both the internet and private networks at high speed. However, WLANs are also being used to provide a service that substitutes entirely for fixed broadband. Not only are WLANs being used to provide hotspot coverage and private networking, but also to deploy broad coverage public access networks. These two modes of deployment are rather different.

In the case of hotspot provision, WLANs are typically used to extend a fixed broadband connection and share the available bandwidth amongst a number of users. In this case, a fixed broadband connection is required to deploy the service and so WLAN access may not be a true independent competitor to fixed broadband. Transmission speeds are only as good as the fixed link used to provide connectivity to the Internet. If this is an ADSL link (as might be used in a typical café-based hotspot), then actual speeds will be limited by the fixed broadband connection, rather than the radio connection.

From 2002, there has been significant roll-out of WLANs in Europe and the United States, as a wireless solution for connecting computers in homes, offices and universities, and by commercial interests creating hotspots:

☐ In June 2003, Gartner reported that some 19.5 million units of WLAN equipment were shipped worldwide in 2002, up 120% from the previous year.[48]
☐ According to the CNET News.com, WiFi *"has taken off as a cheap and effective way to share resources on a network, such as a broadband connection, and it has quickly spawned a commercial hot-spot service industry aimed at delivering bandwidth in high-use areas including hotels, airports and truck stops"*[49]. For example, T-Mobile operated over 2,400 active hotspots in the United States as of July 2003, in locations such as Starbucks cafés, Borders bookstores, and airports.[50]
☐ In total, there were approximately 4,200 active hotspots in the United States at the end of 2002, and IDC expects wireless providers to add more than 55,000 new hot spots in the United States by 2008.[51] IDC also projects that there will be over 32,000 hotspots in Western Europe by 2007.[52]
☐ A June 2003 report by Allied Business Intelligence estimated that the market for WLAN-enabled notebook users could reach 58 million users worldwide by 2008[53]. However, other forecasters are more sanguine: for example, Forrester projects 7.7 million regular users in Europe by 2008, about 15% of lap top owners and 20% of WiFi-enabled PDA owners.[54]
☐ The largest European deployment of WLANs to date is at the University of Twente in the Netherlands, with 650 access points covering 140 hectares to serve the 8,500 students and staff.[55]
☐ Paris is now close to offering widespread WiFi coverage, as Cisco plans to install antennae at the majority of Paris' many Metro stations.[56]

WLANs can also be used to provide broad coverage public access, providing backhaul networking wirelessly through the use of directional antennae. In this

---

[48] Total Telecom (June 2003a).
[49] CNET News.com (July 2003a).
[50] T-Mobile Press Release (May 2003).
[51] T-Mobile Press Release (May 2003).
[52] Cellular Online (June 2003).
[53] Total Telecom (June 2003b).
[54] Forrester (June 2003b).
[55] Total Telecom (June 2003c).
[56] The Inquirer (May 2003).

case, wireless base stations may be connected wirelessly to other wireless base stations. The overall network would be interconnected with the Internet at a number of fixed points using commercial backhaul. In this case the wireless service is *not* reliant on any fixed broadband service to operate.

A number of commercial broad coverage services are already underway. For example, Irish Broadband offers WiFi-based broadband in Dublin. Following "high demand for its products", it plans to roll out service in other Irish cities, using 2.4 GHz base stations interconnected using 5.7 GHz wireless links.[57]

2.3.9   Third Generation (3G) mobile

Mobile communications offer an alternative medium to fixed wireline and wireless infrastructure for accessing the internet and sending and receiving data transmissions. Existing 2G phones using GPRS can be used to transmit data at rates equivalent to a standard analogue dial-up connection, although they can provide an always-on connection. However 3G systems, which are currently being deployed, are capable of much faster transmission rates (albeit to a limited number of users in any single cell area). The European 3G Universal Mobile Telecommunications Service (UMTS) standard provides for rates of 2 Mbps for stationary phones, 344 Kbps for a person walking and 144 Kbps in a moving vehicle, which are comparable with many existing DSL and cable broadband offerings. However, realistic rates at launch for 3G networks may be somewhat less than this.

A key advantage of 3G over other broadband access devices is, by definition, its mobility. Users are not tied to a specific location, and can send and receive large data files anywhere where there is coverage. Although the physical size of handsets imposes limits on users' visual experience of some data applications, this can be addressed by linking handsets to portable computers. The development of 2.5G and 3G technologies is also driving innovation in access devices. For example many mobile operators now market 'data cards', mobile access devices designed specifically for data transmission that can be plugged straight into laptops.

As a potential competitor to DSL and cable, the ubiquity of mobile phones is important. As of May 1 2003, Mobile Communications estimates that there are 307.7 million mobile subscribers in Western Europe, a penetration rate of 78.7%.[58] Although nearly all these subscribers currently use 2G, most European mobile operators are currently rolling out 3G networks. Once 3G networks are in place, the marginal costs of providing data transmissions are small. Therefore, 3G operators will have strong incentives to win customers and maximise traffic by offering attractive services.

---

[57]ZDNet UK (October 2003).

[58]Total Telecom (June 2003d).

For some users, 3G may be a useful complement to fixed broadband services, and the experience of fixed broadband may boost demand for 3G and vice versa. Using both platforms may increase consumers' understanding of what benefits data services offer and so boost demand in general. As experience of data services grows, however, these services may increasingly be substitutes, either at the level of usage decisions, or even at the point of deciding to subscribe at all.

Here, an analogy can be drawn with voice, where there is substantial empirical data of substitution with mobile telephony at the levels of individual calls and access choices, and evidence that this substitution has increased as mobile call charges have declined and mobile phone ownership become ubiquitous.[59] This form of substitution can occur even if prices of fixed and mobile services are rather dissimilar. By analogy, once 3G technology is mainstream, there may be a strong price incentive for consumers with modest broadband demands to use their mobile devices rather than subscribe to an infrequently used fixed service, especially as it becomes increasingly easy to interconnect mobiles and PCs without specialist knowledge. The extent of substitution will be primarily determined by the trade-off between the cost-effectiveness for users of using 3G for additional data communications versus signing up to an entire fixed broadband access package.

The extent of substitution between fixed and wireless data technologies depends on the nature of service and customers' needs. Mobile connections have some vulnerability to link disruption and cell capacity limits, although similar problems also affect fixed broadband technologies to differing extents. More significantly, proposed data rates for initial implementation of 3G are substantially below those for most fixed access technologies, making it unsuitable for some high bandwidth applications. However, mobile operators are already offering bundled services using WiFi hotspots and their future data services offers may be based on variety of underlying technologies, including GPRS, EDGE, 3G and WiFi. Therefore, for many users, mobile solutions will offer sufficient bandwidth in a sufficient variety of locations (with wide coverage at lower bandwidths) to be an effective substitute for fixed services. For fixed and mobile services to compete, it is not necessary for them to have very similar characteristics or for all customers to consider them substitutes; what is required is that a sufficient number of customers (which could be a minority of all customers) find the services substitutable.

---

[59] For example, Horvath and Maldoom (2002) analysed survey data on over 7,000 British telephone users in order to investigate the link between mobile phone ownership and fixed telephone usage. Controlling for underlying taste differences between fixed and mobile users, they found strong evidence of fixed-mobile substitution at both the call and access levels.

2.3.10 'New mobile' technologies

As a substitute for fixed broadband access systems, WLAN and 3G technologies each have drawbacks: WLANs have high speed but limited mobility; and 3G provides wide coverage but is slower than most fixed broadband (at least as it is likely to be initially deployed). However, future developments of these technologies promise to combine the mobility and range of mobile with the transmission speeds of WiFi. Assuming these can be developed as commercial services, such technologies would appear to have the potential to satisfy the broadband access requirements of most users and provide full mobility at the same time.

The future evolution of mobile data services is uncertain, owing to the many different potential technology paths; in particular, it is possible that a number of competing standards could emerge. Mobile operators (and other providers) may offer data services over a mixture of different technologies, reflecting the comparative advantages of different technologies in different situations and the impact of legacy systems. These different technologies may eventually be knitted together to provide seamless service.

A popular description for any mobile technology that offers superior data handling capabilities to those currently available is '4G', though we do not consider this a meaningful term. Technologies identified under this banner may be better described as extensions of existing 3G and WiFi technology. For example, the latest W-CDMA standard (a 3G technology) can potentially offer speeds of up to 10.8 Mbps. We use the term 'new mobile' to describe such technologies.

There are already products coming to market aimed at business and high-end residential users which promise wide-area data access at broadband speeds, using a development of existing WLAN standards to include cell structures and cell handovers. Companies developing technology under this banner include ArrayComm, Broadstorm, Flarion Technologies, IPWireless, and Navini, and trial deployments are already underway in parts of Canada, Germany, Italy, the Netherlands, New Zealand, South Korea, and the United States.[60] Both Flarion and ArrayComm, for example, are developing end-to-end IP networks, with full on-demand capability:

- ☐ Flarion is in talks with a number of mobile carriers, including Nextel in the United States, about deploying its Orthogonal Frequency Division Multiplexing technology on top of current networks.[61]
- ☐ ArrayComm is engaged in the live deployment of its iBurst technology in Sydney, Australia, under the marketing banner of "personal broadband" for

---

[60]The Economist (May 2003).
[61]ComputerWeekly.com (June 2003).

consumers and business.[62] Promising initial speeds of 1 Mbps, its plans to roll out its network across urban Australia, using 5MHz of 3G spectrum purchased in a 2001 auction. Initial pricing is highly competitive: as of June 2003, ArrayComm was projecting a price of 35 Australian dollars per month (20 euros), which compares favourably to other forms of broadband access.

Notably, Arraycomm's technology is suitable for deployment over unpaired frequency allocations (TDD) in and around the bands 1800-2100 MHz, which are owned by mobile operators across the EU but at present not being used.[63] These unpaired blocks have, until recently, been seen as having little value and were envisaged for various in-building and unlicensed deployments of 3G networks. However, it is now clear that these blocks have great potential to be used for data traffic. Moves towards technologically neutral licensing of spectrum are likely to mean that new data services can be deployed within existing spectrum assignments.

For consumers and business users who value both home and remote access to broadband, 'new mobile' technologies could provide a one-stop solution. Ultimately, whether these technologies can attract customers away from fixed broadband access will depend on whether they can be shown to work effectively; whether investors can be found to finance the costs of deploying networks; and whether the end-user price is competitive. It is too early in the development of these technologies to draw firm conclusions. Nevertheless, mobile operators are an obvious source of investment in these services notwithstanding the problems they have experienced with the cost of rolling out 3G networks: they have existing customer bases to market these services to; existing billing systems; and can potentially develop integrated offers with other mobile services.

---

[62] http://www.arraycomm.com.

[63] All 3G operators in Denmark, Finland, France, Greece, Ireland, Italy, Luxembourg, Netherlands, Portugal, Spain and Sweden, plus 3 of 6 operators in Austria, 5 of 6 in Germany and 4 of 5 in the United Kingdom were awarded TDD spectrum.

3 Competition in broadband markets

Broadband services are provided to end-users over many different networks, using a variety of technologies, and by many different companies. In this chapter, we survey the extent of competition both between networks and between companies supplying broadband at the retail level. We draw an important distinction between *'facilities-based competition'*, where providers are using all (or some of) their own infrastructure, and *'access-based competition'*, where providers use access to someone else's network.

This distinction matters because the extent to which a provider has control over its own network determines its ability to control the characteristics of its service, including both cost and functionality. In general, facilities-based competition generates much more scope for product and pricing innovation within a market than does access-based competition.

This chapter is split into three sections. We first explain the distinction between facilities and access-based competition, and describe the different mechanisms for access-based entry. The second part analyses the extent of platform competition and access take-up in EU member state markets and examines the impact this has had on broadband product and pricing innovation. We conclude with a series of OECD country case studies which analyse contrasting development paths in broadband competition.

3.1 Facilities-based and access-based competition

3.1.1 The broadband value chain

Figure 1 shows the broad classes of activity essential to provision of a broadband Internet service. For the moment, we do not concern ourselves with who undertakes each activity; in principle, these could all be undertaken by the provider of the ultimate retail service, or else procured from other suppliers of wholesale services.

Given appropriate peering and interconnection arrangements to access the internet backbone, connectivity must be carried to end-customers. We can roughly divide the provision of this connectivity into two steps: the use of a backhaul network to bring shared connectivity to nodes close to customers (e.g. to a local exchange or a cable distribution node), with some means to link to individual customers (e.g. though the local loop or a cable drop). In practice, the optimal network topology will depend on the details of the technology used, and the distinction between backhaul and local access networks may not be clear cut.

These are the minimum set of activities needed to bring Internet connectivity to the customer; they are also sufficient to form the basis of a simple 'no frills'

Figure 1: Generic broadband value chain

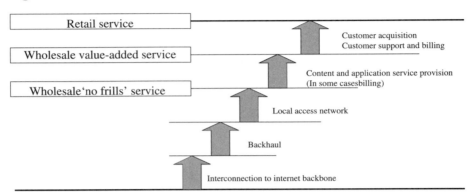

wholesale service. However, any retail offer additionally requires management of the customer relationship, including at least:

☐ marketing and advertising the service to acquire customers in the first place;
☐ providing customer support (which is typically a significant cost given the technical problems that customers may have in setting up computers to use broadband connections); and
☐ billing and credit control.[64]

The provider may choose to provide value-added services in addition to simple connectivity to the Internet. These services may include:

☐ Internet-based content, as for example some ISPs such as AOL offer bundled with broadband access;
☐ Internet-based applications, such as email or web hosting;
☐ bundled software, such as anti-virus or parental control software;
☐ broadcast TV distribution;
☐ video-on-demand; and
☐ voice telephony.

There are various ways in which video and voice services can be delivered. In the case of DSL and cable networks, the physical link to the customer is used to provide both voice and broadcast TV services,[65] reflecting the history of these networks as voice and TV distribution platforms that have been retrofitted to provide broadband. However, it is also possible to provide voice and video over

---

[64]In some cases (e.g. Germany), the billing function is a mandated component of a regulated wholesale product.
[65]For example, in a cable network, certain ranges of frequencies are used for broadcast TV distribution and other ranges for data communications.

the IP layer, allowing these value-added services to be deployed over various underlying network technologies.[66]

For example, voice services can be carried as IP packets (so-called voice over IP) flowing over a broadband data link. They are various options how to split out voice traffic at different stages of the network (e.g. interconnected to the PSTN at the local exchange or nearest switch or else carried further over IP networks and broken out closer to the recipient of the call). In the case of broadcast TV or video-on-demand, additional infrastructure would be required to distribute the content, together with appropriate commercial arrangements to source the content. Both video and voice services running over IP links require appropriate equipment at the customer end to split out the service and present it in an appropriate format for the customer's equipment.

3.1.2 Build or buy?

Already, we can see that there are important commercial choices that a provider of broadband services can make regarding the nature of the service it offers and how it is delivered. As well as potentially being able to vary the physical characteristics of the service (such as bandwidth) through technology and equipment choices, it is possible to bundle various value-added services and to offer varying levels of customer support. A broadband provider needs to decide at which levels of the value chain it will be active, and where it will buy in services from others.

Like many other sectors, there has been considerable debate in the telecoms sector about the where the boundaries of individual firms should lie, and whether the benefits of focus and clear priorities from a narrow range of activities outweigh the costs of the complicated arms-length relationships required between separate businesses. Indeed, many players in the sector have themselves been subject to substantial restructuring in response to changing commercial perceptions of where the right balance is to be found between offering a comprehensive end-to-end service and specialisation in particular aspects of the value chain.

In addition to these organisational concerns, cost conditions are a key driver of the structure of value chains. Where there are scale economies, there may be incentives for activities to be outsourced and provided by players large enough to benefit from those scale economies. Therefore, if the minimum efficient

---

[66]Different services make different requirement of the bandwidth and latency of the IP layer. For example, in the case of broadcast TV, it does not matter if there is significant latency (i.e. delay) provided there is sufficient bandwidth. In the case of voice over IP (and other two-way applications such as video conferencing), it is important to have reasonably low latency; this is difficult to achieve with satellite-based systems owing to the length of the physical path to the customer. Video conferencing is potentially the most demanding application as it requires both low latency and significant bandwidth in both the upstream and downstream directions. With the possible exception of satellite systems, all the technologies we reviewed in Section 2 have the potential to provide VoIP, video conferencing, broadcast TV distribution and video-on-demand.

scale of certain activities is large, there may be pinch points in the value chain where self-provision is inefficient except for all but large players. The PSTN local loop has been suggested to be just such a pinch point; however, as we shall see, there are many methods of deploying broadband other than DSL, and it is evidently not the case that access to existing local loops is essential.

3.1.3   Regulation and the shape of the value chain

Access regulation is a major feature of current regulatory systems for telecommunications. However, it is not the case that regulation is necessarily essential for the efficient organisation of the value chain. Where it is more efficient for an operator to source an input from elsewhere, rather than providing it itself, there will be incentives to conclude an appropriate commercial arrangement. For example, even a monopolistic network operator with unfettered market power may still have an incentive to provide wholesale services to others if they could retail the service more efficiently or reach additional customer groups. Such a provider might price excessively if customers had no alternative, but it has every incentive to organise provision of its service efficiently. Commercial incentives will always have an important role in ensuring efficient organisation of the value chain.

In general terms, regulatory concerns should only arise where there are aspects of the value chain that are essential to provide a service and which are subject to strong economies of scale that limit the number of potential providers. In this case, a pinch point might become a bottleneck, control of which could lead to market power being exercised at the retail level. In such a case, price regulation of the service at the retail level would be an unnecessary remedy, as it may be that most of the activities necessary to provide the service are not subject to economies of scale, are replicable and could be easily subject to competition. Access regulation can be used to relax the bottleneck and permit competition to operate over those other activities in the value chain that are not subject to natural monopoly, whilst at the same time ensuring that scale economies in the bottleneck activity are not lost.

As we discuss in later sections, regulation is imperfect and there are considerable advantages to allowing competition to operate to the greatest extent possible. Therefore, access regulation is only necessary as a response to retail-level market power deriving from natural monopoly (or strong scale economies more generally) in some particular activities within the value chain. In such cases, it provides a less intrusive alternative to direct retail-level regulation. Where retail competition is effective as there are no bottlenecks, there is no beneficial role for access regulation.[67]

---

[67]This principle is part of the new European regulatory framework: retail level remedies should only be used if the underlying competition problem is not addressable using wholesale access requirements.

Regulation has had a very important role in shaping the organisation of the value chain in telecommunications, in that some potential inputs are available on regulated terms. The terms and conditions of regulated access products affect the incentives of providers to be present at the various levels of the value chain. Given that there are many possible broadband provision strategies available to entrants, regulatory intervention that favours one particular strategy may distort these choices. As we shall see, access regulation currently goes further than is necessary to ensure that activities subject to strong scale economies cannot give rise to market power. It is highly debatable whether control of PSTN local loops could be a source of market power in broadband provision given that there are many other platforms, including, but not limited to, cable. However, even if local loops were bottlenecks for broadband provision, access regulation goes much further than necessary to address any such problem, by providing not just access to the local loop, but also to other, largely replicable facilities.

3.1.4 Provision strategies over PSTNs

An entrant wishing to provide broadband services has many approaches available to it, potentially ranging from building its own infrastructure to reselling the incumbent PSTN operator's service. Current access regulation makes available a range of wholesale services that enable entrants to piggyback on existing PSTN networks to varying degrees.[68]

We can distinguish four different forms of network services that can be used for broadband provision:

- full 'metallic' *local loop unbundling* (LLU);
- *line sharing* of unbundled local loops;
- *bitstream access*; and
- *wholesale end-to-end access*.

Full metallic bundling of local loops involves taking the copper pair between a local exchange and an end customer from the incumbent operator and making it available to an alternative operator.[69] The alternative operator needs to provide equipment both at the consumer end (a DSL modem, which might be bought by the customer depending on the contractual terms of the service) and at the local exchange end (a DSLAM). The provider will have choices over what

---

[68] Regulated access is currently limited to PSTN networks, though some NRAs are investigating extension of access requirements to other networks; the NRF does not rule out such extensions of regulation per se.

[69] In some cases, the copper pair does not run directly from the subscriber to the local exchange, but rather first to a remote concentrator unit (RCU). This consolidates lines, which are then trunked back to the local exchange. In this case, the alternative provider would access a sub-loop, i.e. the copper pair from the RCU to the subscriber.

technical solution is used, subject to some general restrictions necessary to prevent interference between copper pairs running closely together.[70]

To provide services to customers, the provider using LLU would also require onward connectivity from the local exchange. This might be provided by an alternative network (owned by the broadband service provider or someone else), or by using various network services procured from the incumbent. Typically, an alternative provider using unbundled local loops might use a mix of solutions to provide backhaul connectivity that vary from location to location depending on which solution was most economical.

Taking over an entire local loop raises the question of what happens to a customer's existing voice telephony service. Given that any need to switch voice provision along with broadband provision might potentially decrease customer switching, line-sharing arrangements have been used. This 'splits' the copper loop, using high frequencies to carry data traffic while low frequencies continue to carry voice traffic. It is then possible to have different providers of broadband and voice telephony services, removing any consumer inertia that might be caused if it were necessary to switch voice telephony provider along with broadband provider. The technology required to implement line sharing is very simple: low-pass filters at the customer's premises[71] and the local exchange separate the voice circuit, blocking interference from the high frequency data signals. There is little difference between the filtering arrangements that would be required if there were a common provider of voice and broadband service from those needed if there are different providers of the two services.

Line sharing raises the additional issue of how the costs of the line should be shared between the voice telephony provider and the broadband provider. However, in terms of delivering broadband services there are few differences in the capabilities of an entire unbundled line and of a shared line. In both cases, the broadband provider has technical choices about the equipment used and hence about the features of the service and the cost of delivering it. In particular:

- different equipment and standards can give different maximum data rates;
- the split of capacity between upstream and downstream links can be chosen differently;
- different equipment and standards can be used to allow longer line lengths; and

---

[70] These restrictions to prevent cross-talk have emerged from collaborative work in international standards bodies between all operators and are implemented by NRAs.

[71] Typically, a customer would simply plug a microfilter into each of his or her telephone sockets. This is a simple procedure that does not require any changes to the wiring of telephone sockets and the customer can easily install the equipment. An alternative is to use a splitter on the exchange line coming into the customer premises. This provides a filtered voice line that can then be distributed to the customers' telephone sockets.

☐ appropriate equipment can allow additional services such as video over DSL and VoIP.

For example, at present there is considerable experimentation with running DSL services over longer local loops. In general, there is a limitation on the length of the copper pair from exchange to customer than can sustain DSL services, and also a trade-off between the length of the line and the maximum data rate than can be sustained, although on-going technical innovations have pushed this forward in recent years (see section 2.3.1).

In contrast, most technical choices leading to differentiation of service features possible using unbundled loops are not open to providers using bitstream access services. With bitstream access, the alternative provider purchases IP connectivity between a handover point and the end customer delivered using the incumbent's equipment; it hands over and receives data packets from the incumbent, who is then responsible for conveying them to and from the end customer. There may be a variety of available bitstream services varying in bandwidth, but not other characteristics. A provider using bitstream access needs to procure onward connectivity from the handover point in a similar way to a broadband provider using fully unbundled local loops. Again, this might be by means of its own network, or through network services bought for other providers.

An alternative provider using bitstream access is unable to adjust any characteristics of its service that are related to the choice of standards or equipment used to provide IP connectivity over the local loop. There are some choices that the provider can make about the bandwidth and reliability of its backhaul network that may affect the overall quality of its service. Therefore, the potential for differentiation of the ultimate retail service is more limited than for a provider making use of unbundled local loops. For example, Tiscali introduced in 2003 a 'midband' service at 150kbps in the UK in response to ntl's similar speed offer. This uses a standard bitstream connection (Datastream), but with greater contention in the backhaul network, thereby saving some backhaul costs relative to a more conventional broadband DSL offer at 512 Kbps. Some flexibility in packaging and pricing is possible with bitstream services, but innovations dependent on control of the delivery platform such as enhanced bandwidth and related services are not possible (e.g. video over DSL).

Some of these apparent disadvantages of bitstream access relative to use of unbundled loops are balanced by the fact that the alternative provider need not incur any of the risks associated with installing its own equipment on the local loop. Procuring services from the incumbent means that a provider using bitstream access can easily and rapidly expand or contract its customer base and faces no risk of technological obsolescence.

A further form of access is resale of the incumbent's entire DSL service. In this case, a reseller would purchase a wholesale equivalent of the incumbent's retail service (what we call wholesale end-to-end access). It would then market

Figure 2: Access services and the broadband value chain

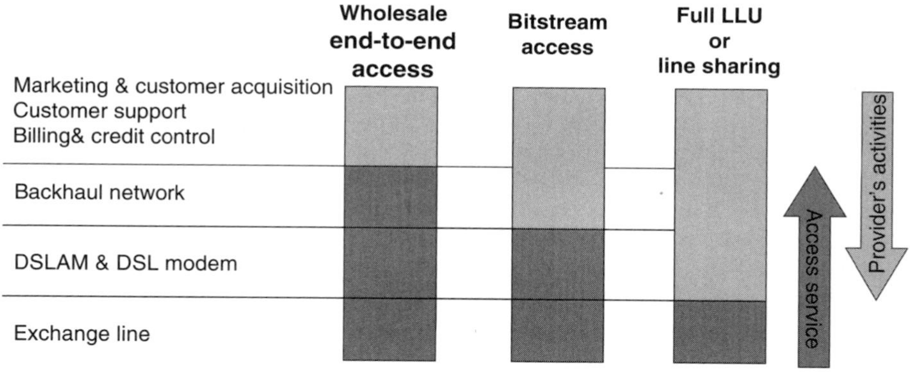

	Wholesale end-to-end access	Bitstream access	Full LLU or line sharing
Marketing & customer acquisition / Customer support / Billing& credit control			
Backhaul network			
DSLAM & DSL modem			
Exchange line			

this service and provide billing[72] and customer support. The characteristics of the service would necessarily be the same as those of the incumbent's offer. In this case, even the flexibility on pricing and packaging possible with bitstream access would be lost.

The relationship between these various access services over PSTN local loops is illustrated in Figure 2. Moving across the spectrum from wholesale end-to-end access (resale) at one end, through bitstream access and onto fully unbundled local loops at the other end, the provider becomes active deeper into the value chain and has greater control over more aspects of the service. With the possible exception of the local loop itself, all aspects of the value chain are replicable. Therefore, provision of unbundled local loops exposes much more of the value chain to competition than does, say, provision of a wholesale end-to-end access service.

3.1.5   Defining facilities-based competition

Throughout this book, we draw a distinction between facilities-based and access-based competition. This distinction matters because, broadly speaking, building facilities (infrastructure) gives fine control over the characteristics of the service offered, whereas utilising access to others' networks does not. Therefore, there is greater scope for value creation amongst firms competing at a platform level relative to those relying on access products.

This said, building out competing networks in situations where there are substantial minimum efficiencies of scale may not be viable. However, as we shall see, there is little to suggest that any aspects of broadband provision are durable natural monopolies. To the extent the local loop may be difficult to replicate in rural areas, unbundling is likely to be a sufficient remedy to address this.

---

[72] In Germany, there is an obligation on the incumbent to provide access to its billing system.

Distinguishing between facilities and access-based competition is not entirely straightforward. The clearest example of facilities-based competition is that of multiple, vertically integrated platforms providing closely substitutable services entirely over their own infrastructure, for example broadband service provision by cable and DSL network operators. This is what we call end-to-end *'platform competition'*. In this case there are multiple providers of closely substitutable services with each exerting control over the significant aspects of its value chain, thereby determining the features and cost of its services subject to competitive pressure. Platform competition can be *intra-modal* (e.g. two different mobile telephony companies competing amongst themselves), where there are multiple platforms with similar technologies, or *inter-modal* (e.g. DSL versus cable), where there are platforms with significantly different technologies, but which provide retail services that are closely substitutable for end-users.

By contrast, where a company relies entirely on reselling other operators' wholesale end-to-end products[73], this is clearly access-based competition. However, in between these two extremes, there is typically a hierarchy of service options, varying according to the extent to which a provider builds infrastructure or relies on the purchase of network services[74] from other operators. Certain types of access product require users to deploy a significant amount of own infrastructure and therefore may be described as examples of partial facilities-based competition. We provide a simplified illustration of these distinctions in Figure 3.

3.1.6 The incentives to build infrastructure

Building infrastructure gives fine control over the characteristics of the service offered. In the case of broadband, these characteristics include:

- cost (and hence the retail price);
- the service mix (e.g. ability to offer voice and/or video services cost effectively alongside data connectivity by using appropriate terminal equipment at the customer end);
- bandwidth (including its allocation between upstream and downstream links);

---

[73] By a **wholesale end-to-end product**, we mean a wholesale version of a retail product offered by a carrier. The provider would typically resell this product, providing its own customer support and billing. The characteristics of the wholesale product (e.g. quality of service, availability and so on) would be exactly mirrored in the retail product. For example, in the UK, BT's IPStream wholesale broadband product mirrors its own retail broadband offer and is resold by ISPs such as Freeserve and AOL to provide their own branded services.

[74] By a *network service*, we mean a service provided by one operator to another for the purposes of providing network connectivity that does not correspond to a retail service; rather it is just one of many elements needed to provide the ultimate retail service. For example, bitstream access to an end customer is a network service, as to offer a retail service of any type the provider would need other infrastructure or network services to provide onward connectivity from the local exchange.

Figure 3: Different categories of competition in broadband

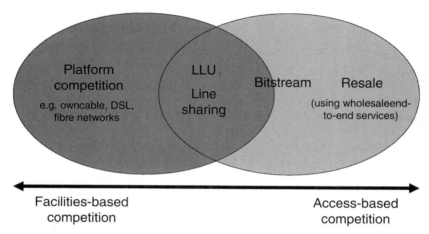

☐ latency (i.e. delay that may affect specific applications such as VoIP and video conferencing); and

☐ availability and service quality guarantees.

Choices over all these aspects of the service are present up to the point when the investment is made. However, making an infrastructure investment entails a substantial commitment as:

☐ it may be difficult to change the characteristics of the service subsequent to making the investment;

☐ the option to wait and see if better technological solutions subsequently become available may be lost;

☐ assets are likely to be largely sunk[75] and their costs are unlikely to be recovered if the service were discontinued or if demand is not as great as originally forecast; and

☐ investment in capacity may only be possible in lumps and subject to significant lead times, making it difficult to respond to unexpectedly high consumer demand.

In contrast, the use of an access service gives much less choice over service characteristics. In the case of resale of a wholesale end-to-end product, there

---

[75] Few assets are entirely sunk, in the sense that their investment costs are completely unrecoverable. However, most telecoms assets are at least partially sunk in that they have little second-hand value and there may be few alternative uses. The degree to which an asset is sunk must be assessed relative to the degree of uncertainty in the commercial environment. For example, in the very long run most assets will depreciate and have little value. Therefore, if anticipated sufficiently far in advance, it may be possible to change technologies or exit a market at little cost. In practice, the commercial environment in telecoms is likely to change rapidly relative to the lifetime of assets.

may be no choice over the service characteristics at all. However, whether using a wholesale product or combining various network services, an operator gains other forms of flexibility not possible with an infrastructure investment. In particular, an access-based entry strategy:

- makes little commitment to the market, as they are few costs that are not re-coverable on exiting the market (i.e. costs are largely scaleable and economies of scale much smaller than with infrastructure based operations);
- provides the ability to respond rapidly to unexpected increases or decreases in consumer demand, without sacrificing service quality and without any additional costs associated with holding reserve capacity;
- is not tied to a particular technology; and
- maintains the option to make an infrastructure investment at a subsequent date once technology choices are mature and likely consumer demands known.

These factors mean that an access-based entry strategy is very likely to have lower risks than an infrastructure-based entry strategy. (Of course, there is always the risk that a new regulatory agenda might sweep away the former access regime.) Providers of innovative services face substantial uncertainty: there may be competing technologies and standards, with the winners difficult to forecast; consumer demand may be highly unpredictable. Access-based entry strategies provide flexible ways to manage these risks, at the cost of less flexibility in the design of the service offered.

In general, there is clearly a trade-off between the flexibility and scaleable provided by access-based entry and the ability to set service features provided by infrastructure investments. The terms of this trade-off will change over the life-cycle of a new service. When a new service is initially offered, it may be uncertain what features of the service will be attractive to customers. Access services provide a valuable option to free-ride on the early development of a new service and see what features of the service customers value and what the most cost effective means of delivering the service might be. Consumer take-up for a new product is likely to be difficult to forecast, and so the flexibility provided by access services to scale supply up and down quickly is of great value. In contrast, the ability provided by infrastructure investment to change the features of services is of limited value, not least as it may be uncertain what features of possible services customers would value. Therefore, for new services, the terms of this trade-off are strongly tipped in favour of access-based services.

As new services mature, the terms of this trade-off shift. It becomes clearer what features of new services customers value and what are the best technologies, standards and equipment for delivering these services. Likely take-up can be predicted from experience so far. Indeed, it may be clear for the first time that the new service is likely to succeed. Therefore, as services mature, the flexibility and scalability benefits of access-based entry become somewhat less impor-tant and the ability to change service characteristics and offer differentiated propositions to customers becomes more important. The balance tips back towards infrastructure investment, but the trade-off still critically depends on the terms on which access is made available.

3.2 The current state of broadband competition

Across OECD countries, broadband access is mainly provided by two platforms: DSL and cable. Their relative share of broadband subscribers varies significantly from country to country. For example, cable leads in the Netherlands, United Kingdom and United States, whereas DSL leads in France, Germany and South Korea. Fibre networks have made significant inroads in the Swedish and Italian markets, but elsewhere alternative access technologies have not yet delivered on their potential. Overall, market share data provides *prima facie* evidence of significant competition between DSL and cable customers in most OECD countries. Analysis of pricing and marketing behaviour also indicates that there is direct competition across delivery platforms.

Broadband penetration is often portrayed as disappointingly slow by commentators. However, actual take-up has been rapid compared to many other new technologies. At end-2002, average penetration across the EU was over 8% of households, less than three years after introduction. By comparison, in most EU countries, mobile penetration only reached this level in population terms in 1997, around four years after the launch of GSM services and over a decade after the launch of analogue services. Similarly, the ITU has observed that U.S. broadband growth *"has far outstripped"* mobile growth at a comparable stage of development, and *"is likely to reach the 25 per cent penetration mark more quickly than either PCs or mobile telephones did."*[76]

Broadband has continued its rapid expansion in the 18 months to end-June 2004. Based on the latest ECTA data, EU-wide penetration climbed to over 18% of households in mid-2004, a 130% increase in subscribers over 18 months.[77] Based on the latest FCC data, high-speed lines connecting homes and small businesses to the Internet increased during the first half of 2004 to 30.1 million, representing roughly 25% of all U.S. households.[78]

3.2.1 Platform competition

The current position of DSL and cable is illustrated in Figure 4 and Figure 5, which show the recent evolution of broadband subscriber take-up by access platform across the 15 EU member countries and in the United States, respectively. In the EU, DSL is the largest platform with just over 80% of subscribers at mid-2004, up from about 70% at end-2002. By contrast, in the United States,

---

[76]ITU (September 2003).
[77]ECTA.
[78]FCC (June 2004).

Figure 4: Broadband platform subscribers in the EU 15

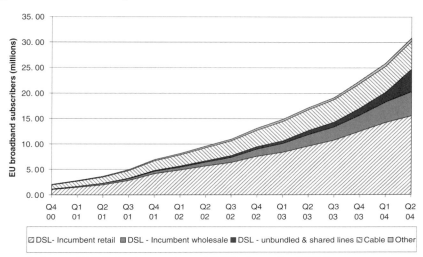

Source: Informa (2003) for data up to end-2002, thereafter ECTA

Figure 5: Broadband platform subscribers in the United States

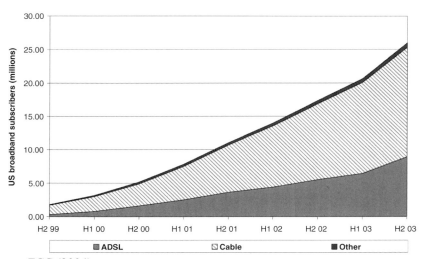

Source: FCC (2004)

cable led with a 64% market share at end-2002. Both platforms have enjoyed rapid growth in subscribers over recent years, with national growth rates of 100% or more per annum common. The fact that cable has a commanding lead in the United States and DSL has a commanding lead in the EU suggests that neither platform is technologically superior to the other.

Figure 6: Broadband subs per 1,000 households, end-2002

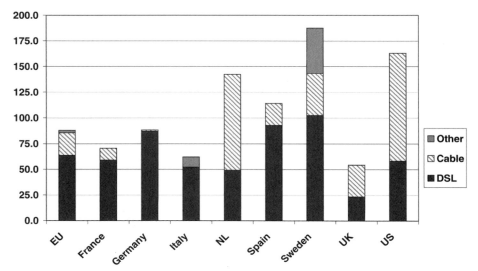

Source: Data from Informa (2003); Idate (2002); Strategy Analytics (2003)

The EU data disguises significant variation between national markets, as illustrated in Figure 6 and 7. At end-2002, cable subscribers accounted for the majority of broadband connections in Austria (60%), the Netherlands (66%), Portugal (70%) and the United Kingdom (56%) at end-2002. By contrast, DSL was the majority access platform in Belgium (59%), Denmark (67%), France (84%), Germany (98%), Italy (90%), Luxembourg (96%), Spain (81%) and Sweden (55%). This wide variety in relative cable/DSL market shares can be observed across OECD countries. For example, cable led DSL in Australia (56%), Canada (58%) and the Czech Republic (99%), whereas DSL had the larger share in Japan (67%), South Korea (63%) and New Zealand (90%), as of mid-2002.[79]

Over the 18 months to June 2004, all types of platform have enjoyed rapid growth in subscriber numbers. However, in Europe, DSL has generally grown faster than cable, owing to its larger footprint. For example, DSL has overtaken cable in terms of market share in Austria and the United Kingdom. By contrast, in the United States, cable's market lead has held steady.

In all OECD countries where broadband has taken off, DSL has established itself as a national delivery platform. However, this is not always true of cable, for two reasons:

---

[79]OECD (2002), page 14.

Figure 7: Broadband subs per 1,000 households, end–June 2004

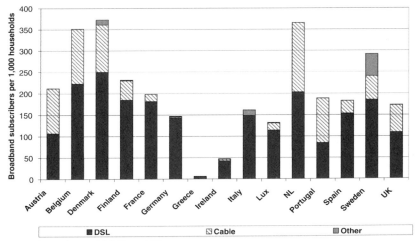

Source: ECTA (June 2004) and Eurostat

☐ Whereas DSL is ubiquitous, cable roll-out varies significantly from country-to-country (not least owing to historical factors to do with the roll-out of television services);

☐ Existing cable infrastructure often requires upgrading to carry broadband and this additional investment has not always been forthcoming (see section 2.3.2).

Figure 8 plots cable television penetration against cable's share of national broadband markets for EU and North American countries. As might be expected, there is a positive relationship between the two, which indicates that existing cable penetration is an indicator of cable broadband success. However, this is not the only driver of cable broadband take-up as, for example, the upgrading of cable infrastructure is important. For example, the strong position of cable broadband in Austria and the Netherlands can be linked, in part, to substantial new investment by UPC in upgrading its networks (see the case study of UPC in Annex II). The disproportionate success of cable broadband in Portugal has also been facilitated by new infrastructure built with broadband services in mind, although this is also because Portugal Telecom initially promoted this platform ahead of DSL. By contrast, cable broadband penetration in Germany is negligible, despite extensive cable infrastructure. This reflects the failure of domestic companies to invest in upgrading the infrastructure, which in turn can be linked to the unusual ownership structure and regulatory obstacles to industry consolidation.[80] We explore this issue further in the case study of Germany in Annex I.

---

[80] Frankfurter Rundschau (June 2003).

Figure 8: Cable TV penetration and share of broadband, end-2002

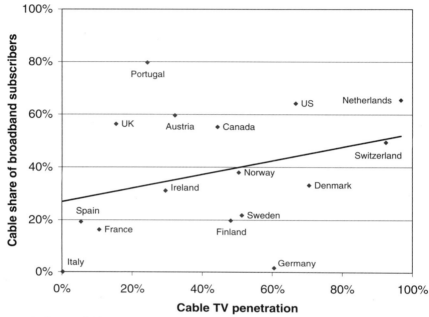

Source: Informa (2003)

In most other EU countries where there is low cable broadband penetration, this reflects the limited extent of cable infrastructure. However, in at least two of these countries, there are notable examples of new build:

☐ Italy has negligible domestic cable infrastructure and satellite dominates television. However, new entrant FastWeb has been aggressively rolling out FTTH in urban areas (see case study in Annex II), and has enjoyed significant success in winning broadband market share.

☐ The Spanish cable industry is a late developer in European terms, but Spain is one of the few countries where there is currently significant new roll-out of cable. New entrants Ono and Auna only began roll-out in 1998 but the number of homes passed had reached 38% by mid-2002[81]. Ono launched broadband services in December 1999 and is deploying a network designed to offer a triple-play of TV, telephony and Internet (see case study in Annex II).

To date, other delivery platforms have made relatively little headway in most broadband markets. Table 3 provides some examples of other broadband platform technologies being used in Western Europe. Most of these are small

---

[81] 5,438,885 homes passed, according to the Misnisterio de Ciencia y Tecnologia.

Table 3: Examples of alternative broadband platforms in Western Europe (end-2002)

Country	Type of platform	Number of subscribers†
Denmark	FWA	1,211
Ireland	FWA	5,600
Ireland	Wide-area WLAN	N/A
Italy	Fibre to the home	110,000
Italy	Satellite	65,000‡
Norway	WiFi & FWA	1,020
Spain	Powerline	3,000
Sweden	Fibre LAN	190,000
United Kingdom	Satellite	4,000
United Kingdom	FWA	2,500
United Kingdom (Scotland)	Powerline	N/A

†May include more than one provider; ‡May 2002, one-way satellite only
Sources: Informa (2003); ETNO (2003); Netsystem website

scale, and typically aimed at either niche markets (e.g. the UK satellite operation) or still at an experimental stage (e.g. the Spanish and UK powerline operations). However, there are some notable success stories, most prominently FTTH entrants FastWeb Italy and B2 in Sweden, which had 16% and 24% of the broadband access market respectively at end-2002, demonstrating the potential for technologies other than DSL and cable (see section 4.2 and Annex II). Also in Italy, satellite operator NetSystem claimed an impressive 65,000 subscribers in non-DSL areas by May 2002, although this is only a one-way satellite service; the return path is by analogue modem.[82]

There have also been a number of failures. Notably, many of the FWA (WLL) who launched from 1999 onwards have failed, victims of over-aggressive roll-out target and over-ambitious subscriber targets. These companies include Broadnet, FirstMark, Callino, LandTel, Associated Com and Winstar in France and Germany[83], and Liberty Broadband in the United Kingdom. Meanwhile, Bredband Benelux, the Belgian sister company of Sweden's B2, which launched in mid-2001 with a target of 400,000 connections, went bankrupt with just 475 customers.[84]

One other area where there is significant 'alternative' network roll-out is 3G mobile. As of June 2004, there were over 1.5 million 3G subscribers spread

---

[82]www.netsystem.com.
[83]Idate (2002).
[84]Paul Budde Communications (June 2003), page 7.

across Austria, Denmark, Italy, Sweden and the United Kingdom.[85] This number is set to expand rapidly, with leading MNOs, such as Vodafone, launching 3G services in late 2004. Most early service offerings have been focused on providing voice and video, rather than broadband data transfer. Hence, 3G has not yet had an impact on the broadband subscriber market. However, this is certain to change. All the major European incumbent MNOs already market GPRS for data transfer over their 2G networks, which can be used as a substitute for narrowband internet access. Using 3G to provide such services at broadband speeds is an obvious step forward.

3.2.2   Take-up of access products

Rather than develop their own delivery platforms, many alternative providers of broadband services use access to existing networks. In EU member states, much access-based entry to date has been on the basis of regulated access obligations on telephony networks. Cost-based unbundled local loops and line sharing are available in all EU states, as a result of the 2000 Unbundling Regulation, although NRAs have considerable discretion over terms and conditions. The basis for pricing bitstream access and wholesale end-to-end services varies substantially from country-to-country: as of 2003, some EU countries did not mandate access in these areas (see Table 5).

The resale of and bitstream access to wholesale DSL lines from incumbents is currently much more prevalent across the EU than take-up of full LLU and line sharing (see Figure 9 and Figure 10), notwithstanding the more limited extent of regulation in this area. According to the June 2004 ECTA Scorecard (see Table 6), there were:

- □ 4.8 million incumbent wholesale lines (bitstream and resale) provided by other operators/ISPs, up from a combined total of 1.8 million in March 2003; and
- □ 1.25 million unbundled lines[86] and 1.18 shared access lines, up from 423 million and 77 million respectively in March 2003.

In absolute terms, the largest volumes of resale or bitstream-based entry can be observed in large EU countries where regulated access terms are available, namely France, the United Kingdom, Italy and Spain. However, significant resale entry can also be observed in some countries where entry terms have been commercially negotiated, notably Austria, Belgium and Portugal (in Belgium, Belgacom is obliged to make a reference offer). There are also examples of ISPs negotiating access deals with cable companies; notably, in the Netherlands, the ISP Wanadoo provides broadband services over both KPN's DSL network and rival Casema's cable network.

---

[85]Baskerville (2004).

[86]These are unbundled lines used for broadband deployment, rather than all unbundled lines.

Figure 9: DSL connections by type of provider, EU15 June 2004

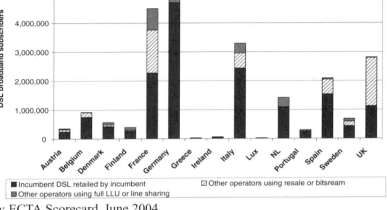

Source: ECTA Scorecard, June 2004

Figure 10: DSL connections by type of provider, EU15 March 2003

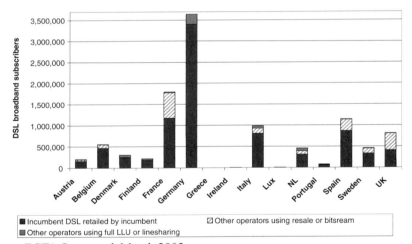

Source: ECTA Scorecard, March 2003

With respect to wholesale access, Germany is an unusual case. According to the ECTA scorecard data, there are no wholesale lines in Germany. However, this is somewhat misleading, as although Deutsche Telekom does not offer inter-connection at the ATM level, it does offer interconnection at the IP level. This means that the subscriber line stays with Deutsche Telekom but the customer is free to select the ISP. As of mid-2003, around 850,000 (24%) out of 3.6 million DSL subscribers in Germany used alternative ISPs.

Table 4: Access prices for full LLU and line sharing (euros)

Country	Full LLU		Line sharing LLU	
	One-off charge	Monthly rental	One-off charge	Monthly rental
Austria	54.5	10.9	109.00	5.45
Belgium	54.86	11.86	54.86	2.32
Denmark	44.80	8.30	35.25	4.15
Finland*	216.00	14.60	160.00	7.00
France	78.70	10.50	78.70	2.86
Germany	70.56	12.48	74.91	4.77
Greece	36.12	10.60	141.89	6.89
Ireland	121.52	16.81	123.41	9.00
Italy	32.00	8.30	44.50	2.80
Luxembourg	91.13	15.79	168.78	7.54
Netherlands	79.01	13.50	89.19	5.60
Norway	139.50	17.83	74.00	9.83
Portugal	82.50	11.96	149.80	7.82
Spain	20.00	12.30	26.97	4.77
Sweden	Up to 168.35	11.47	71.06	5.47
UK	131.00	15.08	174.00	6.57

*weighted average
Sources: Cullen International, Q1 2003; Ovum, March 2003; Telecom Italia

Table 6 shows that only seven of the EU15 have significant take-up of LLU and shared lines (more than 5% of all broadband lines): Denmark; Finland; France; Germany; Italy, the Netherlands and Sweden. With the exception of France and Sweden, these are the same countries that had significant LLU take-up in early 2003. Often, the activities of a single entrant have had a substantial impact on take-up of LLU, where such access is being used as part of a strategy to offer value-added services to customers. For example, as of March 2003, HanseNet (Germany, LLU), FastWeb (Italy, LLU); and CyberCity (Denmark, shared lines) accounted for 18%, 56% and 52% of all unbundled lines in their respective countries. In the remaining eight Member states, unbundled lines accounted for fewer than 2% of all broadband lines. We discuss possible explanations for the generally low take-up of LLU across Europe, especially when compared to bitstream take-up and resale in section 5.4.3.

Looking across the EU as a whole, a narrow majority of LLU take-up is of fully unbundled lines, rather than shared lines, despite shared lines being generally cheaper (see Table 4). However, this is almost entirely due to the large number of fully unbundled lines in Germany and Italy, where there are particular considerations. In Italy, FastWeb takes fully unbundled lines, but does not use the

Table 5: Availabillty of resale and bitstream access in selected European countries, 2003

| | Availability of: | | | |
| | Resale | Bitstream | | |
Country	wholesale end to-end service	Handover at parent ATM switch	Handover at ATM switch nearest DSLAM[†]	Legal basis and /or pricing rule
Austria	No	No	Yes	Commercially negotiated
Belgium	No	Yes	No	Reference offer required
Denmark	Yes	Yes	Yes	To be included in standard interconnect offer, at cost-related pricesXS
France	Yes	Yes	No	Prices set by NRA at a level "sustainable for efficient new entrants"
Germany	No	No*	No	
Greece	No	No	No	
Ireland	No	Yes	Yes	
Italy	Yes	Yes	Yes	Retail minus, with margin approx 50%
Luxembourg	No	No	No	
Netherlands	Yes	Yes	No	Reference offer required
Norway	Yes	Yes	Yes	Reference offer required
Portugal	Yes	No	No	
Spain	Yes	No	Yes	Retail minus pricing
Sweden	Yes	Yes	Yes	
Switzerland	Yes	No	No	Reference offer required
UK	Yes	Yes	Yes	Retail minus pricing

†Reduced backhaul requirements relative to handover at a parent ATM switch;
*available if alternative operator uses its own IP network.

Table 6: Take-up of wholesale and LLU access offers for DSL broadband across EU states, June 2004

Country	No. of DSL lines	No. of incumbent DSL lines						No. of OLO lines used for broadband					
		Total		Retailed by incumbent or its ISP		Wholesale (resale or bitstream)		Total		OLO fully unbundled lines		OLO shared access lines	
		No.	%	No.	%	No.	%	No.	%	No.	%	No.	%
Austria	355,718	320,700	90.2%	249,400	70.1%	71,300	20.0%	35,018	9.8%	35,000	9.8%	18	0.0%
Belgium	916,071	908,638	99.2%	747,875	81.6%	160,763	17.5%	7,433	0.8%	4,795	0.5%	2,638	0.3%
Denmark	562,112	484,110	86.1%	427,322	76.0%	56,788	10.1%	78,002	13.9%	49,884	8.9%	28,118	5.0%
Finland	400,000	306,600	76.7%	277,100	69.3%	29,500	7.4%	93,400	23.4%	61,800	15.5%	31,600	7.9%
France	4,490,487	3,759,767	83.7%	2,270,407	50.6%	1,489,360	33.2%	730,720	16.3%	13,066	0.3%	717,654	16.0%
Germany‡	5,350,000	4,700,000	87.9%	4,700,000	87.9%	0	0.0%	650,000	12.1%	650,000	12.1%	0	0.0%
Greece	22,927	21,845	95.3%	10,245	44.7%	11,600	50.6%	1,082	4.7%	932	4.1%	150	0.7%
Ireland	56,880	55,500	97.6%	44,955	79.0%	10,545	18.5%	1,380	2.4%	280	0.5%	1,100	1.9%
Italy	3,292,258	2,955,000	89.8%	2,435,802	74.0%	519,198	15.8%	337,258	10.2%	337,100	10.2%	158	0.0%
Lux.	20,493	19,752	96.4%	18,101	88.3%	1,651	8.1%	741	3.6%	741	3.6%	0	0.0%
NL	1,419,700	1,089,590	76.7%	1,086,536	76.5%	3,054	0.2%	330,110	23.3%	32,500	2.3%	297,610	21.0%
Portugal	297,154	292,864	98.6%	260,339	87.6%	32,525	10.9%	4,290	1.4%	4,290	1.4%	0	0.0%
Spain	2,086,172	2,043,728	98.0%	1,535,179	73.6%	508,549	24.4%	42,444	2.0%	40,302	1.9%	2,142	0.1%
Sweden	685,967	587,200	85.6%	434,000	63.3%	153,200	22.3%	98,767	14.4%	10,972	1.6%	87,795	12.8%
UK	2,807,850	2,794,000	99.5%	1,123,600	40.0%	1,670,400	59.5%	13,850	0.5%	7,580	0.3%	6,270	0.2%

Source: ECTA Scorecard, June 2004; ‡Does not include subscribers connecting to non-incumbent ISPs at the IP level, of which there were approximately 850,000 in Germany as of mid-2003

Table 7: Monthly subscription rates for selected broadband products of incumbent DSL and cable operators in EU countries, July 2003

All prices in euros; Max download speeds in kbps	Incumbent DSL operator & selected product	Leading cable operators & selected products		DSL price as % of	
				Max cable price	Min cable price
Austria	**Telekom AonSpeed 1 GB**	chello	**LiWest 24SPEED Privat standard**		
Monthly fee	40.62	49.05	42.15	83%	96%
Speed	512	600	768		
Belgium	**Belgacom Skynet Go**	chello	**Telenet mono**		
Monthly fee	39.54	39.95	41.95	94%	99%
Speed	3000	600	3000		
Denmark	**TDC Ubregraen- set bredband**	Telia Stofa FlatRate 512			
Monthly fee	58.5	57.16		102%	102%
Speed	512	512			
France	**Wanadoo eXtense 512 k**	chello Noos	**NC internet performance**		
Monthly fee	45.42	44.05 39	40	103%	116%
Speed	512	512 512	512		
Germany	**Deutsche Telekom**	**Primaspeed Pro**	**Ish Internet**		
Monthly fee	49.98	39	39.9	125%	128%
Speed	768	1024	2000		
Ireland	**eircom i-stream**	ntl Always-On 600			
Monthly fee	54.45	40		136%	136%
Speed	512	600			
Italy	**Tin-it Tin-It Alice pro**				
Monthly fee	36.95 54.95	N/A		N/A	N/A
Speed	256 640				

Table 7: (cont.)

Netherlands	KPN Planet Internet	chello	Casema	Essent		
Monthly fee	52.25	49.95	49.95	47.95	105%	109%
Speed	768	1500	800	2000		
Portugal	**SAPO ADSL.PT**	**TV Cabo Speed-on**		**Cabivisau**		
Monthly fee	34.99	35		45.50	100%	130%
Speed	512	640		512		
Spain	**Telefonica**	**ONO**		**Auna**		
Monthly fee	39.07	39.03		30	100%	130%
Speed	256	300		300		
Sweden	**Telia 500**	**Com Hem**	**Tele2 Kabel**	**chello**		
Monthly fee	41	32.09	27.22	38.16	107%	151%
Speed	500	512	512	640		
Unitedm Kingdo	**BT Openworld**	**ntl**		**Telewest**		
Monthly fee	43.05	35.88		42.83	101%	120%
Speed	500	600		512		

Notes: Selected products only, excludes special offers. DSL prices exclude cost of renting phone line; cable prices exclude discounts for subscribing to other services or rental for others services where this is essential to obtain broadband.
Sources: Company websites, surveyed by DotEcon, 11 July 2003

low-frequency part of the line, choosing instead to provide voice services using VoIP. Although taking a shared line would be cheaper, FastWeb presumably chooses not to do this, as it would risk sharing the line with an alternative voice provider who would compete with its own VoIP service. Therefore, the decision to use fully unbundled lines is presumably a commercial one intended to develop its VoIP services. By contrast, in France, the Netherlands and Sweden, take-up of shared lines in 2003-04 has significantly outpaced take-up of fully unbundled lines.

3.2.3   Price competition and product differentiation

The European broadband consumer market since 2002 has been characterised by two major trends: price reductions and increased differentiation in product offerings. Both are consistent with the maturing of broadband into a mass-market product; these trends are similar to those observed in the mobile telephony market during the late 1990s and early 2000s. Competition between DSL and cable operators for subscribers appears to be an important driver of both price decreases and product differentiation.

Almost all European markets experienced significant broadband price reductions since 2002. For example, Forrester Research found that broadband prices across EU countries fell by an average of more than 20% during 2002 (based on a comparison of the lowest available offerings of more than 128 kbps downstream).[87] The largest declines occurred in the United Kingdom (52.5%), Austria (49.2%) and the Netherlands (42.2%), all countries where both DSL and cable companies have been investing heavily in rolling out broadband services.

shows a snap shot of monthly subscription charges for selected broadband services in July 2003 offered by incumbent DSL and cable operators in EU countries, taken from company websites. Where operators offer more than one broadband product, we have attempted to select products with similar speed and usage restrictions (nevertheless, care should be taken in drawing conclusions about relative pricing, as service offerings vary). As would be expected in a situation where cable and DSL operators are competing directly for customers, there appears to be a tendency for their prices to both decline and converge. In eight of the twelve countries surveyed, the prices charged by the incumbent DSL operator and at least one of the main cable operators are now within 10% of each other.

The United Kingdom provides a useful example of the way in which platform competition has led to both a reduction and convergence in broadband access prices (for further detail, see the case study in Annex I). Figure 11 shows the evolution of monthly subscription charges for broadband access from leading UK providers. A number of key features stand out:

☐ In the absence of competition from DSL, cable providers ntl and TeleWest initially charged quite high prices.
☐ The cable operators responded to the launch of BT's ADSL product in mid-2000 by introducing price cuts totalling around 50% from their launch levels. BT has subsequently cut its wholesale access prices for DSL, facilitating competitive prices cuts by leading ISPs.
☐ Perhaps the most striking feature of Figure 11 is the way in which prices of the nine leading broadband providers have converged as the market has matured. Most notably, between March and December 2002, the range of the highest to the lowest price fell from over £20 to less than £6 (excluding ntl's 128/150 kbps offering).

The importance of competition across DSL and cable in contributing to these prices falls has been widely recognised. For example, Peter Waller, UK Deputy Director General of Telecommunications, commented in June 2003 that:

---

[87]Forrester (June 2003a).

Figure 11: UK monthly suvscription charges for broadband access from leading UK providers (excluding VAT)

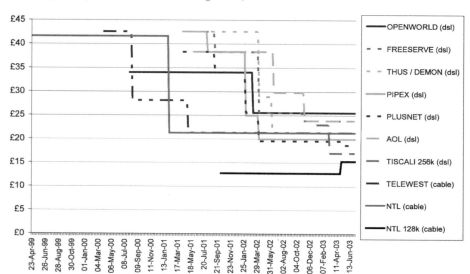

Source: BT and company websites (NB Prices for BT Openworld, ntl and Telewest from launch dates; others from April 2001)

"Service providers in the UK are offering competitive broadband to consumers through a choice of platforms including a number of DSL and cable providers, resulting in a six per cent drop in broadband prices in the last six months"[88]

The UK now has a particularly competitive retail market, owing to the profusion of ISPs offering broadband access via BT's wholesale ADSL product. Nevertheless, it is apparent that the key step changes in price competition have been the actions taken by the cable operators and by the incumbent BT. Price changes by independent ISPs that essentially resell BT's product have, unsurprisingly, had a much smaller impact, their room for pricing innovation being inevitably constrained by their limited ability to influence the cost base and service characteristics of their products.

The convergence between cable and DSL prices for broadband is also apparent in relation to other delivery platforms aimed at the mass market. Table 8 shows a selection of monthly subscription offers from operators using alternative platforms. Notably, FastWeb and Bredbandsbolaget, Europe's only large-scale, private fibre operators, price their products at comparable levels to the standard offer of the local incumbent DSL provider. Similarly, the operators of new Powerline and WiFi offerings in the United Kingdom have pitched their standard products at similar prices to the ISP of incumbent ADSL provider BT. By

---

[88]Europemedia (June 2003).

Table 8: Monthly subscription rates for selected broadband products using alternative plarforms, July 2003

Provider & product (country)	Platform	Max download speed	Monthly sub	Premium (discount) to incumbent DSL offer∗
Bredbandsbolaget (Sweden)	Fibre	10 Mbps	320 Kr (35 euros)	(15%) (15%)
FastWeb (Italy)‡	FTTH	10 Mbps	67 euros	(4%)
Strato (Germany)	Satellite	1.6 Mbps	7.49- 29.99 euros +	na
Tiscalisat (Germany)	Satellite	400 Kbps	92 euros	100%
Tiscalisat (UK)	Satellite	400 Kbps	£59.99 (87 euros)	207%
Liberty Broadband (UK)†	FWA	512 Kbps	£39.99 (58 euros)	33%
Scottish Hydro-Electric (UK)	Powerline	2 Mbps	£29.99 (43 euros)	0%

Sources: Company websites, July 2003 (except Liberty Broadband Sept 2002)
Notes: *Based on comparisons with offers in Table 7; ‡Product includes telephone line (comparison based on tin.it pro broadband subscription plus cheapest line rental with Telecom Italia); †No longer available, as the company has stopped trading

contrast, satellite services are typically more expensive, which reflects their current niche market proposition targeted at customers who cannot receive broadband by other means. One notable exception is German satellite Strato which has a series of subscription packages starting at as little as 7.49 euros per month but with extra charges per MB downloaded which vary depending on the priority you require when traffic is congested. FWA operators appear to be struggling to develop a viably priced product, as illustrated by the failure of Liberty Broadband in the United Kingdom, which a contemporary press article attributed to "competitive market conditions.".[89]

With platform competition driving prices down, non-price product differentiation is likely to become increasingly important. This is evident in the increasing diversity of products offered by European operators. Most initial broadband offers by DSL and cable operators were based on the standard model for dial-up

---

[89]ComputerWeekly .com(january 2003)

charging: all-you-can-eat access (subject to certain caps) in return for a fixed monthly fee. Subsequently, however, they have experimented with a variety of different pricing and product offerings:

☐ *Multiple product offerings.* Many companies now offer a variety of broadband products, usually differentiated on the basis of maximum download speeds. For example, in France, Wanadoo (DSL) offers products with download speeds of 128, 512 and 1024 kbps, while cable companies UPC chello and NC Numericable both have products at 128 and 512 kbps. Some companies have also introduced products with data usage charges instead of (or with reduced) fixed monthly fees.

☐ *Special offers.* Many operators are attempting to gain customers through price discounts. For example, at the time of the survey above, Tin-it (Italy DSL) was offering a 20% discount off its monthly subscription rates for the first year and free installation (normally 154.80 euros); ntl (UK cable) was offering free installation (normally £75-50); and BT Openworld (UK DSL) was offering the first month rental free.

☐ *Extras.* Various 'extras', such as multiple e-mail addresses, portal access, and web hosting are usually included in the product. For example, all KPN's Planet Internet (Netherlands DSL) ISP residential ADSL offerings include five e-mail addresses and 25MB of webspace. Similarly, its cable rivals UPC and Essent both offer five e-mail addresses, plus 10MB and 25MB of webspace, respectively. Meanwhile, BT and Telefónica have enjoyed some success with introducing cheap 'no frills' broadband connections without any such extras.[90]

☐ *Double-play and triple-play offerings.* By linking broadband access to telephony and/or television packages, operators can boost overall take-up of services and differentiate themselves from rivals with more restricted offerings. For example, FastWeb (Italy fibre) offers combined broadband and telephony packages, with television as an optional extra, while TeleWest (UK cable) offers a £4.99 discount off its broadband monthly subscription to users who also take its telephony service.

Importantly, most of these options for product differentiation are available to companies irrespective of platform.[91] When one company introduces a new product that is successful, rivals can and often do replicate their offers, especially at the low-end of the market, where new offerings are unlikely to require new infrastructure. For example, in the Netherlands in mid-2002, KPN introduced a cut-price 34.90 euros, 256kbps product in parallel with its standard 768 kbps offering. The largest cable company, UPC, did not immediately

---

[90] Forrester (June 2003).

[91] The most difficult aspect to replicate will typically be the double or triple play strategies of rivals on other platforms (i.e. for DSL to offer video services or cable to offer voice), as this may require new network investment. We discuss the impact of double and triple play offers on competition in Section 1.8.5.

respond, probably owing to concern that it would cannibalise its own higher-speed product. However, after losing market share, it introduced a new 300 kbps product at 34.95 euros a month. The other main cable operators have also introduced products at similar speed levels.

3.3   Summary of country case studies

To supplement our analysis of competition in broadband markets, we undertook case studies in mid-2003 of seven countries with very different competitive structures:

- □ Germany;
- □ Netherlands;
- □ Republic of Ireland;
- □ South Korea;
- □ Sweden;
- □ United Kingdom; and
- □ The United States.

A summary of the main observations from each study is provided in Box II below and the full case studies can be found in Annex I. Our main observations from these case studies are as follows:

- □ There are many examples of vigorous competition between operators using different platforms, usually but not exclusively cable and DSL, for example: the Netherlands; Sweden; South Korea; United Kingdom; and the United States. Competition between alternative platforms, rather than between providers using access products, stands out as the key driver of price and product innovation by operators.
- □ The Netherlands shows that where there is extensive cable rollout there are few competitive problems. Competition between DSL and cable platforms is intense.
- □ Amongst alternative delivery technologies, FTTH (led by Italy and Sweden), WLANs/WiFi (led by South Korea and the United States) and 3G (all countries) appear to have the most promising prospects, both in competition with and as complements to existing DSL and cable networks.
- □ Regulatory interventions can have a detrimental impact on the development of platform competition or broadband penetration or both. Countries where regulatory errors appear to have been made include Germany (ownership rules making cable broadband upgrades difficult), Ireland (delays in DSL roll-out owing to a dispute over access terms) and the United States (very cheap access terms creating disincentives for DSL roll-out). Meanwhile, the Netherlands and South Korea, in particular, appear to have benefited from relatively light regulatory intervention, especially in the first few years of market development.

☐ In the aftermath of the telecoms bubble economy, there is uncertainty about the prospects for further roll-out and upgrades of competing platforms. The regulatory environment – especially the use of subsidies and the terms of access to networks – is likely to have a significant impact on business cases for facilities investment.

We develop these points in more detail in chapter 5.

Box II: Summary of main observations from the mid-2003 case studies of broadband competition

Germany

☐ Very little platform competition, with DSL having a 98% market share at end-2002.
☐ Ubiquity of cable television across Germany suggests there is considerable scope for platform competition. However, regulatory-induced problems with ownership structures have prevented upgrading.
☐ Lack of platform competition stands out as a key reason why broadband penetration lags behind European leaders, such as Netherlands and Sweden.
☐ Some evidence of alternative providers using LLU as a way of entering the market with a partial facilities-based strategy, creating competition on a regional basis.

Netherlands

☐ Cable networks established an early lead in broadband penetration, forcing incumbent KPN to accelerate DSL roll-out.
☐ Highly competitive broadband market characterised by high penetration, low prices and product innovation, notwithstanding late entry of service providers using access to KPN's network.
☐ Further upgrading of cable networks may be threatened by government initiatives to open access to cable and roll-out a national fibre network.

Ireland

☐ Irish broadband penetration lags well behind all other EU countries (except Greece), despite above average Internet usage.
☐ Performance is partly the result of late DSL roll-out. However, it also reflects the lack of platform competition and a regulatory environment that favours wholesale access over facilities-based competition.
☐ Ireland is unlikely to catch up with other EU economies for the foreseeable future without new facilities entry, which looks unlikely in the present regulatory environment. Irish broadband penetration lags well behind all other EU countries (except Greece), despite above average Internet usage.

South Korea

- South Korea is the world's leading broadband market in terms of broadband penetration.
- Platform competition – led by three rival DSL and cable providers – has played a key role in stimulating demand through low prices and service innovation.
- A combination of limited access regulation and government stimulation of both infrastructure and demand has helped stimulate penetration.
- The geographical distribution of the population and existing infrastructure are particularly favourable for the roll-out of fibre, cable and DSL (including VDSL) services. However, the way that consumers use the internet is similar to users in other OECD countries, suggesting much of Korea's success in terms of penetration is replicable in Europe.

Sweden

- Europe's most competitive broadband market, with many customers enjoying a choice of DSL, cable or fibre LAN.
- Amongst the lowest prices and highest penetration rates in Europe.
- A test bed for the development of fibre optic LANs both as a competitor and complement to DSL and cable.
- Government subsidies are being used to promote broadband take-up but are also a potential source of uncertainty for private operators.

United Kingdom

- The introduction of broadband in the United Kingdom lagged other leading OECD economies and was initially characterised by high prices
- Since mid-2001, intense competition between DSL and cable providers has pushed prices down and driven rapid penetration growth
- Low prices and rapid growth are expected to continue for the foreseeable future, with DSL overtaking cable as the leading delivery platform

United States

- Competition between cable and DSL has been a key determinant of market growth and falling prices.
- Asymmetric regulation has held back roll-out of DSL, enabling cable to consolidate its early lead in terms of broadband market share.
- Despite cheap access to incumbent networks, competitive entry by many CLECs has proved unsustainable, owing in large part to excessive spending on customer acquisition.
- 2004 could see increasingly aggressive competition between DSL and cable players bundling voice, data and video services.
- WiFi poses a potential new competitive threat to existing broadband players.

4 New entry and market outlook

In this chapter, we examine the scope for new entry in broadband markets and the general outlook for competition. The first part identifies the main dynamics that affect broadband entry decisions, including the potential positive and negative implications of regulatory intervention on entry incentives and thus competition. In the second part, we summarise a series of case studies of entrant broadband providers in OECD countries (the full case studies can be found in Annex II). These studies highlight the scope for successful facilities-based entry in EU markets and the benefits that they can bring in terms of product and pricing innovation. However, they also reveal the threat to the business case for new facility-based entry posed by public policy interventions that favour mandated cheap access and/or particular technologies. In the third part, we examine the outlook for broadband competition in the EU, drawing on industry forecasts to develop a central scenario, then examining upside and downside risks. Although industry forecasts are quite downbeat about the prospects for new facilities-based entry, they largely extrapolate current trends based on a weak investment climate and do not consider the impact of new mobile technologies. The upside potential for facilities-based competition appears considerable, but is critically dependent on the emergence of regulatory frameworks that do not discriminate in favour of access-based entry.

4.1   Entrant choices

Entrants in the broadband market face a number of choices:

- ☐ whether or not to enter the market;
- ☐ whether to build facilities, lease unbundled network access from an incumbent, resell an incumbent's service, or engage in a combination of these; and
- ☐ what type of platform/technology to offer service over (if a facilities-based structure is selected).

Entrants weigh these choices on the basis of business case analysis. The decision to enter a market can be thought of as the decision to invest resources in that market. Any profit-maximizing firm's investment decision will depend on a calculated risk – that is, a firm must weigh the probability that it will earn an excess return from the investment against the risk of investment loss. A corporate finance manager will generally make an investment only if they can construct a business case for the investment has a positive expected net present value (NPV), which is to say, if the sum of the expected cash flows generated by the asset during each future time period, discounted at the project's weighted average cost of capital (WACC), is positive.[92]

Investment opportunities are often mutually exclusive, so there are often a number of positive expected NPV projects that a firm will not undertake. The firm will choose the investment option that generates the *highest* expected NPV, even though the forgone investment option may also offer a positive expected NPV. A firm that is debating between facilities-based entry and access-based entry, for example, will weigh the trade-off between the flexibility and scalability provided by access-based entry and the ability to set service characteristics provided by infrastructure investment. As access-based entry tends to be less risky than infrastructure investment (see discussion in section 3.1.6), this type of entry may offer a higher expected NPV even if its overall upside potential is lower than for infrastructure investment.[93]

For an entrant, the NPV of investment in broadband, in turn, depends on a large number of factors, such as market dynamics, deployment costs and technology constraints, and capital dynamics. A further critical factor affecting the expected NPV of broadband entry is the current and prospective regulatory environment.

4.1.1   Why entrant decisions matter

Entry decisions matter because, all else being equal, entry will increase competition in the market. Generally, entry will enhance consumer welfare by lowering prices and by increasing the range of available service offerings. Entry can also place pressure on firms to be more efficient, which may lead to further consumer gains. Often, a single entrant can have a significant impact on both the price and adoption rate of broadband service in a particular market. In some cases, an entrant will have an impact that extends beyond its service area. For example, in Sweden, the launch in 1999 of a 10 Mbps FTTH service by facilities-based entrant B2 for only 22 euros per month pushed Swedish DSL and cable providers to respond by lowering their prices to similar levels, even though B2's service area was limited (see case study below).

All entry, however, is not the same. The long-run benefits to consumers from facilities-based entry, in which the entering firm constructs its own network over which it delivers broadband service, generally significantly exceed those from non facilities-based entry, in which the entering firm provides service to consumers over an incumbent's network. We will discuss this at length in section 5.2. Entrants typically have available a spectrum of entry opportunities ranging from pure resale (in which an entrant merely resells the services of an incumbent) to the construction of an entirely new network. An entrant may also pursue a mixed strategy, in which it constructs some infrastructure on

---

[92]Brigham, Gapenski, and Daves (1996), page 216; Razavi, Brealey and Myers (1996) page 14.
[93]For an explanation of the relationship between conventional NPV investment rules and option valuations, see Dixit and Pindyck (1994).

its own and leases certain network elements from an incumbent. Facilities ownership typically requires much more investment, but provides a broadband entrant with greater flexibility over its products, prices, and costs. Furthermore, an entrant credibly commits itself to the market by making the investments in sunk assets associated with a facilities-based strategy, whereas a reseller may be able to exit the market relatively painlessly in response to a change in market conditions. Facilities-based investment is thus much more likely to offer sustained competition to incumbent carriers.

4.1.2   Factors affecting entry choices

A number of factors affect a firm's decision to enter a market and the type of strategy it employs. These factors can be grouped under four main headings:

- □ market dynamics – consumer profiles and behaviour, and the number and type of projected competitors;
- □ deployment costs – other factors that affect capital and operational expenditure;
- □ capital availability – access to and cost of capital; and
- □ the regulatory environment.

In the following subsection, we explore how regulatory initiatives could accentuate or distort resulting investment incentives for operators. Our main observation is that with European broadband markets still at an early stage of development, there are considerable opportunities for existing and new entrants to build viable businesses, based on facilities or access-based strategies. However, the uncertainty about the future direction of broadband technology and consumer demand for related services makes choosing the right strategy difficult. In particular, although facilities-based entry strategies offer much greater upside revenue potential, this is balanced by significantly greater risks than for access users. Given the cautious attitude within capital markets towards telecoms investments at present, this means that regulatory intervention (or even perceptions of future regulatory intervention) could have a pronounced effect on entrant activity over this period.

Market dynamics

Projected revenues as well as some key cost categories (such as marketing) are closely tied to expectations about consumer demand and the extent to which this subscriber acquisition will be contested between operators. Residential and business demand for broadband services is projected to grow strongly across all EU countries (see section 4.3.1) and this is likely to be a key driver of entry over the next five years. However, at the same time, entrants are likely to face an increasingly crowded competitive landscape.

Key market dynamics determining entry choices will include:

☐ **Projected demand for high-speed Internet.** The absolute size and growth
  rates of broadband markets vary widely across the EU. A number of factors
  underpin these differences:

  1. Surveys of high-speed internet take-up suggest that overall demand for
     broadband is closely correlated with income levels, which reflects the
     fact that consumers do not currently consider broadband to be an essen-
     tial good.[94] The wealthier European markets, such as Denmark and the
     Netherlands, can be expected to remain amongst the leading economies
     in terms of penetration.
  2. Other factors usually linked to broadband take-up include age, education
     and computer/internet awareness. Younger generations are typically more
     likely to use broadband services. This may tend to restrict the ability
     of European countries to match the success in broadband penetration of
     South Korea, where the population is much younger (just 10% over 60 and
     25% under 15).[95] Education and PC/internet penetration are fairly strong
     across the EU, but a few countries – notably Sweden – have exceptionally
     youthful profiles, which suggest they will remain European leaders in
     broadband.
  3. Cultural differences may also affect the willingness-to-pay of consumers.
     For example, the less prominent the primary language of a particular
     set of consumers is on the Internet, the less value those consumers will
     place on Internet access of any kind. Academic studies have also shown
     that some countries are more receptive to new products than others. For
     example, Tellis, Stremersch and Yin (surveying 150 products across 16
     Western European countries) observed that the average take-off time for
     new products in Scandinavian countries is half that of Mediterranean
     countries.[96]

Notwithstanding these differences, over the next five years, all the EU countries
(with the possible exception of Greece) are expected to experience very rapid
broadband market expansion. These will make them all potentially attractive
markets for entrants, as it tends to be easier for entrants to build brand awareness
and acquire new customers in an expanding market. For the leading broadband
economies, the next five years may be particularly crucial as market penetration
could rise to above 50%, meaning that entrants who launch after this period
may find it harder to build market share.

☐ **Availability of broadband content and demand for high-bandwidth services.** More innovative broadband services, such as on-line gaming and

---

[94]Hausman (2003).
[95]Enders Analysis (2002).
[96]Trellis, Stremersch & Yin (2003).

video-on-demand, have so far made only a very limited impression on European consumers. However, in Japan and South Korea, demand for such services has boomed. IDC believe that the availability of more broadband-specific content will stimulate European demand for broadband in general and more bandwidth in particular.[97] The extent to which demand for such services will take-off in the next five years is somewhat uncertain, but growth would most obviously promote new facility-based entrants, as such companies (witness FastWeb in Italy and B2 in Sweden) are most obviously likely to combine the technology and flexibility required to develop this market.

☐ **Existing competition.** The number and type of existing competitors in a market clearly has a big impact on an entrant's expected profits in a broadband market. Facilities-based entrants, who require significant market share to recoup large sunk costs, are most likely to target markets where competition is currently limited or pursue market segments which appear underserved or both. Some of the most successful broadband economies, such as the Netherlands, Sweden and Belgium already have quite crowded fields. While this does not preclude new entry, it will increase the importance for new entrants to be able to differentiate themselves from competitors, either through new services or marketing spend. However, there are still a number of leading EU economies where the incumbent operator faces limited competition at present, notably Germany. Such countries are particularly likely targets for new entry. Indeed, the successes of FTTH operator FastWeb (Italy) and cable company Ono (Spain) illustrate the scope for new facility-based entrants to challenge incumbents where competition was hitherto limited. By contrast, the failure of FTTH operator Bredband Benelux in Belgium shows how much harder it is to launch in markets where there already several competing platforms.

☐ **Projected competition.** Expectations about other entry will also affect the decisions of entrants. Business cases for facility-based entrants are typically particularly sensitive to assumptions about the number of competitors, given the need to gain market share and revenues to cover sunk costs. For access users, this is less of a threat, given that their investments are more scalable. As a result, the potential threat of multiple competition from new entrant access users is an important factor affecting the business case for new facility entry.

☐ **Cost of customer acquisition.** The more crowded the competitive field, the greater the likely cost of customer acquisition, including advertising, special promotions (e.g. free installation) and other marketing activities. In the short term, consumers benefit from these greater information flows and price reductions. However, such benefits may be lost in the medium term if the cost of customer acquisition rises to the extent that the business case of many entrants becomes unviable. This appears to be what has happened in many U.S. regional markets, where low access prices attracted what now appears to be excessive, unsustainable entry.

---

[97]IDC (2003), page 17-20.

☐ **Synergies from other operations.** An established telecommunications or media firm may already possess the customer base or general business knowledge necessary for successful entry into the broadband market. This is most obviously reflected in the success that cable companies and incumbent telephony providers have had in penetrating European broadband markets. Similarly, new entrants may increase their chances of successful entry by exploiting synergies between the provision of multiple services. For example, ONO entered the Spanish broadband market in 1998 by deploying a cable network that allowed it to bundle internet access with telephony and television services. Attempts to exploit synergies both within and across markets may encourage two significant trends in entry over the next five years:

1. Cable and fibre companies will push triple-play strategies (combining internet, telephony and television and possibly other videocommunication services), and DSL operators will respond by launching video-over DSL services. The development of new broadband technologies, such as VoIP, will make it possible for a much wider array of platforms to provide multiple services. New technology may also facilitate the entry of mobile operators as direct competitors for broadband subscriptions.

2. Successful companies in national markets may seek to exploit their expertise abroad through new entry or foreign takeovers or both. Early signs of this potential trend include FT's takeover of UK ISP Freeserve and Telecom Italia's purchase of HanseNet.

Deployment costs

Many of key factors that determine deployment costs – such as urbanisation, topography and labour – are largely pre-determined.

Key factors affecting deployment costs and thus entry choices will include:

☐ **Degree of urbanisation.** Most broadband technologies, especially fixed-line ones, can be deployed much more cost effectively in densely populated areas. Many of the countries with high levels of platform competition are also those high urbanisation rates, e.g. the United Kingdom (90%) and South Korea (83%). A related factor affecting deployment costs is the percentage of the population in a given market who live in multiple-dwelling units (MDUs), where residences can share a common line from the network. Spanish broadband entrant ONO considers that it has been able to deploy its network more cheaply than comparable companies in part because its service area has a high urban population density with a significant portion of MDUs.[98] In South Korea, which leads the world in broadband penetration, 60% of the population lives in MDUs.[99]

---

[98]Cableuropa (2003).
[99]Enders Analysis (2002).

☐ **Topography.** It is cheaper to deploy wireline broadband technologies to a land area that is flat and continuous than to an area that is mountainous or that is significantly 'interrupted' by water (such as a series of small islands).[100] Although water does not pose as much of a cost constraint on wireless networks, uneven topography does makes wireless networks more costly.

☐ **Cost of labour.** A broadband entrant must hire employees for its business and (depending on its strategy) employ workers to construct its physical network infrastructure. Owing to local economic factors, changing labour laws and the degree of unionisation, the cost of labour can vary significantly across countries. The United States National Research Council, together with a number of other research bodies, notes that fibre installation costs *"ultimately are tied to the cost of labor."*[101]

☐ **Cost of network construction.** An entrant that wishes to deploy its own wireline broadband network will typically have to trench (dig and lay wires) under city streets and other existing infrastructure. Local planning laws, and street and building lay-outs can have a big impact on the cost of trenching in that city. A potential entrant that can avoid trenching for all or part of its network will have a significantly greater incentive to invest in deployment. For example, Italian broadband entrant FastWeb was able to avoid significant trenching costs by using an existing network of ducts, passing over 1.5 million homes, that had been constructed for defunct cable television project.[102] Similarly, Spanish broadband entrant ONO realized significant savings by building portions of its network above ground.[103]

☐ **Technology.** The relative cost of and type of services that can be delivered over different technologies will have a big impact on entrant choice between different types of facility entry and access use. Relative costs and the type of services that can be offered are essentially driven by two factors: technological advance; and technology penetration, which drives economies of scale in production. With respect to penetration, it is apparent that cable, DSL, and fibre technology will enjoy advantages in terms of economies of scale over the next five years. However, the pace of technological change is sufficiently fast that these cost advantages could be at least in part offset, most obviously by advances in wireless technology.

☐ **Cost and availability of backhaul.** The availability and price of access to other networks to provide backhaul has an impact on entrant's build or buy decisions. In certain instances, cheap backhaul may encourage complemen-

---

[100] Indeed, in its 1998 Annual Report, Commonwealth Telephone Co. cited the fact that its service area (located in Pennsylvania of the United States) is located *"in the midst of mountains, rivers and streams"* as one of the primary reasons that it had *"one of the most defendable incumbent local exchange carrier franchises in the industry."*

[101] Committee on Broadband Last Mile Technology, Computer Science and Telecommunications Board, Division on Engineering and Physical Sciences & National Research Council (2002), Introduction.

[102] Cisco Service Provider Solutions (2002).

[103] Cableuropa (2003).

tary facilities entry. For example, in Sweden, B2's FTTH business case is in part based on linking its own local networks to municipal optic networks.

Capital availability

The surge in demand for broadband in recent years in many EU economies has coincided with a pronounced downturn in capital market sentiment towards the telecoms sector in general and internet-related businesses in particular. This has made it very difficult for both existing and potential entrants to obtain the funding necessary to support their network roll-out plans. Facility-based entrants are particularly vulnerable owing their large upfront funding requirements and the associated higher investment risks. A number of broadband market entrants have failed – for example, many of the FWA operators in France, Germany and the United Kingdom – or been forced into bankruptcy protection – for example cable companies, UPC, ntl and Telewest.

The change in the funding environment is one factor explaining why platform competition varies so much both between and within EU countries. Most obviously, where cable companies invested heavily during the boom years in upgrading networks to carry broadband, some consumers have reaped the benefits of resulting competition (even if some of these companies have subsequently faced cash crises). Unfortunately, other areas where new building started later did not benefit from boom-driven investment to the same extent.

Against this background, the outlook for the next five years is rather uncertain. There are signs of a fragile recovery. For example, the three cable companies mentioned above are all expected to emerge from bankruptcy protection in 2003, helped in large part by operational success in attracting broadband subscribers. Meanwhile, the WiFi sector is enjoying something of a mini-boom, with extensive investments in hotspots across Europe, mirroring similar advances in the United States. However, with memories of the recent telecoms slump likely to remain strong in the medium term, any recovery is likely to be vulnerable to exogenous shocks, such as a high-profile market failure or adverse regulatory rulings. Indeed, the Economist in June 2003 ran a short report speculating whether WiFi could be the next dotcom bubble.[104]

4.1.3   Impact of regulatory conditions on entrant choices

The purpose of supply-side regulatory intervention may be either to facilitate competition by increasing the attractiveness of entry,[105] or to control the market power of an incumbent broadband provider. Regulatory intervention can affect

---

[104] The Economist (June 2003).

[105] A government could conceivably intervene on the demand side of the broadband market by providing consumers with broadband credits or subsidies, or by facilitating the development of compelling broadband content.

the entry decisions of firms by altering the expected NPV of various entry options. Regulation or subsidies targeted at a particular type of technology or type of entry may distort investment incentives for other technologies and types of entry. For example, a hypothetical subsidy for cable broadband providers would decrease the incentives for entrants to invest in DSL technology. The net effect of selective regulatory intervention on consumer welfare may be negative, especially in cases where resale or leased access is promoted at the expense of facilities-based competition.

Regulatory intervention can affect a broadband entrant's investment incentives either direct or indirectly:

1. Direct effects

☐ Regulatory intervention has the potential to alter the relative return on investments from access and facilities-based investment strategies and therefore to encourage entrants to pursue one type of entry at the expense of the other. This may have the result of decreasing investment in new facilities.

☐ Some entrants use a combination of facilities investment and access products. For example: FastWeb uses DSL over unbundled lines to reach areas not covered by its FTTH network; and Bulldog, a UK operator, provides DSL services over unbundled lines in London, but uses bitstream access in other parts of the country to extend its reach and reap economies in marketing. For such operators, the relative costs of access products and new facilities are critical in the decision to further develop their own networks. If access prices are set too low, such entrants will be encouraged to delay or even scrap plans to extend their network, with the result that consumers will be denied the more extensive services that are available over the companies' own networks.

☐ A regulatory policy that allows entrants to lease access to the local loop from an incumbent on a short-term basis provides the entrant with "*the right but not the obligation*" to use those network elements indefinitely.[106] The entrants' leasing option spares them the risk associated with the sunk costs of a network construction by the incumbent. If the value of the option is not incorporated into the price of leased access, an entrant will have an incentive to postpone or forgo altogether investment in its own facilities and network.[107] We consider the need to reflect option values in access prices in detail in section 5.3.3.

☐ Studies have demonstrated that subsidisation of the non facilities-based approach through artificially low leasing rates decreases the total number of new facilities-based lines constructed because the substitution effect (existing entrants substituting from constructing lines to leasing lines) outweighs the

---

[106] See Hausman (2000).

[107] See Hausman (2000); Crandall, Ingraham and Singer (2004). For an application of real options analysis to telecommunications investment, see Alleman and Noam (1999); Hausman and Sidak (1999).

output effect (access to unbundled lines inducing new entrants who engage in a mix of leasing and construction).[108]

□ The threat of future regulation can cause similar distortions to actual regulation. The absence of clear commitments for regulatory forbearance on new services in existing EU frameworks leaves facility-based entrants potentially exposed if they are successful. In Europe, regulators have generally not made commitments regarding forbearance of regulation on new services, so a facilities-based entrant has no assurances that it would not become the victim of access regulation, itself, if it should become successful. Similarly, if future access terms are uncertain, entrants may be encouraged to pursue bitstream or resale entry rather than using full unbundling or shared lines, as being active in less of the value chain requires less investment and exit is easier.

2. Indirect effects

□ Access regulation and subsidies can have a big impact on the likely evolution of competition in a broadband market. Actual or expected entry by one set of entrants may undermine the business case for entrants pursuing a different entry strategy. This might be detrimental to overall welfare if, say, a new facilities-based entrant was deterred from rolling out its network because the market had become crowded with ISPs reselling an incumbent's DSL services. For example, in Spain, Ono's next phase of cable network roll-out involves increasingly marginal areas, where even a small reduction in demand owing to competition from resellers could potentially undermine its business case.

□ Perceptions of regulatory policies, including both current frameworks and possible future initiatives, can also have a big impact in investment sentiment towards a particular sector. If regulation is seen as favouring a particular type of entry strategy or technology, then investors are likely to favour entrants pursuing such approaches. Thus, any bias in regulatory policy is potentially accentuated. Second, regulatory uncertainty may discourage investors from funding broadband entrants in general.

In summary, regulatory intervention can have a significant effect on the investment decisions of potential broadband entrants, particularly at the margins. There exists a particular danger of regulatory bias against facilities-based competition because an entrant who constructs its own facilities will take longer to enter a market than an entrant who merely resells the services available from an incumbent provider. Regulators in search of a 'quick fix' to what they

---

[108]Using an econometric model on state-level U.S. data, Crandall, Ingraham and Singer (2004) found that decreases in UNE rates decrease the total number of new facilities-based lines. They concluded on the basis of the available data that the number of facilities-based lines in the United States would have increased by between 98,000 and 524,000 if the U.S. UNE rates were increased by 10 percent. Crandall, Ingraham & Singer (2004) *supra* note 107, page 13-14.

view as high broadband prices may, by encouraging non-facilities based invest-ment in activities such as resale and LLU leased access, distort the business cases of potential facilities-based entrants. Indeed, there is strong evidence that unbundling policies can discourage facilities-based investment.[109]

4.2 Entrant case studies

In Annex II, we present case studies undertaken in mid-2003 of entrant operators in European and North American markets:

☐ Bredbandsbolaget (B2), a Swedish fibre operator;
☐ e.Biscom (FastWeb), an operator in Italy using FTTH and DSL over unbun-dled lines;
☐ HanseNet, an operator in Hamburg, Germany, using DSL over unbundled lines;
☐ Ono, a Spanish cable operator;
☐ UPC (chello), a cable operator offering broadband in nine European coun-tries; and
☐ selected U.S. competitive local exchange carriers (CLECs).

A summary of the main observations from each study is provided in Box III. Our main findings from these studies are as follows:

☐ The success of companies such as B2, FastWeb and Ono illustrate the poten-tial for new entrants pursuing a facilities-based strategy to challenge and win market share in broadband internet provision from fixed-line incumbents.
☐ Non-DSL entrants, such as B2, UPC chello and FastWeb, have typically played a key role in driving price and product competition within their local markets, illustrating the advantages of platform competition between DSL and cable/FTTH. B2 and FastWeb, in particular, stand out as arguably the most innovative operators in Europe in terms of new services.
☐ Some entrants are using local loop unbundling as a complement to facilities-based strategies. Notably, HanseNet uses unbundled lines to connect cus-tomers to its local network, while FastWeb and B2 use DSL over unbundled lines to reach homes where it is not yet cost effective to extend their fibre networks to the home.
☐ However, the relatively unsuccessful experience of access regulation in the United States highlights the distortions in entrant behaviour that result if access terms are set too generously. There is strong evidence that access policies deterred new facilities investment and encouraged the emergence of access-focused CLECs whose business models were ultimately unsustain-able.
☐ Looking forward, regulatory interventions and subsidies pose threats as wells as opportunities to facility-based entrants. These threats include competition

---

[109] See, for example, Crandall, Ingraham & Singer (2004), supra note 107.

from other entrants enjoying cheap access to incumbent networks; uncertainty over whether regulators might attempt to extend access regulation to cable and fibre networks; and the risk that subsidies may favour alternative technologies.

Box III: Summary of main findings from the mid-2003 case studies of entrant broadband operators

Bredbandsbolaget in Sweden

☐ New entrant using fibre LAN technology to deliver a 10 Mbps symmetric broadband service to the home.

☐ Aggressive pricing and product offering has been a key driver of competition in the Swedish broadband market.

☐ Demonstrated potential residential demand for very high speed services. However, business model remains somewhat uncertain, not least owing to reliance on interconnection with government-funded municipal optical networks.

e.Biscom (FastWeb) in Italy

☐ e.Biscom uses optical fibre networks to deliver a combination of telephony, high-speed internet access and innovative new broadband services, such as video-on-demand, through its subsidiaries FastWeb in Italy and HanseNet in Hamburg, Germany.

☐ In July 2003, it announced plans to sell HanseNet to Telecom Italia, which will ease the company's debts and free up capital to invest in developing its Italian network.[110]

☐ Where it has not yet deployed its FTTH network, it supplies services via DSL over unbundled lines. This has enabled it to more rapidly acquire customers and better manage its network roll-out costs than would have been the case with a pure fibre play.

☐ FastWeb has enjoyed impressive subscriber and revenue growth, illustrating the potential for new entrants using a facilities-based strategy to challenge incumbents with large broadband market shares.

HanseNet in Germany

☐ HanseNet uses its own fibre network and DSL technology over unbundled lines to deliver voice, data and video services to businesses and residents in the Hamburg area of Germany.

☐ Its strong operational performance demonstrates the potential for a new entrants using a facilities-based strategy to mount a viable challenge to

---

[110] e.Biscom (July 2003).

Deutsche Telekom's leading position in the German telephony and broadband markets.

□ Backed by Telecom Italia, it appears possible that HanseNet's success in Hamburg could be extended to other parts of Germany.

ONO in Spain

□ Established in 1998, Ono has rapidly rolled out a regional cable network purpose built to supply a combination of telephony, broadband internet and television services.

□ In the regions where it operates, it has gained substantial market share, establishing itself as the leading competitor to Telefónica for telephony and internet services. Despite a challenging operating environment, analysts believe it has consolidated itself as a viable market player.

□ Ono's success illustrates the potential for new entrants pursuing a facilities-based strategy to challenge and win market share in broadband internet provision from fixed-line incumbents.

UPC chello in nine European states

□ UPC has invested very heavily in upgrading its network to provide two-way communications, enabling it to develop new services, in particular broadband internet. However, its aggressive pan-European acquisition policy has also left it heavily indebted and financially weak.

□ In the regions where initial upgrades have been completed, its chello broadband products are highly competitive and often enjoy higher market shares than comparable DSL offers from incumbent ISPs.

□ UPC is a potential role model for other cable operators whose networks require upgrading to compete in the broadband market. However, the business case for UPC and other cable companies to invest further in their networks may depend critically on regulatory frameworks which do not penalise successful facilities investment.

United States CLECs

□ The FCC, under the auspices of the Telecommunications Act of 1996, mandated that competitive local exchange carriers (CLECs) have access to incumbent local exchange carriers' (ILECs') networks at regulated wholesale rates that were set below the ILECs' historical costs. The unbundling regulations are asymmetric in the sense that they do not apply to facilities-based CLECs or to cable telephony operators that offer broadband services.

□ The FCC's unbundling rules and state UNE-P rates discouraged CLECs from investing in their own facilities because the low unbundled rates increased the NPV of leasing access to incumbents' lines relative to building new lines.

□ In general, those CLEC entrants in the United States that relied primarily on unbundling have not provided a sustainable source of competition, and most have failed.

4.3   The future evolution of broadband competition

4.3.1   Industry forecasts

The next five years will be a crucial phase in the evolution of competition within EU markets. During this period, broadband is expected to evolve into a truly mass-market product, with household penetration across Western Europe rising from below 9% at end-2002 to 30-50% by 2008. Based on the experience of South Korea, the world's most developed broadband market, it is likely that market growth will slow significantly beyond this point and that there will be relatively few high value users not already signed up to a particular provider. This will make it harder for new entrants to establish themselves, as their business cases must be much more heavily dependent on inter-provider churn rather than organic growth to win market share.

We reviewed the broadband market projections (made in 2002-03) of five major forecasters: Datamonitor, Forrester, Idate, IDC, and Strategy Analytics. Although there is significant variation in their numbers, some key themes can be identified across the forecasts. These can loosely be termed the 'central scenario' for platform competition in the European broadband market. This central scenario is a plausible if somewhat conservative picture of the future:

1. **DSL** will remain the leading delivery platform across Europe. It will also gain ground in countries where it has lagged cable, especially the United Kingdom, where limited roll-out (51% of homes passed) will constrain the relative growth prospects of cable. If Europe follows a similar path to South Korea, then there will be increased use of high bandwidth DSL technologies (VDSL), where local conditions allow.
2. **Cable** will experience strong subscriber growth across Europe (with the exception of Italy). Cable is expected to expand its share in a number of countries where DSL has hitherto been overwhelmingly dominant. For example, Strategy Analytics projects cable market share to increase from 2% to 35% in Germany and 16% to 37% in France, from 2002-08. However, this growth will largely be driven by upgrading of existing cable infrastructure rather than virgin build.
3. **Fibre** will be the leading alternative delivery platform, with significant roll-out in urban areas in a number of EU states. For example, Idate projects that the market share of metro ethernet (fibre) across Western Europe will triple to 6% in the five years to 2007. Although pure fibre plays are not expected to break the hold of cable and DSL over the medium term, the picture is somewhat blurred as many new cable and DSL upgrades will involve installing fibre closer to the home.

4. **Other** fixed access delivery platforms are not expected to have a mass market role. Satellite and FWA are expected to consolidate their positions as niche technologies, serving rural and business markets respectively. The forecasters do not expect powerline to take off.

In relation to the development of broadband competition more broadly, a number of other projections deserve highlighting:

1. As penetration rises and growth slows, churn rates are expected to increase as companies compete to lure customers away from each other. Forrester expects churn rates to rise above 20% in countries with broadband penetration over 15%, compared to current churn of around 5-10%.[111]
2. In an effort to minimise churn, there will be increased pressure on companies to differentiate their services. Datamonitor highlight the potential benefits from providing access to content, such as music, video and games, high bandwidth products already very popular in South Korea.[112] Forrester emphasise the role of bundling, linking broadband access to other services, such as fixed and mobile voice, WLAN home networking and advanced services, such as video telephony.[113]
3. In this competitive environment, many resellers are expected to struggle. As IDC notes: *"It is hard for reselling ISPs to differentiate themselves, as the product features are set by the limited range of wholesale offers available. Moreover, as the wholesale prices are set all reselling ISPs to a large extent face a similar cost structure, so that pricing differentiation is hard too."*[114] Forrester expect the ranks of reselling ISPs to thin over the next 18 months.[115]
4. There is somewhat more optimism about the prospects for access-based entrants that have some control over the facilities that they are using. Nevertheless, the forecasters all expect incumbent PTOs to maintain a leading role in broadband service provision, helped by their scale advantages at both the network and service levels.

Forecasting the development of a new sector that is subject to rapid technological change is inherently uncertain. The forecasts highlighted above are generally plausible but by no means certain. Three main criticisms can be directed at the 'central scenario' developed from our assessment of industry forecasters:

1. *It is essentially an extrapolation of current trends.* Consensus forecasts in any industry typically extrapolate recent developments into the future. The forecasts for broadband development are no exception; broadly speaking, they simply extend recent trends, subject to allowances for well-understood constraints on market growth, such as local factors affecting receptiveness

---

[111]Forrester (June 2003), page 11.
[112]Datamonitor (March 2003), page 8.
[113]Forrester (June 2003), page 11.
[114]IDC (2003), page 17.
[115]Forrester (June 2003), page 10.

to new services, and constraints on cable penetration implied by limited roll-out and current financial problems. In practice, the future rarely turns out this way, especially in industries subject to rapid technical change. Typically, positive or negative shocks will alter the growth path. An alternative way of analysing potential future trends is to consider a range of plausible scenarios, and to assess their relative likelihood based on an analysis of possible drivers of such developments. We discuss alternative scenarios and possible drivers in the next subsection.

2. ***Inconsistency in expectations on competition.*** There is an inconsistency between the emphasis which forecasters place on competition driving service innovation and their moderate pessimism about the prospects for entrants to compete with incumbent PTOs. The former conclusion is an implicit acknowledgement that incumbent PTOs will face substantial facilities-based competition, given that this is widely acknowledged as the key stimulant of product and price innovation. The most obvious immediate source of this competition is cable companies.

3. ***No consideration of new mobile technologies.*** The forecasts are generally fairly pessimistic about the prospects for other platform technologies to develop as mass market rivals to DSL and cable. However, their analysis of alternative platforms is typically limited to FTTH, satellite, FWA and powerlines. They do not give proper consideration to the potential impact of new mobile technologies on the broadband access market. In particular, they fail to consider the potential role of high-bandwidth 3G services as a substitute for fixed broadband links. This is a potentially serious oversight given that: the latest W-CDMA standard (a 3G technology) can potentially offer speeds of up to 10.8 Mbps; and such services could be offered by MNOs, who (unlike other new entrants) already have the scale economies in networks, service staff, and billing systems necessary to provide a sustainable competitive challenge to DSL and cable operators.

4.3.2 Scenarios for future broadband competition

Using the 'central scenario' of European forecasters as a starting point, in this subsection, we identify alternative scenarios for the development of the European broadband market and analyse possible factors that might affect growth. The central scenario generally paints a positive picture about platform competition based on existing infrastructure but is rather pessimistic about the scope for new facilities operators to win market share. We identify more positive scenarios as ones in which there is greater facilities-based competition driving product and price innovation. More negative scenarios would be ones in which facilities-based competition is even more restricted than presently envisaged.

What are the possible developments that could result in greater facilities-based competition? Four main possibilities stand out:

1. *Extensive new cable roll-out.* Investment in new cable is stalled in many European countries as cable companies have been in financial difficulties since the bursting of the telecoms bubble. Forecasters expect these problems to continue. However, with cable broadband companies such as ntl, UPC and Ono all enjoying strong revenue growth from broadband, and cable equipment costs continuing to fall, the business case for new investment is improving. If a compelling business case for triple-play (voice, television and internet) can be established, akin to the success of the cable operators in the United States, cable is particularly well placed to benefit.

2. *Extensive new fibre roll-out.* Forecasters project only very modest fibre roll-out, mainly because they are pessimistic that the benefits of increased bandwidth will be enough to justify the investment cost. However, this could change if demand for high-bandwidth applications takes off. Notably, there is substantial new investment in fibre in Japan and South Korea, the two countries where such demand is most advanced. In the United States, ILEC investment in FTTH is expected to take-off following the FCC's ruling that it will not be subject to access regulations.[116]

3. *New mass market fixed technology emerges.* Could FWA, satellite, power-line establish themselves as mass market propositions in Europe? This would require a significant fall in their deployment costs. Possible drivers of this could include technological change or economies of scale from their deployment in developing countries, where the poor state of fixed-line telecoms infrastructure means that these technologies already have more compelling business cases than in Europe.

4. *Mobile technologies emerge as substitute for fixed access products.* As discussed above, forecasters generally ignore convergence between mobile and fixed-line data solutions. However, mobile appears to have real potential as a substitute for fixed links. Developments of 3G and WLAN technology are set to offer data rates equivalent to existing fixed-access packages.

What are the possible developments that could result in less facilities-based competition? Again, there are four main possibilities:

1. *Access-based entry crowds out facilities-based investment.* Forecasters are generally pessimistic about prospects for ISPs using access-based entry, especially resale. However, the prospects for entry of this type hinges very much on whether regulated access is available and the price at which resale is made available. Evidence from the United States suggests that mistakes in setting regulatory access can grossly distort investment flows in favour of access-based entry over facilities.

2. *Investment in DSL upgrades stalls.* A widespread assumption amongst forecasters is that European PTOs will continue to upgrade the local loop for DSL, reaching the vast majority of national populations. This looks a reasonable assumption given that such plans are typically well advanced. However,

---

[116]Cambridge Strategic Management Group (2002).

DSL roll-out could yet be stalled if shocks to the policy framework for broadband – such as very generous access terms or subsidies that favour other technologies – degrade the business case.

3. *Investment in cable upgrades stalls.* Many of the forecasters, most notably Strategy Analytics, expect cable companies to gradually upgrade remaining one-way television networks to broadband. This is clearly something that cable companies would like to do. However, given that many have precarious finances, such programmes appear vulnerable to adverse capital market or regulatory shocks.

4. *No significant investment in fibre.* Even the modest investment in fibre that most forecasters anticipate might not appear in the event of an adverse investment shock. Moreover, the business case for fibre investment is heavily predicated on demand for high bandwidth taking off. If this demand is weaker than expected or if one of the European FTTH operators (B2 or FastWeb) were to fail then the business case for new fibre could be severely set back.

We summarise these positive and negative scenarios and their potential drivers in Table 9 and Table 10. These are not exclusive and some could occur in parallel. Indeed, often they have common drivers. In particular, the following six drivers stand out as being likely to be influential in determining the ultimate development path of European broadband markets:

☐ *Technological change.* New technical developments could significantly alter the relative prospects for different broadband delivery platform. The scope for new platforms, such as mobile broadband, to take off, could be boosted significantly be new innovations.

☐ *Critical mass deployment.* The current advantages of cable and DSL as delivery platforms derive in large part from their superior global scale economies in equipment costs. These scale economies are potentially replicable if other technologies also obtain a critical mass. In this context, other technologies, such as FWA and powerline, may be better placed than DSL or cable for deployment in developing countries (such as China or India), where fixed line infrastructure is limited. Such deployment could bring down costs in general, making them more competitive in EU markets.

☐ *The investment climate.* The prospects for both upgrading of existing facilities and new build depend heavily on the availability of finance. In the aftermath of the technology and telecoms bubbles, it is not surprising that current forecasts are fairly pessimistic about funding. However, as the tech bubble itself shows, investor sentiment can change very quickly, notably in response to other drivers, such as technological innovations and the regulatory framework.

☐ *Demand for high bandwidth applications.* Prospects for fibre in particular, but also for further upgrading of cable and DSL, depend heavily on the outlook for demand for high bandwidth applications. Within Europe, this is currently quite limited. However, the Korean model suggests that demand could rise very rapidly once broadband penetration reaches a critical mass.

Table 9: Alternative scenarios that could *boost* broadband market development

Potential developments deviating from the 'central scenario'	Likelihood	Possible drivers
1. Extensive new cable roll-out	Medium likelihood – Investment in new cable is currently stalled in most European countries but this could change if existing cable operations continue to demonstrate strong cash generation	□ Compelling business case for bundling □ Improvement in investment climate □ Lighter-handed broadband regulation, especially with respect to access obligations and overall prices
2. Extensive new fibre roll-out	Medium likelihood – Superior technology to DSL and cable in search of a compelling business case. Also, many cable and DSL networks use fibre networks	□ Demand for high bandwidth applications takes off □ Improvement in investment climate □ Lighter-handed broadband regulation, especially with respect to access obligations and overall prices
3. New mass market fixed technology	Low likelihood – FWA, satellite and powerline established as niche delivery technologies but no evidence to date that they are viable as mass market propositions	□ Critical mass deployment □ Improvement in investment climate □ Lighter-handed broadband regulation, especially with respect to access obligations and overall prices
4. Mobile technologies emerge as substitute for fixed access products	High likelihood – Extensive investment in 3G, WiFi and 'new mobile' services is taking place, with widespread roll-out likely in the medium term	□ Mobile applications launched which offer data rates equivalent to fixed access packages □ Incremental price of adding broadband access to mobile offerings is competitive with fixed access

Table 10: Alternative scenarios that could *impede* broadband market development

Potential developments deviating from the 'central scenario'	Likelihood	Possible drivers
1. Access-based entry crowds out facilities investment	Medium likelihood – Resale and bitstream access regulation becoming more prevalent in EU	☐ Strong domestic pressures on NRAs to grant generous access terms to incumbent DSL networks ☐ Excessive entry at resale level drives up customer acquisition costs to unsustainable levels
2. Investment in DSL upgrades stalls	Low likelihood – Programmes for DSL in most EU countries are already well underway	☐ Access regulation undermines business case for new facilities investment ☐ Government subsidies create uncertainty and/or favour other platforms (e.g. fibre) ☐ Consumers unresponsive to bundling offers
3. Investment in cable upgrades stalls	Medium likelihood – Required funding may not materialise if financial market confidence in telecoms does not improve	☐ Access regulation undermines business case for new facilities investment ☐ Government subsidies create uncertainty and/or favour other platforms (e.g. fibre)
4. No significant investment in fibre	Medium likelihood – Requires substantial upfront investment costs	☐ Demand for high bandwidth applications fails to take off in medium term ☐ Access regulation undermines business case for new facilities investment

☐ *Receptiveness of consumers to bundling*. Many commentators believe that bundling broadband with related products, such as voice and television, can help companies differentiate their products and win market share. Cable and fibre technologies, in particular, are suitable for offering bundled services, and the business cases for new roll-out might benefit from consumer responsiveness in this area. Mobile technologies may also be able to expand their market share by linking broadband data to more traditional mobile services.

☐ *The regulatory framework*. Regulation can have a critical impact on the investment incentives for new entrants. In some cases, LLU may be used by facilities-based entrants to enhance their business cases, which may bring benefits where platform competition is weak. However, ill-conceived access regimes may undermine the case for new investment; in particular, mandated bitstream and especially resale access products could encourage access-based entry at the expense of new facilities investment. Meanwhile, government initiatives to promote broadband, such as infrastructure or demand subsidies, could skew the development path if they champion particular technologies over others.

From the perspective of a policymaker seeking to foster faster broadband deployment, an understanding of these drivers in critical. Intervention in the market through access regulation and/or subsidies can have big impact on other market drivers, such as industry choices between technologies and investment sentiment towards entrants, with unintended consequences for general market development. We address this issue in greater depth in section 5.3.

5 Analysis of competition in broadband markets

In this chapter, we analyse the appropriate market definition for broadband and assess the relative merits of facilities and access-based competition, in light of the evidence presented in chapters 3 and 4. We observe that broadband services delivered over different platforms have similar characteristics and are close substitutes for each other, but are rather different from narrowband services. Therefore, it is appropriate to consider the need for, and the appropriate design of regulatory policy, against the background of a separate market for broadband services comprising all (actual and potential) delivery platforms.

We show that facilities-based competition brings benefits that are not achievable through access-based competition, and that platform competition is demonstrably feasible. In any case, even where platform competition is only emerging, LLU (if priced appropriately) should be sufficient to act as a competitive safeguard (and should avoid distorting new entrants' choices in favour of access-based competition).

These arguments are supported by empirical evidence showing a strong positive relationship between platform competition and broadband penetration, but no corresponding evidence that access-based entry has stimulated penetration. We also find evidence that regulated bitstream access and resale tends to crowd out facilities-based competition.

5.1 Defining the market

The new European regulatory framework is strongly based on competition law principles and seeks to identify relevant markets in which there might be competition problems requiring regulation. Thus, the first step in applying this framework is to identify relevant markets based on the substitutability of products and services (see Annex III for a brief introduction to general principles of market definition).

We have already seen in section 2.1 that broadband provides much greater functionality than narrowband. There is reasonable evidence that the extent of substitutability between narrowband and broadband services is insufficient to suggest that they lie in a single relevant market. However, what about broadband services delivered over different platforms? Are these all in the same relevant market? We show in this section that broadband delivered over different platforms compete strongly, regardless of issues such as the ability of cable networks to offer triple play services (TV, telephone and broadband).

Although there is geographical heterogeneity in competitive conditions in broadband provision, pricing is typically geographically uniform, so the benefit of more strenuous competition in some areas is passed to all customers. Further, the issue of geographic heterogeneity in competition should not be overstated, as broadband services can be and are being deployed in fringe areas with low population density.

Despite the needs of small businesses being quite different to those of residential customers, both groups can be served by the same broadband delivery platforms. SME demand for broadband is a potentially significant driver of take-up rather than constituting a distinct customer segment.

5.1.1   Substitution between different platforms

Whereas broadband and narrowband lie in separate relevant markets, broadband services provided over different platforms provide generally similar experiences for the end-customer and must be considered as belonging to the same relevant market. We start by considering substitution between DSL and cable, where there is a variety of evidence from disparate sources and different countries that these platforms compete strongly.

Substitution between DSL and cable

Consumers view DSL and cable modem service as being close substitutes. According to a consumer poll conducted by Harris Interactive in 2000, "subscribers saw little difference between DSL and cable modem services."[117] Similarly, close to half of those surveyed in a study by the Yankee Group and the Satellite Broadcasting and Communications Association who had an interest in broadband service expressed no preference between DSL, cable, or satellite service.[118] McKinsey and J.P. Morgan assert in their 2001 broadband industry report that consumers do not differentiate between various broadband technologies: "most consumers are platform agnostic – or more precisely, *platform ignorant.*"[119]

DSL and cable operators appear to be keen to combat this ignorance, including information on the relative merits of DSL and cable services on their websites and extolling the virtues of their own particular technology and/or service relative to their competitor's. For, example:

☐ NTL Ireland's website claims that its broadband service is "faster", "better" and "cheaper" than any other residential broadband service provider in Ireland. It illustrates this claim with a table comparing key characteristics of its Always-On 600 service with incumbent DSL provider eircom's i-stream starter product.[120]

---

[117]CyberAtlas (December 2000).
[118]Yankee Group (March 2001).
[119]McKinsey & Co. and J P Morgan H&Q (April 2001).
[120]www.ntl.com/locales/ie/en/athome/internet_cable.html (September 2003).

☐ Telefonica has a webpage entitled 'ADSL vs. cable' which compares them on the basis of a number of metrics, such as line sharing, speed and security.[121]

However, what these comparisons really show is how similar the products are[122], and how cable operators and DSL providers are in direct competition for their customers.

Substitutability of cable and DSL is also evident in the pricing strategies of European providers. We have already seen in section 1.1.1 that:

☐ there has been convergence of prices for broadband over DSL and cable;
☐ innovation in providing new services on one platform has lead to a response by the other platform, with similar services being introduced; and
☐ price changes by one platform produce a competitive response in the pricing of the other platform.

This is compelling evidence of competitive interaction between DSL and cable.

As in EU countries, DSL and cable broadband providers in the United States view each other as competitors. For example, AT&T (now Comcast) promotes its cable modem service to both business and residential customers as a competitor to DSL.[123] According to Comcast's 2001 Form 10-K filing with the Securities and Exchange Commission, Comcast considers DSL to be its most important competitor in the provision of mass-market broadband Internet access services.[124] Indeed, Comcast refuses to air local DSL advertisements on its cable television networks because it perceives DSL to be competitive with cable modem service.

A measure for the extent to which DSL and cable are substitutes is the cross price elasticity of demand between the two services. Two academic studies[125] have estimated the cross price elasticity of demand for DSL in the United States with respect to a change in the price of cable. Using econometric techniques to analyse data on the choices of thousands of broadband and dial-up customers across the entire country, the authors conclude that there is a statistically significant and positive relationship between the price of cable modem services and the demand for DSL. This shows that cable modems constrain the pricing of

---

[121] www.telefonicaonline.com/on/es/micro/adsl/v2/home/index.html (September 2003).

[122] One significant criticism often levelled at cable by DSL providers is that shared use of bandwidth means that cable customers may suffer reduced speeds during busy periods; however, cable operators can and do resolve this problem by adding new infrastructure capacity, splitting congested fibre nodes.

[123] Applications for Consent to Transfer of Licenses and Section 214 Authorizations from MediaOne Group, Inc., Transferor, to AT&T Corp., Transferee, CC Dkt. No. 99-251, AT&T Reply Comments at 80 (filed Sept. 17, 1999) (calling DSL services *"the most obvious competitors of broadband cable modem services"*).

[124] Comcast Cable Communications (2001).

[125] Crandall, Sidak and Singer (2002a); Rappoport, Kridel, Taylor and Duffy-Demo (2001), Table 10; see also Rappoport, Kridel and Taylor (1999).

DSL service, and hence that DSL does not constitute a product market distinct from cable.

The U.S. FCC initiated a proceeding to investigate whether substitution between cable and DSL is sufficient to find incumbent DSL providers non-dominant in the supply of broadband services. In its analysis, the FCC considers whether the firm or firms at issue has market power by virtue of a more favourable cost structure or greater resources.[126] In February 2003, the FCC voted to discontinue the unbundling of the high-frequency portion of the copper loop for DSL service for new customers in one year and for all customers in three years.[127] This vote ended the former "line-sharing" rule that compelled the incumbent local exchange carrier (ILECs) to lease at regulated prices the upper frequencies of their copper lines to rivals such as Covad.[128] Although the FCC has not ruled formally on the issue of dominance, the agency's decision to end unbundling of components for DSL service provision demonstrates that the FCC does not believe that the ILECs possess market power. Indeed, as of December 2002, the ILECs' share of the residential broadband Internet access market was approximately 36%, roughly *half* of AT&T's share of the U.S. interstate long distance market when the FCC declared AT&T to be non-dominant.[129]

Fibre as a substitute for DSL and cable

A typical FTTH broadband service is able to offer all the features provided by DSL and cable platforms, including voice telephony services and TV/video distribution. For example, Fastweb in Italy offers a triple-play package. FTTH offers a proposition that, from the customer's perspective, is very similar to cable and DSL, even if the underlying delivery technology is different.

Despite having the potential to provide greater bandwidth and functionality than cable and DSL in the long term, fibre services are offered and priced in competition with cable and DSL, given that at present few applications require such massive bandwidth. For example, as of July 2003, Fastweb's FTTH offer was priced at a slight discount to Telecom Italia's Tin-It pro DSL offer (see Table 8).

In new-build situations, the costs of digging trenches (where necessary) and running cables are the same for fibre as for copper loops, creating strong incentives to install fibre in anticipation of future bandwidth requirements. Therefore, the extent of competition from fibre is strongly dependent on the extent of new building and the extent of urbanisation. In the long term, as new high-bandwidth applications emerge, FTTH may have advantages over cable

---

[126]FCC (1995).

[127]FCC (Febuary 2003a).

[128]FCC (November 1999).

[129]FCC (June 2003b), Table 5.

and DSL, increasing the competitive pressure on those platforms to modernise their networks.

3G services as a substitute

Although mobile data services such as GPRS (also called 2.5G) only match the data rates achievable on fixed analogue connections, 3G services are being deployed that will provide data rates comparable with those on some broadband services. As discussed in section 3.2.1, as of late 2004, most leading MNOs in western Europe have either launched 3G services or have firm plans to so in 2005.

Future developments in mobile data services are uncertain and it is likely that there will be a mix of competing technologies. Nevertheless, fears expressed by some commentators in 2002-03 about 3G roll-out being permanently stalled were misplaced. In the longer run, mobile operators are likely to have good incentives to deploy 3G technology both to increase the range of services offered and to make more efficient use of scarce radio spectrum. Moves towards liberalisation of radio spectrum licensing in the EU are likely,[130] which may ultimately allow mobile operators to reuse existing spectrum currently used for 2G services for 3G.

A lack of available handsets, often blamed to be an impediment to roll-out, is likely to have only a limited effect. Clearly, manufacturers typically seek reasonable certainty of demand for new features at a sufficiently large scale (at a global level) before committing to developing new handsets. Until handsets become available in sufficient supply, it can be difficult for mobile operators to market new services. However, this co-ordination problem is common in the introduction of new services, and is usually overcome. Recent experience with GPRS and MMS shows that once the handset bandwagon is rolling, take-up of new services by customers can be rapid; there is now widespread availability of these new mobile services and take-up of compatible handsets within a year or so of introduction.

The potential future of 3G services is best illustrated by the case of Japan, where the take-up of advanced mobile data services is ahead of the EU. Following a trial in May 2001, NTT DoCoMo began the full-scale commercial rollout of FOMA, the world's first 3G mobile communications service, in October 2001. Based on w-CDMA standards, FOMA provides high-speed packet-based data communications with speeds of up to 384 Kbps. This is comparable with fixed broadband. At June 2003, coverage was almost 93% of Japan's population The range of services offered via FOMA has greatly increased since its introduction and includes: i-motion (which combines audio and video to deliver movie previews and more); and a multi-access service (which allows subscribers to simultaneously use their mobile phones for calls and data communications).

---

[130]For a detailed discussion of the scope for trading and liberalisation of radio spectrum in the EU, see Analysys, DotEcon and Hogan & Hartson (2004).

Novel services targeted at corporate users such as remote monitoring for construction sites or daycare centres, and remote learning systems via videophone are also being promoted. NTT DoCoMo intends to expand the FOMA coverage area, expecting to reach 97% of Japan's population by March 2004[131], while simultaneously enhancing the quality of services.

Despite concerns about delay in roll-out following the large licence fees paid in 3G auctions, it is reasonable to expect growing 3G deployment and take-up over time across the EU. Even if data rates available in the EU do not match those available in Japan (as some mobile operators only anticipate deployment at 196 Kbps), 3G will provide an alternative to mid-band to low-end fixed broadband services. As 3G handsets are deployed, an increasing number of mobile customers will have the potential to use high-speed data services though their handsets.

Once widely available, these mobile data services will compete with fixed broadband services in the same way that mobile voice services now provide a significant competitive constraint on fixed voice. Although initial take-up of mobile phones may have been driven by particular users' needs for mobility, the falling price of mobile voice telephony relative to fixed services has led to significant substitution. At the same time, growing demand for access due to increased use of the Internet has been met in part by migration of voice traffic onto mobile phones to free existing fixed lines. For example, a 2002 econometric study based on extensive market research data found statistically significant evidence not only substitution of fixed calls by mobile calls, but also replacement of entire fixed lines by mobile phones. The extent of substitution has grown over time.[132]

Substitution of fixed data traffic by mobile services can be expected to emerge in a similar manner. Like early mobile voice telephony, mobile data is at present being marketed primarily at particular customer groups such as mobile workers and business customers. However, falling prices, easier to use products and improving content should encourage broader adoption, turning this into a mass-market product in the same way as mobile telephony is now ubiquitous.

Substitution between fixed and mobile data services may occur in unexpected ways. For example, someone with a 3G handset who is an occasional user of data services might find it more cost effective to use a mobile connection rather than incur the expense of installing and maintaining a fixed connection. This is analogous to substitution of fixed access lines by mobiles by low users (such as those who are rarely at home, or who use mobile telephony for second homes). Therefore, 3G may play an important role not just for those with particular needs for mobility, but also for occasional broadband users. Although 3G provides a less cost effective platform for, say, broadcast TV distribution or video-on-

---

[131]NTT DoCoMo (2002).
[132]Horvath and Maldoom (2002).

demand than cable, FTTH or DSL platforms, there are classes of user who are likely to find 3G a reasonable substitute for fixed services.

Further, the cost structure of 3G is likely to lead to a strong competitive dynamic, with large increases in network capacity and mobile operators in search of revenues to generate from that capacity. As has happened with voice telephony, mobile operators may find themselves with network capacity that needs to be filled up and may offer tariffs aimed at encouraging exactly such substitution behaviour from fixed services.[133]

New and niche technologies as substitutes

We have seen in section 2.3 that there are a variety of other technologies capable of delivering broadband and, thus, offering an alternative to cable, DSL, and FTTH propositions.

For example, there has been renewed interest in fixed wireless broadband, where a number of European countries have sold or plan to sell spectrum at 3.5 GHz. For example, in the United Kingdom, PCCW acquired a national licence that it is using to roll-out a wireless broadband service (under the trading name UK Broadband) using technology from IP Wireless. Fixed wireless effectively provides a wireless local loop and could deliver services very similar to those provided over DSL and cable.

WiFi technologies are attracting much interest and have the potential to be used to provide a nomadic alternative to fully mobile data services such as 3G. Given the low costs and general availability of equipment for WiFi, this is likely to provide a significant degree of competition for 3G for some classes of user (e.g. a laptop user requiring a sporadic rather than permanent connection to the Internet). Just as with 3G, such nomadic WiFi services have the potential to compete strongly with broadband for particular groups of users. WiFi has the added advantage that its data rates are greater than 3G and comparable with most broadband services.

However, in addition, WiFi also has the potential to be deployed as a means of connecting customers to an underlying backbone network[134] and effectively to provide a wireless local loop. WiFi is already being used to provide broad coverage public access networks. Used in this way, WiFi has more in common with fixed wireless access. Data rates can easily match or exceed those currently available on DSL or cable given sufficient backhaul capacity.

Wireless technologies are characterised by low costs of joining customers to the network once the network infrastructure is in place. For example, once a fixed

---

[133] For example, Orange has at various times offered tariffs in the United Kingdom that have been marketed as fixed-line replacements. One2One (now T-mobile) at one time offered discounted off-peak prices aimed at filling otherwise underutilised network capacity.

[134] Wireless bridging can also be used to provide some core networking through WiFi links, rather than needing backhaul.

wireless base station is in place, joining a customer simply requires installation of an antenna and terminal equipment at the customer's home or premises. A broad coverage network based on WiFi does not even require this, as the customer will typically be able to connect with off-the-shelf equipment (wireless LAN adaptors are now built into many laptops as standard).[135] Therefore, wireless network operators have strong incentives to win customers and traffic. Once network infrastructure is in place, the incentives to seek out revenues to cover the sunk costs of network build are strong as few additional costs are incurred from adding customers.

5.1.2   The position of regulators

There appears to be widespread acceptance amongst regulators, international bodies, and consumer associations that broadband should be recognised as a single market regardless of the type of delivery platform. In particular, many such institutions make explicit acknowledgement that providers of cable modem and DSL services compete directly for subscribers and that this competition is highly beneficial for consumers. This is notwithstanding the fact that many such bodies also advocate very different regulatory regimes for the provision of DSL and other broadband access technologies.

The promotion of platform competition in broadband provision has been enshrined as a key EU economic goal. The explanatory memorandum published with the EU Commission's Recommendation on relevant product and service markets within the electronic communications sector states that:

> "Looking ahead, the eEurope 2005 Action Plan promotes a **multi-platform approach to broadband deployment**, driven by strong competition between services provided over competing platforms. Competing network infrastructures are essential for achieving sustainable competition in networks and services in the long term."[136] [emphasis added]

Documents published by EU and other national regulators generally recognise – either explicitly or implicitly – that there is competition across platforms for broadband subscribers. For example:

□ ART (France): *"Internet access via cable plays a key role in allowing competition for residential high-speed. Although available in France with geographically limited coverage, it is, for the time being, the only infrastructure **competing with ADSL** for the general public."*[137] [emphasis added]

□ ComReg (Ireland): *". . . the Government wishes to ensure the widespread availability of open-access, affordable, always on broadband infrastructure*

---

[135] At the time of writing, Intel is strongly marketing its Centrino chipset for laptops, which provides built-in 802.11 wireless networking with low power consumption.

[136] European Commission (February 2003a), page 6.

[137] ART (March 2003).

and services ... on the basis of utilisation of **a range of existing and emerging technologies** and broadband speeds"[138] [emphasis added]

☐ In its 2002 annual report, RegTP (Germany) describes cable modem, powerlines, and satellite as *"competitors"* to DSL in the provision of broadband services.[139]

☐ CMT (Spain): *"el mercado de servicios de acceso de banda ancha comprendería, en principio, multiplicidad de alternativas tecnológicas, entre las cuales se encontrarían las tecnologías xDSL, cuyo exponente más actual y paradigmático es el ADSL (Asymmetric Digital Subscriber Line), el cablemódem y el bucle de abonado inalámbrico WLL (Wireless local loop) cuyos exponentes principales son el LMDS y el MMDS"* ["the market for broadband access includes, in principle, multiple alternative technologies, among which are xDSL technologies, whose more paradigmatic example is now ADSL (Asymmetric Digital Subscriber Line), cable modem and WLL (wireless local loop) whose most relevant instances are LMDS and MMDS"].[140]

☐ Oftel (United Kingdom): *"Broadband is always-on, high speed Internet access. There are different ways of accessing the Internet using a broadband connection. Most people use a connection via their existing telephone or cable line. However, broadband is also available using other technologies including radio, satellite and powerlines."*[141] Since January 2001, Oftel (now part of Ofcom) has published a bi-annual survey comparing prices for broadband services in the United States and selected EU countries. These studies explicitly compare prices for both DSL and cable modems. In later surveys, Oftel begun surveying prices for alternative broadband access technologies, including FWA and satellite.

☐ The FCC (United States) has suggested that different broadband platforms are substitutable: *"We recognize that residential high-speed access to the Internet is evolving over multiple electronic platforms, including wireline, cable, terrestrial wireless and satellite. By promoting development and deployment of multiple platforms, we promote competition in the provision of broadband capabilities, ensuring that public demands and needs can be met."*[142] [emphasis added] Similarly, the FCC concluded that the relevant product market for the proposed merger between America Online and Time Warner was the market for mass-market broadband services.[143]

☐ The Ministry of Information and Communication (South Korea) has referred to *"fierce competition"* among broadband service providers and includes firms that provide DSL, cable, and wireless broadband access in official

---

[138]ComReg (June 2003c).

[139]RegTP (February 2003), page 19.

[140]CMT (2002), page 49.

[141]Oftel (August 2003).

[142]FCC (March 2002).

[143]FCC, AOL / Time Warner Order.

reports detailing the number of broadband service subscribers in South Korea.[144]

Similarly, studies and position papers on broadband development from relevant international bodies and consumers associations also tend to emphasise the importance of platform competition, both within and across technologies:

☐ OECD: *"The most fundamental policy available to OECD governments to boost broadband access is infrastructure competition".*[145]

☐ ITU: *"Competition is the key to driving prices down and increasing the broadband options available to consumers. The most successful economies in terms of broadband penetration have strong competition both among providers of the same broadband technologies, and between providers of different broadband technologies."*[146]

☐ INTUG: *"There is good evidence that where services using cable modems compete with xDSL then this is a considerable stimulus to market development. Competition between these technologies appears to be beneficial."*[147]

Notwithstanding this emphasis on platform competition, most regulators and other international bodies also concurrently advocate regulatory regimes that promote broadband service competition through various regulatory obligations on incumbent PTOs to provide access to their infrastructure. This has resulted in many OECD countries adopting highly asymmetric regulatory regimes with respect to broadband provision via DSL and other technologies, despite there being strong substitutability between these platforms.

5.1.3   Geographical markets

Residential customers typically require broadband service at a given location and can only choose amongst the options available at that location. Further, not all broadband technologies can be feasibly deployed everywhere and certain technologies are more appropriate to particular geographical areas. Therefore, competition in broadband is not geographically homogeneous.

Nevertheless, at present, most DSL and cable modem provision is offered at geographically uniform prices (where these services are available). This is usually a matter of practice, rather than a result of any explicit regulatory requirement. The broadband marketplace is still in the early stages of development and at present there may be competitive advantages from uniform pricing in terms of marketing and raising consumer awareness of the service. Clearly it is possible that broadband providers might at some time choose to set different prices depending on location. Indeed, a maturing market and toughening competition

---

[144]IT Korea (2002).
[145]OECD (October 2001), page 4.
[146]ITU (2003), page 1.
[147]INTUG (2001).

may force geographically differentiated pricing as a result of costs varying across customers within the coverage areas of providers; maintaining uniform prices in such circumstances might otherwise give profitable opportunities for cream-skimming of lower cost customers.

However, even with geographically differentiated prices, it is not necessarily the case that there are different relevant geographical markets. Careful case-by-case analysis is needed to determine this. NRAs have to date largely ignored the geographical elements of market definition, with the danger that undue attention is given to small fringe geographic areas where competition may be limited by low demand and high costs, and insufficient attention to core areas (already encompassing the majority of the population in most countries) where competition is already or potentially effective.

Geographical variation in competitive conditions should not in itself be cause for concern by policy makers. Competition is already effective in significant areas and there is every indication that these areas can be enlarged:

☐ We have already seen that platform competition is clearly feasible, both between cable and DSL and between established and new platforms. In many countries, the large majority of customers already can choose from competing cable and DSL offers.
☐ Given an appropriate policy framework, there are incentives for existing platforms to be rolled out further and for new networks (such as FTTH) to be deployed.
☐ New developments, particular in wireless networking, offer a cost effective means of deployment even in rural areas with low customer densities.

Table 11 shows DSL coverage and cable homes passed in a variety of countries. In the absence of a coherent public source of data on footprints, it is difficult to determine exactly where DSL and cable coverage areas overlap. However, a reasonable working assumption is that areas with cable coverage will often have DSL coverage (as cable coverage will typically be concentrated in urban areas), but not necessarily the reverse. Sweden and Italy additionally have fibre networks, which overlap with DSL coverage, and to a lesser extent with cable coverage.

On this basis, the upper bound on the proportion of the population who at present have a choice of platform is the smaller of the coverage of DSL and of cable/FTTH combined. We show this upper bound in Table 11.

In practice, the actual overlap may be lower than this upper bound to the extent that:

☐ cable is offered in areas where DSL is not available;
☐ existing cable infrastructure may require upgrading to carry broadband; therefore, the overlap of cable and DSL may not represent overlapping coverage of cable and DSL broadband offers.

Table 11: DSL and cable coverage in selected EU states and the United States, end-2002

	DSL coverage (% of lines)	Cable homes passed (% households)	Fibre homes passed (% households)	Upper bound on overlap
Austria	77%	53%	-	53%
Belgium	95%‡	100%	-	95%
Denmark	95%	77%	-	77%
France	86%	51%	-	51%
Germany	90%	86%	-	86%
Ireland	50%	88%	-	50%
Italy	68%	11%	6%	17%
Luxembourg	89%	100%	-	89%
Netherlands	85%	94%	-	85%
Portugal	61%	93%	-	61%
Spain	89%	38%*	-	38%
Sweden	75%	65%	7%	72%
United Kingdom	63%	62%	-	62%
United States	62%	97%	-	62%

Notes: ‡% of population, not lines; maximum overlap calculated as the higher of DSL coverage and cable & fibre homes passed. *Data from Informa implies that this figure is only 15%, but this is at odds with official Spanish data.
Sources: Informa World Broadband Database; *Broadband Access for Business*, OECD, Dec 2002; NCTA (www.ncta.com); Ministerio de Ciencia y Technologia (Spain)

Nevertheless, where upgrades have taken place, actual overlap should be reasonable close to this upper bound. This assertion is backed up by the limited company data available. For example, BT estimates that, as of March 2003, approximately 50.9% of its DSL lines were in areas covered by cable. Given that BT only wins a share of broadband connections in areas with cable, this indicates that a significant majority of areas served by BT are also served by cable broadband. In the United States, cable operator Comcast (which has over 4 million cable modem subscribers) estimates that DSL services from either SBC or Verizon are available in 77% of its broadband operating market.[148] Overall, we can conclude that in most cases, over half of the population (and often a large majority) is served or could be served by both cable and DSL platforms, without virgin network build.

---

[148] Internetnews.com (May 2003); Subscriber numbers from CNET News.com (July 2003b).

Customers within the overlap have an effective choice of provider at present. However, this does not imply that competition is restricted to within the area of the overlap, as we must also consider supply-side substitutability.[149] A platform can be expected to increase its coverage to areas not currently served in response to a significant, non-transitory increase in the price of another platform in those areas. Thus, the *potential overlap* of the services is larger than the actual overlap. It is the potential overlap, rather than the actual overlap that determines the extent to which platforms compete.

For example, even where cable networks have not been upgraded, their presence gives rise to scope for supply-side competition and provides a potential competitive constraint on DSL pricing that could become operational quickly. For example, in Germany, although there is very little broadband competition for DSL from cable at present, potential overlap between DSL and existing cable networks is over 80% of households.

Not only may cable networks be upgraded, their coverage may also be extended, though is likely to have a longer lead time. Although Italy and Spain stand out in Table 11 as having relatively low overlaps between cable/fibre and DSL, the situation in these countries is changing; both have companies that are actively extending their cable and fibre networks at the moment (see case studies on FastWeb and Ono in Annex II). New build and extending coverage are important aspects of competition in these cases. Therefore, it is the potential overlap between platforms that determines the extent of competition rather than just the current overlap.

In addition to the wireline platforms (DSL, cable and FTTH), there is both actual and potential competition from wireless networks (3G, WiFi, fixed wireless access, 'new mobile' and satellite). All these platforms have the ability to reach into areas with low population density where it may be costly to roll out wireline broadband networks.[150] Some of these networks (3G, WiFi and 'new mobile') provide mobile or nomadic service across their entire coverage area. Once a decision has been made to provide service in a particular area, all customers located in that area can be connected at little or no additional cost. Therefore, competition from wireless networks is likely to have the effect of driving wireline networks to offer to more customers and increase their coverage areas.

Given these competitive dynamics, there are good reasons to expect broadband provision to push into rural areas over time. There are technologies available

---

[149] see Annex III for a brief discussion of market definition principles.

[150] A good example of the ability of wireless networks to reach into low population density areas is provided by developing countries, where they are being heavily promoted by development agencies as a means of deploying Internet access, bypassing wireline networks entirely. Details of the United Nations Information and Communication Technologies Task Force's recent wireless initiative can be found at http://www.unicttaskforce.org/WiFi/.

(especially wireless) that should allow sustainable competition between multiple platforms even in fringe areas with relatively low population densities. Geographical heterogeneity in competitive conditions is, therefore, not a concern in itself. Public policy concerns only arise to the extent to which variation in cost and demand conditions mean that platform competition could not be sustained in fringe areas because of a combination of low demand and high costs of provision, for example, because scale economies mean that only one network would be feasible. Worse still, the balance between demand and cost might be so adverse that no network might be feasible without subsidy.

In the event that there were fringe areas that could not sustain competing platforms because of high costs or low demand, a regulatory requirement for geographically uniform pricing would not in itself provide a solution, as there would be little or no incentive to provide service in such areas. This is an important difference to narrowband where universal service obligations (going back to the time of state-controlled monopoly provision of voice telephony), determine the roll-out. Even if similar obligations were to be imposed on broadband providers (which in itself is questionable), geographically uniform pricing is unlikely to work for broadband. Given the competitive dynamics in an emerging and fast-growing market, there is little reason to expect that a sufficient margin could be sustained in low-cost areas (e.g. urban and metropolitan areas) to subsidise supply in high-cost rural areas. To the extent to which there are fringe areas that are too expensive to serve with broadband, but which public policy judges should be served, this needs to be addressed with competitive neutral subsidy measures, as we discuss in chapter 6.

5.1.4   Customer segmentation

In defining the market for broadband, a further consideration is the extent to which there may be separate markets for different types of customers. Two customer segments would be considered as separate markets if they had distinct needs that are met by different products, and relatively little substitution is observed between the products in the event of relative price changes, either on the demand-side or on the supply-side.

In the case of broadband, business customers often have distinct requirements from residential users, such that lower grade broadband products are unsuitable. Consequently, looking at demand substitutability alone, it would be appropriate to identify distinct markets for business and residential customers.

Whereas consumers are typically interested in broadband services for quicker download speeds and entertainment purposes, business demand often requires high upstream speeds to be able to quickly send large files to customers and to host content of various forms.[151] Large businesses will typically require

---

[151] For example, in contrast to residential customers who are typically only concerned about downloading content and can be allocated dynamic IP addresses, SMEs may require static IP addresses for hosts to be addressable from the Internet.

dedicated leased lines (e.g. a T1 connection) to meet their requirement, as their bandwidth demands are too great to be met through DSL or cable platforms; and hence are clearly a distinct market. For SMEs, the situation is less clear cut, as their needs may be serviceable using DSL or cable technology. Nevertheless, it is often insufficient for a broadband provider to simply offer its residential service to SMEs on an 'as is' basis; rather, providers typically offer much more extensive menu of premium broadband services than that available to residential consumers.[152] Furthermore, it is often necessary for providers to sell SME services through direct sales forces.[153]

Despite residential and SME segments having different needs, there is a supply-side substitution as it is possible to deploy services over a common platform for both residential and SME users. The extent to which the SME market is differentiated from the residential market on the supply side in terms of provider overlap varies between countries, depending on whether DSL, cable modem and FTTH services are available and whether they are aimed at business markets as well as residential. In its Third Broadband Report, the FCC[154] noted that high-speed cable modem service in the United States is typically available only to the residential market:

> "Cable networks were originally deployed to provide video programming and other programming services to residences throughout the United States. While some residences are located in areas where there are large and small businesses alike, most businesses were originally, and still are, not wired for cable service. This leaves cable operators less capable of providing cable modem services to many business districts without additional system build-outs. In addition, cable's shared network characteristics make it difficult for providers using currently deployed cable modem technology to guarantee the consistently high speeds and other advanced features that some business customers require."[155]

However, in many EU countries (e.g. Spain and Italy), business and residential areas are much less distinct, meaning that network roll-out unavoidably reaches both type of customers, even if it is initially aimed primarily at residential. Moreover, where DSL or cable is being upgraded with fibre closer to the end user, enabling higher-grade residential products, the scope for these to meet the demands of SMEs is increasing. In Italy, FTTH operator FastWeb has been

---

[152]McKinsey & Co. and J.P. Morgan (April 2001).

[153]For example, Verizon (2003b) stated that *"[b]ecause of the increasing complexity of communications services and business needs, small and medium-sized businesses now require one-on-one consultations with Verizon sales representatives to sort out which products and services they should have."*

[154]Of the three relevant US federal regulatory – the DOJ, the FTC, and the FCC – only the DOJ fails to restrict its definition of the relevant product market to residential broadband as opposed to all broadband.

[155]FCC (February 2002), Appendix B23.

very successful in winning both residential and business customers with its symmetric high-bandwidth network.

Demand from businesses located outside urban areas may also drive roll-out of alternative wireless and satellite platforms, with spin-off advantages for residential customers. Many FWA and wide-area WiFi initiatives are aimed at rural and semi-rural areas, where business demand is insufficiently dense to attract DSL or cable roll-out, but customers are not large enough to justify dedicated leased lines. In remote or sparsely populated areas, the relatively greater need of businesses for bandwidth and advanced services makes them excellent potential customers for two-way satellite services, which uniquely do not require a critical mass of potential customers in a particular local area to make serving that area commercially attractive.[156]

5.1.5 Double and triple play

One area where it may be potentially difficult for all providers to replicate each others' offers is in relation to double and triple-play offerings. DSL service may be offered alongside voice services, either by the incumbent PSTN operator, or an operator using unbundled local loops. Cable networks typically offer cable modems alongside broadcast TV and voice telephony services. Although PCs provide the ability to use VoIP and video services over IP connections, most consumers will require a seamless service with voice and TV signals presented on standard interfaces to which they can connect telephones and televisions. In this regard, cable networks have the benefit of already supplying broadcast distribution, to which voice telephony and broadband access can be added. Industry analysts, such as Datamonitor, Enders and Strategy Analytics have all cited this as a potential significant advantage for cable operators.

Discounts and incentives may be offered to those who take up bundles of services. For example, both ILECs and cable firms have offered discounts for bundled services in the United States. In 2003, Verizon offered discounts of 5 US dollars off the price of DSL in many areas when DSL is purchased in a bundle with other telecommunications services, and SBC also offers discounts on DSL when purchased as part of a larger telecommunications package.[157] Comcast also offers discounts to consumers who subscribe to both its cable television and cable modem services.[158] Many European providers employ similar discounts (see section 1.1.1).

---

[156]FCC (February 2002), Appendix B45.

[157]Telephony (May 2003); Boston Globe (May 2003), explaining that Verizon had lowered the price of DSL service to $34.95, but that customers who purchased DSL as part of a "Freedom bundle" with other telephone services would pay only $29.95.

[158]CNET News.com (April 2003).

One might suspect that bundling somehow impairs broadband competition based on the fact that certain tying arrangements have been found to be anti-competitive in some situations. Such a suspicion is unjustified for two reasons.

First, as Judge Richard A. Posner explains, *"[t]he traditional objection to tying arrangements is that they enable a firm having a monopoly in one market to obtain a monopoly in a second one."*[159] Although the possibility of competitive harm involving such a monopolist is debateable, wherever a broadband provider faces competition bundling is unlikely to have any anticompetitive effects.[160]

Second, bundling is distinct from – and far less restrictive than – tying: whereas tying involves conditioning the sale of one product on the purchase of another, bundling merely involves discounting the price of a set of products, when those products are purchased together. Bundling promotes competition by forcing other broadband providers to lower prices or offer promotions in response.

For example, assume that a given area is served by both a cable and DSL broadband provider, and that each broadband provider offers service for a monthly price of €25.00. Now assume that the cable provider typically offers cable television service for €30.00, but now decides to bundle television and broadband service for €50.00. That decision by the cable firm will affect different consumers in different ways:

☐ consumers who are both cable modem and cable television subscribers will experience an additional consumer surplus of €5.00 per month;
☐ existing cable television consumers who value broadband service at above €20.01 but below €25 will now subscribe to the bundle of both services;
☐ existing cable broadband customers who value cable television service above €25.01 but below €30 will subscribe to the bundle of both services;
☐ consumers who previously subscribed to neither service but who value the combined services above €50.00 but below €55 will now subscribe to the bundle of both services.

The DSL provider in this scenario would stand to lose those of its customers who also subscribe to cable television service, and would be unlikely to attract consumers who value the bundled cable package at or above €50.00 *and* value cable television at or above €25.02. Nonetheless, any consumer who valued cable television service below €25.00 would not find the cable bundle an attractive option. If the DSL provider wanted to avoid losing customers, it would have to lower its own prices for broadband, or develop its own bundled package that consumers would find equally attractive. Thus, the effect of bundling is

---

[159] Posner (2001).

[160] If the broadband provider had durable market power in another market, this would need to be addressed at source by appropriate regulation within that market; this should not be a concern for policy toward broadband.

to *promote*, rather than hinder, competition.[161] Bundled rebates can only be anticompetitive if the size of the bundled rebate offered by the cable provider, when fully matched by the DSL provider, causes the DSL provider to price its service below average variable cost and thereby induce exit. Therefore, bundling practices on DSL and cable platforms should not raise competition concerns providing platform competition is effective.

In addition, technological convergence is rapidly eroding any distinctive capability that particular platforms might have in the delivery of particular content. For example, in Italy, Fastweb is providing a triple play proposition with broadband, voice telephony and video services over fibre. The deployment of video services over DSL is feasible and the main impediments to date have been regulatory (specifically whether incumbent PSTN operators offering such services might be subject to regulatory obligations such as access requirements).[162] In the case of a provider with limited geographical footprint (within which we include national PSTN operators), the principal difficulty in offering video and TV services is likely to be access to content, rather than technological limitations. Voice over IP is rapidly maturing as a technology and provides a route to offer voice services regardless of platform (subject to modest bandwidth and latency requirements). Such systems are now routinely used by corporate organisations with internal networks carrying both voice and data traffic.

5.2   The desirability of facilities-based competition

Facilities-based competition brings benefits that are not achievable through access-based competition. There are many examples of competition between platforms in broadband provision. Therefore, platform competition is demonstrably feasible. In any case, LLU (if priced appropriately) is sufficient to act as a competitive safeguard even if platform competition is only emerging.

5.2.1   Competition vs. regulation

Facilities-based competition leads to competition over many more aspects of a service than access-based competition. Where services are heavily dependent on regulated access to other networks, the characteristics of the service and its cost are mostly determined by the characteristics and pricing of the access service. With access-based competition, outcomes are strongly determined by the terms of access regulation, rather than by the choices made by the provider under the discipline of competition.

---

[161] For a recent extensive review of the economics of tying and bundling, see Nalebuff (2003). This emphasises that bundling can be used in a variety of ways, both pro-competitive and anti-competitive.

[162] Although prior regulatory restrictions on offering video services in some countries have been removed (e.g. those previously imposed on DSL operators in the United Kingdom), there is still uncertainty about what approach NRAs might take to such new services.

There is general consensus that, where feasible, competition has many advantages over regulation. Regulation is only an imperfect proxy for competition and, therefore, it is essential that regulation should not replace competition where it is feasible. The Framework Directive is explicit about this: *"It is essential that ex ante regulatory obligations should only be imposed where there is not effective competition."*[163] Only where cost and demand conditions are such that multiple competing players cannot be sustained may there be a role for regulation in controlling market power (to the extent that this is not addressable by competition law).

Indeed, were regulation perfect and able to replicate exactly the outcome of competition, it would make little difference whether services were delivered by competition between platforms vying to offer attractive and cost effective services to their customers, or by an all-knowing regulator able to judge what customers needed and how best to deliver it. However, in practice regulation cannot achieve the same outcomes as effective competition.[164] Regulators have little information about either customers' needs or the most efficient ways of meeting them, information that is revealed only by the process of competition itself.[165]

There are a variety of benefits from competition that regulation cannot reproduce. These include:

☐ *greater incentive to minimise costs*;
   Regulatory systems necessarily trade-off control of market power and the incentives to reduce cost. For example, if it were possible to regulate a retail price exactly at cost (which is unlikely given imperfect information about what the 'true' level of costs might be), this would maximise allocative efficiency (in that all users willing to pay more than cost would purchase the

---

[163] Framework Directive, European Parliament and Council (2002), Article 27.

[164] There is a considerable body of economic theory that considers the differences in the outcomes achieved by competition and by regulation. One strand of this literature emphasises the informational limits that prevent regulators achieving efficient outcomes by decree. Baron and Myerson (1982) provide an early formal model of these informational limits on regulation. Given the presence of informational limits, regulators need to design incentive mechanisms to edge toward efficient outcomes, for example price caps with reviews only at intervals in order to generate incentives for cost reduction. Incentive regulation must provide the regulated firm with some rents (even if only temporary) in order to incentivise efficient behaviour. These rents would typically be eliminated in a true competitive market. Therefore, even optimal regulation is at best an imperfect substitute for competition. See Laffont and Tirole (1993) for an extensive survey of the principles of incentive regulation.

[165] The idea that competition is important in revealing and aggregating information, thereby producing efficient outcomes that no individual could by themselves achieve, dates back to Hayek. This is often ignored in simple economic models. For example, a textbook model of perfect competition would assume that every producer knew the most efficient production technique and that competition led to prices equal to this production cost. However, in practice the most significant benefit of competition may be in discovering what the most efficient production technique is.

service, and new entrants would provide the service only if they were more efficient than the regulated incumbent). However, there would then be no incentive for the regulated firm to reduce cost, as this would produce an equal reduction in price and no increase in profits. Price caps reviewed at intervals strike a compromise between cost reduction incentives and allocative efficiency, in that regulated firms can enjoy the benefits of cost reduction through higher profits until the next periodic price review, when prices are lowered to pass the benefit of lower costs on to consumers.[166]

☐ *increased internal efficiency;*
Competition generates information about internal efficiency, as the relative performance of competing firms with similar demand conditions and input costs can be compared. This information can be used to set internal performance targets and to incentivise managers. In turn, this increases the internal efficiency of firms and reduces costs.[167]

☐ *Darwinian selection of efficient technologies and methods;*
Competition occurs over many dimensions, not just price. Operators compete over the methods and technologies that they use to deliver their services. These choices affect the features, quality and cost of services. Successful methods and technologies displace unsuccessful ones, either by unsuccessful firms exiting the market or, more often, through diffusion of new methods and technologies from pioneers to all providers.[168]

☐ *increased diversity for customers; and*
Competition implies that there are multiple providers of a service. This diversity may be of value in itself to the extent to which retail customers enjoy a choice between various differentiated services.[169] Diverse offerings of network services may lead to variety at the retail level (e.g. different quality of service or bandwidth), but even where it does not, it provides greater redundancy for operators reliant on network services.

☐ *knowledge spillovers increasing aggregate productivity.*
In the case of innovative sectors such as telecommunications, there may be significant external, economy-wide benefits to there being a variety of platforms and technologies. Each new technology is a potential starting point for the development of new technologies and techniques. Multiple platforms and technologies allow more rapid 'search' for new innovations across the economy as a whole and avoid a technological monoculture. New views of economic growth that are now highly influential in macroeconomic policy

---

[166]See Baumol and Klevorick (1970) for a discussion of periodic regulatory reviews.
[167]See Vickers (1995).
[168]For example, Vickers (1995) emphasises the benefits of competition in terms of discovering efficient production techniques.
[169]Customers can be assumed to place some value on the diversity of the products they buy. For example, see Dixit and Stiglitz (1977).

have emphasised the importance of these knowledge spillovers in promoting innovation and growth.[170]

Although these are all general benefits of competition over regulation, they arise to a much greater extent from facilities-based competition than from access-based competition. Not all forms of competition in the telecommunications sector are equally good at delivering these benefits. In the case of access-based provision, competition can only operate in respect of the value that each provider adds to the regulated access service, as each provider makes use of the same underlying access-service and has no control over its costs or its characteristics. In contrast, platform-based competition exposes the entire value chain to the forces of competition. This implies that there are benefits from encouraging facilities-based competition.

5.2.2 Can platform competition be effective?

Regulation is only necessary in situations where competition is not feasible because of the presence of significant scale or scope economies, limiting the number of providers who can coexist sustainably in the market. In such a case, a limitation on the number of feasible providers may lead to concerns about the exploitation of market power and create the need for regulation.

This raises the question: how many competing network providers are required to achieve effective competition in broadband provision? The simple answer is the more competing platforms, the better, provided that all have potentially viable business cases. However, there is no reason why most of the benefits of competition cannot be realised with just two competing operators, as is evident from observing the intense competition between cable and DSL operators across EU and U.S. markets. For example, in the United States, competition between just two providers in each local service area – one cable modem provider and one DSL provider – resulted in severe price declines, from 89 US dollars per month in 1999 to 29 US dollars per month in 2003. Further, potential competition and the threat of entry can have a strong disciplining effect on existing players.

Looking at EU markets, residential users in urban areas often have a choice of two platforms (usually DSL and cable) at present. In some areas, alternative platforms, such as FTTH, FWA and broad-area WiFi have been or are being rolled out; however, as these have to date largely been focused on filling areas where there is either only DSL or no other platform, they have rarely as yet increased choice beyond two platforms (Sweden, where some residents can chose between cable, DSL and FTTH is an exception). Many users also have

---

[170] Innovation and knowledge spillovers are now seen as being central to the process of economic growth. Aghion and Howitt (1992) present a model of *"creative destruction"* in which new innovations generate growth. Innovations generate benefits not just for the innovator, but also for others by generating starting points for further innovation.

the option of satellite, but as this currently is typically priced above DSL and cable broadband, it is not a significant competitor in urban areas.

Considering first those areas where there are two platforms, it is evident from our findings in section 1.1.1 that competition between cable and DSL networks has brought significant benefits to consumers in terms of product and price innovation, for example through the launch of multiple broadband service packages, the profusion of special offers for new subscribers and the launch of double and triple-play strategies. Customers treat these two platforms as being highly substitutable and so providers must respond to each others' pricing initiatives and service innovations. Even disregarding competition from other platforms, where there is significant overlap of DSL and cable, competition is intense.

Platform competition is clearly having results, as demonstrated by the facts that:

☐ take-up of broadband across the EU as a whole is running ahead of compara-ble products at similar levels of development, such as mobile and PCs, despite there being the same or smaller numbers of 'networks' (see section 3.2);
☐ the decision of the FCC to terminate line sharing demonstrates a clear vision on the FCC's part that competition is feasible and should be allowed to develop; and
☐ our analysis of cross-country penetration in sections 5.4.1 and 5.4.2 pro-vides strong evidence that platform competition drives penetration, but no corresponding evidence that access-based entry helps. Similarly, a DrKW Research report in September 2003 observed that *"the markets with the most active cable competition, not those with the lowest prices, saw the greatest penetration increase."*[171]

While the emergence of a third or fourth network in the future might bring even more benefits, through further pressure for product and price innovation, it would be highly mistaken to consider that where there are two main network operators, this situation is uncompetitive.

Those EU markets where there is currently only one significant network op-erator potentially provide greater concern, since competitive incentives for incumbents to lower prices and introduce new products or tariff packages is likely to be more limited. However, even in these areas, there is still market pressure on incumbent operators.

Given that EU incumbents generally pursue nationwide product and pricing strategies, competition in just a few regions will encourage incumbents to in-troduce product and price innovation that benefits all regions. Most importantly, the threat of new entry – for example, from cable upgrades in Germany or new cable and fibre build in Italy and Spain – should provide a strong incentive for incumbents to behave competitively.

---

[171] DrKW Research (September 2003).

Nevertheless, in the short-medium term, there may be concerns that roll-out of competing networks may not be fast enough to impose sufficient competitive pressure on an incumbent. This may be addressed through LLU, which potentially can enable alternative providers to replicate many of the benefits of platform competition, without undermining the incentives for rolling out alternative infrastructure, provided that access prices are set appropriately. Therefore, DSL supply is subject to intra-modal competition, both from actual providers using unbundled loops and through potential entry. For example, HanseNet in Hamburg has introduced an innovative range of products and taken significant market share from Deutsche Telekom, in much the same way as cable operators have succeeded in other regions of Europe.

In addition to actual competition between existing networks, potential competition from new platforms is a significant competitive constraint. We have outlined a variety of emerging technologies in section 2.3. Given the actual examples of alternative infrastructures being deployed to compete with traditional DSL and cable offers, this competitive threat is real. In addition, the potential for existing alternative networks to develop and extend their coverage areas is an important constraint on the pricing of services delivered over DSL or cable. Wireless networks, in particular, can exert a strong competitive constraint on pricing as, once deployed, they are available to all customers within the coverage area and the incremental costs of serving additional customers are low.

At present, there are a number of different technologies for delivering broadband, all with the potential to take-off and become mass-market products. It is unclear which approaches will ultimately succeed, with the result that the possibility of rapid dislocating change in the marketplace is ever-present. Therefore, innovation is an important aspect of competition within the emerging broadband marketplace.[172] Any assessment of competitive conditions in broadband must take account of innovation in platforms and services as an important part of the competitive dynamic.

Market trends are all in the direction of encouraging competition. Demand for broadband is growing as consumers learn about its benefits and there is increased provision of content interesting to a wide audience. Not only does growing demand increase the number of feasible competing platforms, it also creates a competitive environment without switching costs, where suppliers compete to win and retain new customers not presently tied to any particular provider. The broadband market is subject to the strong competitive dynamic often seen when new services are introduced (e.g. as when dial-up internet access or mobile telephony became mass-market products).

In totality, these factors suggest that broadband provision has little in common with narrowband telephony, where concerns about incumbent PSTN control of the local loop, which until the advent of cable telephony was thought not

---

[172] See Teece (2001) for a discussion of innovation markets.

to be replicable, have shaped policy. In contrast, there are many examples of competitive provision of broadband services that does not rely on the local loops of the incumbent PSTN. The local loop is demonstrably not a bottleneck in broadband provision. Even if there are transitional concerns arising in cases where cable networks are not widespread and alternative infrastructure still developing, LLU is sufficient by itself to address this.

One specific concern about competition between a small number of platforms is that there may be collusive outcomes, even if these emerge from tacit parallelism, rather than explicit coordination. This should not be a material concern for regulatory policy. First, cost and demand conditions in broadband provision are such that the incentives to compete for customers are strong, which would tend to undermine any collusive outcome. Fast-growing markets with strong incentives to win and retain customers are not normally susceptible to tacit collusion, and therefore this is very unlikely to be a problem. Second, there is no reason to expect that regulation would be in any way better suited to address issues of tacit collusion (and, in fact, many regulatory instruments such as transparency and non-discrimination may be counter-productive), than existing competition law. Thus, dealing with the risk of tacit collusion is not obviously an area where competition law would be insufficient, and ex-ante regulation would therefore be justified.[173]

5.3   Access to networks

5.3.1   The role of access regulation

Where there are strong economies of scale or scope at one level of a network, particular assets may be difficult or costly for entrants to replicate. However, other aspects of the value chain may be easy to replicate. Therefore, there may be the potential for competition at some levels of a value chain, but not at others. Regulated access is intended to address exactly this situation. By allowing access to aspects of the value chain that are impossible to replicate profitably, entrants can compete over the other aspects of the value chain, putting pressure not just on the pricing of the overall retail services but also on costs and characteristics of replicable activities. Access may need to be regulated in such cases to control market power resulting from control of difficult to replicate assets.[174]

---

[173]The Framework Directive is explicit that regulation is only justified where the application of competition law would fail to address the competitive problem at hand.

[174]Note that in this example, access regulation would be sufficient to address market power and additional retail level price controls or other remedies would not be necessary. This is another principle of the Framework Directive – that retail level remedies should not be used where there are wholesale level remedies available that are sufficient to address whatever the underlying competition concern might be.

However, in the case of broadband provision, it is difficult to see what assets or capabilities are non-replicable. There are already many cases of competing platforms, in which case it must be that *all* the activities required to provide broadband are largely replicable. Therefore, the general case for access regulation being needed for broadband is empirically weak.

Nevertheless, particular concerns may arise where cable coverage is limited and, therefore, competitive constraints on incumbent operators providing DSL services may be weak. The wide range of emerging broadband technologies suggests that such concerns should at most be transitional. In any case, it is only the local loop that is potentially difficult to replicate, not any of the other activities required for broadband provision. Therefore, the case for access regulation extends at most to unbundling of local loops. In particular, bitstream access and all forms of reselling open up not just the local loop, but also many other easily replicable activities.

It is tempting for regulators to use multiple forms of access regulation just in case there might be a problem and some asset or capability of the incumbent might turn out not to be easily replicable by entrants. However, this approach is fundamentally flawed as regulated access always has a potential downside; that incentives for an entrant to self-provide assets or capabilities that it can procure through access will be undermined. Obviously where these assets or capabilities cannot be replicated due to scale economies, there is no such loss. However, where access regulation applies to assets or capabilities that are replicable, there will be a loss, as competitive pressures that could otherwise have operated at that stage of the value chain may be lost. As we have already discussed, this is the reason why facilities-based competition is preferable to access-based competition, where the former is feasible.

Unnecessary forms of access regulation will inevitably cause distortions. First, as we discuss below, it is very far from the case that current access pricing methodologies used by regulators set efficient access prices. There are strong theoretical reasons why current access prices undermine investment incentives. Empirical evidence shows this to be the case, for example with bitstream access and resale crowding out take-up of LLU and building of alternative platforms. Second, even if the methodology for access pricing were appropriate, it is inevitable that there will be considerable uncertainty over the necessary inputs for calculating efficient access prices, and so the outcome will be uncertain. This risk is asymmetric in its impact (as we show below) and will depress investment incentives.

5.3.2   Access pricing and the benefits of competition

At present NRAs use a variety of approaches to pricing access services used to provide broadband. The Unbundling Regulation 2000 establishes cost-oriented prices for access to unbundled loops. The preamble to the Unbundling Regulation explains the obligations:

> "Costing and pricing rules for local loops and associated facilities (such as collocation and leased transmission capacity) should be transparent, non-discriminatory and be objective to ensure fairness. Pricing rules should ensure that the local loop provider is able to cover its appropriate costs in this regard plus a reasonable return. Pricing rules for local loops should foster fair and sustainable competition and ensure that there is no distortion of competition, in particular no margin squeeze between prices of wholesale and retail services of the notified operator."

Costs of particular elements are assessed by NRAs on a forward-looking LRIC basis. This effectively considers the costs of providing a given service using modern equivalent assets and assuming that networks are configured optimally to meet these demands. This green-field approach ignores significant costs associated with managing demand uncertainty that arise both prospectively and retrospectively. For example, there are costs associated with building network facilities to insure against uncertain future demand and ensure that adequate quality of service is maintained. In a competitive market, these costs are considerable. Further, even with good management, it is seldom the case that network configuration is optimal at every point in time given the demand it is currently serving. Rather, unavoidable inefficiencies arise from network assets being sunk (so costly to reconfigure), and forecasts of demand and of the relative costs of different techniques being incorrect ex post. In the case of advanced services such as broadband, demand and technological conditions are inevitably difficult to forecast as many services are untested, and so the costs associated with managing uncertainty are material.

Regulated bitstream access services are priced by European NRAs in a variety of ways, including cost-based regulation and retail-minus regulation. Retail-minus regulation seeks to establish an access price by subtracting off the costs of the access provider's activities unused by the access seeker from the price of the access provider's own retail service. Providing that there is not market power in the setting of retail prices, costing the value-added to the access service and subtracting this off the corresponding retail price may be a simpler exercise than trying to cost the access service directly. Such an approach also has the benefit of possibly including some of the costs due to the risks of uncertain demand and technology that occur in practice, but which are omitted by the LRIC approach.

In practice, the distinction between retail-minus and cost-based regulation is not as large as these considerations would suggest. Access prices set by retail-minus regulation generally face an additional constraint from competition law, in that the margin between retail and access prices should not be too small, else the incumbent may be subject to complaints of predatory behaviour from entrants.

Such complaints have occurred in many EU states. This means that retail-minus regulation may in practice produce outcomes more similar to simple cost-based regulation, in that the latter provides that benchmark against which such predation tests are applied. In particular, pricing above this level is often taken as prima facie evidence of margin squeeze at the retail level.

Regardless of the details of how access prices are set (which vary from case to case), the LRIC methodology has a pervasive impact on access prices, both explicitly and implicitly. This framework is heavily grounded in the notion of access prices being set to ensure "efficient bypass", i.e. that an alternative provider has incentives to use its own facilities only where this is cheaper than using the incumbent's facilities. Moreover the incumbent's facilities are costed assuming an optimal network built to meet given demand using the best available techniques.

For example, consider a single network service that is not subject to scale or scope economies, implying there is a constant unit cost of the service. Efficient bypass is achieved by setting an access price at unit cost. In more realistic scenarios, this access price would also need to reflect lost scale and scope economies.[175] Access pricing in this theoretical example would appear to promote allocative efficiency, in that entry only occurs when it is efficient, reducing end-to-end costs.

However, such access prices based only on the static notion of efficient bypass are very likely to be too low, taking into account dynamic effects. Higher access prices would encourage facilities-based competition and give rise to social benefits (i.e. cost reduction pressure, diversity and selection pressure) that are unachievable through regulation. This argument suggests that socially optimal access prices are higher than those that are based only on considerations of efficient bypass.

There are important differences between broadband and narrowband voice telephony in this respect. In the case of voice telephony, there is little scope for service differentiation from replicating local loops and significant scale economies to be lost. Therefore, in the case of traditional voice telephony there may be little benefit from bringing in facilities-based competition across the entire value chain unless a significantly different service can be offered (e.g. mobile telephony). However, in the case of broadband, innovation and service differentiation are of much greater importance, and so the overall benefits of facilities-based competition relative to regulated access-based competition are much greater. Therefore, even if access pricing based on efficient bypass were appropriate for traditional telephony, as the dynamic benefits of facilities-based competition relative to access-based competition were relatively small, this is clearly not the case for broadband.

---

[175] See Laffont and Tirole (2000) and Armstrong (2001).

5.3.3   The costs of risk

Access pricing based on efficient bypass principles is wrong for broadband as
it leaves out these significant dynamic benefits of facilities-based competition.
However, a further problem is that current access pricing methodologies do not
properly account of risk and uncertainty. Access prices provide very considerable commercial flexibility to entrants and the resource costs of this flexibility
are not reflected in the access price. By using access, an entrant is able to
provide services without making any long-term commitment to remain in the
market. The scale of the entrant's operations can be rapidly adjusted (both up
and down). The entrant can avoid making any commitments to using a particular technology. These are all valuable commercial options, which current
access pricing policy provide for free to entrants.[176]

In contrast, providing these commercial options has significant resource costs
for the access provider. Networks must be dimensioned to carry traffic, including traffic resulting from uncertain demand for access services. Investments
must be made in specific technologies, with the associated risk of obsolescence, to provide these services. These are real resource costs, which are not
reflected in access prices. Effectively, there is a transfer of risk from the access
user to the access provider that is not costed.

It might be argued that the costs of an incumbent PSTN operator bearing
these risks are negligible. However, this is not the case for advanced services
as there is considerable uncertainty about both demand and about the best
technologies for deploying services. Moreover, any such argument suggests that
the incumbent is always better able to bear the costs of risks associated with new
services and uncertain demand than a new entrant; put differently, an argument
that the incumbent has a natural monopoly in risk-bearing. This is simply
a throwback to old arguments that telecoms networks are intrinsically natural
monopolies, which have been clearly disproved by the enormous progress made
in liberalisation over the last two decades.

5.3.4   The asymmetric impact of uncertainty on incumbents

So far, we have assumed that regulators are able to set access prices so as to
prevent inefficient bypass. We have seen that there are problems caused by failure to consider the costs of risk and the wider social benefits of facilities-based
competition. However, even if all these problems were addressed and access
prices were set on the 'correct' basis, it is still the case that unnecessary access
regulation (in the sense of providing access to replicable assets or capabilities
of the access provider) will necessarily be distorting.

In practice, regulators have imperfect information about costs, both their levels
and their structure (i.e. the extent of scale and scope economies). Therefore,

---

[176]See DotEcon (2001); and Hausman, Chapter 12 in Madden and Savage (2000).

there is considerable noise around regulatory determinations and even with an appropriate methodology for determining access prices, they would rarely be precisely at the efficient level. Imperfect information in regulation and noise in access price setting has important practical impacts on the access provider's incentives.

Consider a simple example. Suppose that the regulated access price for a network service was set at 10, but with imperfect knowledge of the efficient access price.[177] Suppose that there was an evens chance that the efficient access price could be 9 or 11, rather than 10. Notice that 10 is not a bad guess at the efficient access price – it would be correct on average – but lack of information limits the ability of the regulator to determine the efficient access price precisely. If the efficient access price were 11, the current price would promote inefficient access-based entry and lead to losses for the access provider. However, if the efficient access price were 9, this would lead to reduced entry and take-up of the access service. Therefore, there is no countervailing upside benefit for the access provider from the access price being set too high that offsets the downside risk of the price being too low. Even if the access price that the regulator sets is correct on average, introducing noise into regulatory determinations strictly decreases the incumbent's incentives to provide infrastructure in the first place.

This suggests an important precautionary principle. Access prices are always imperfectly set and subject to noise, further depressing infrastructure invest-ment incentives and forgoing the benefits of competition relative to the case of a perfectly set, efficient bypass promoting access price, which we know is too low anyway. Therefore, regulatory imperfections need to be reflected in a further uplift of access prices; the greater the noise in access price setting, the greater this uplift needs to be. Even with the most enlightened setting of access prices, access regulation should not be applied to assets or capabilities that are replicable, even on a 'just in case' basis.

5.3.5 Complementarity of access and infrastructure building

So far we have seen that there are a variety of strong arguments to suggest that access prices as currently set are not optimal. They only take account of very short run static considerations; they ignore the external benefits of competi-tion, the costs of risk and the problem of noise in regulatory determinations. Facilities-based competition in broadband is at risk of being crowded out by access-based entry that relies on access-prices that are too low.

However, some commentators (for example, Paltridge[178]) have suggested the reverse – that lowering access prices relative to the level that promotes efficient

---

[177]NB. We already know that this price excludes external benefits of infrastructure competition and so is probably too low, but let us ignore this for the moment.
[178]OECD (2001).

bypass might actually *encourage* infrastructure competition. For example, a 2002 Oftel statement takes this position:

> "Initiatives to enable local loop unbundling and carrier pre-selection could be seen as moves away from infrastructure competition. This is not the case. These initiatives are more a recognition that getting rid of entry barriers to promote infrastructure competition will enable investment to take place but eventually this build will tail off. Once the infrastructure is built, there will be other opportunities in the market (such as LLU and CPS) which Oftel has responded to in a way that does not undermine any incentives to further investment."[179]

This argument rests on a very strong assumption that cheap access encourages entrants into the market who subsequently invest in infrastructure. However, there are few theoretical reasons to expect entrants to behave in this way. If it is more cost effective to enter using regulated access rather than to invest, then it is also likely to be the case that access provides the cheapest means of expanding as well.

It is difficult to see what factors might strongly tip the business case of an access-based entrant back towards infrastructure investment as its business develops. One possible factor could be better information about demand and cost conditions, which might encourage a commitment to building infrastructure, rather than using access services to wait and see how the market might develop. However, it is doubtful that an entrant would learn much specifically as a result of access-based entry to the market. It is true that the entrant learns about market conditions over time, in particular likely customer demand for its services, and also possibly what aspects of service customers particularly value. However, as an access-based entrant, it does not learn about costs and technology, whereas a facilities-based entrant would. Therefore, it is unlikely that learning about market conditions is sufficient to tip an entrant into making a subsequent infrastructure investment when cheap access is available.

Even if it were the case that greater certainty resulting from information gathered about market conditions leads to later infrastructure investment, it is unlikely that this information would be gained only as a result of entering the market with an access-based business. Simply sitting on the sidelines and monitoring market developments from outside is likely to gather similar information to participating as an access-based entrant. Therefore, even if subsequent infrastructure competition does occur, it is very likely to be the result of the market maturing and players having a more certain investment environment by virtue of the evolution of the market alone, rather than because they were present at early stages of the market as access-based providers. In this case, there is no sense in which initial access-based entry provides a toe-hold that encourages later infrastructure investment; rather infrastructure investment, if

---

[179] Oftel (April 2002), Chapter 1: paragraph 1.14.

it occurs, is a product of changing market conditions. What is certain is that at each and every point in the lifecycle of a new service, the lower access prices are set, the less incentive there is to invest in infrastructure.

Therefore, it is much more logical to see access as a substitute for investment, rather than as a complement. U.S. experience bears this out. Entry has been based on highly discounted, compulsory access to local loops. Entrants have not subsequently switched over to infrastructure investment as the incentive to use access is too great. Indeed, as their business practices have become established and reliant on access, there is likely to be some resistance to switching over to alternative business models, especially those based on infrastructure investment.

In the EU, the prices of unbundled local loops are generally higher than in the United States and so the problem is a different one. Resale and bitstream access has crowded out both investment in platforms and more limited facilities-based competition based on unbundled local loops. No provider using resale or bitstream access has switched into facilities-based provision. Therefore, bitstream access and resale are not generally complementary to facilities-based competition (either full platform competition or more limited facilities-based provision based on LLU).

There are some benefits to competitive carriers in using LLU alongside a platform-based strategy. Some platform-based providers have used mixed strategies of both using their own platforms and unbundled local loops (e.g. FastWeb in Italy). This mixed strategy can increase coverage and spread some common costs of marketing and central overheads across a larger coverage area. However, if unbundled loops are priced too cheaply, this risks undermining the incentives of providers using such mixed deployment strategies to extend the reach of their platforms.

Using bitstream access to extend the coverage of a mass-market retail service is likely to have little benefit apart from that of enjoying limited scale economies in marketing. However, there may be some niche markets where bitstream access is beneficial to a facilities-based provider. Some business customers may have very geographically fragmented data networking requirements, e.g. in banking or other sectors with many small branch offices. It may be difficult for even an infrastructure-based entrant to provide the entire portfolio of services such a business customer might require. In such cases, bitstream access may be used alongside infrastructure to provide service offers over wide geographical areas that certain business customers might require.

In summary, even if there are some very specific circumstances where there are complementarities between access and certain types of investment, it is very far from the case that access-based entry naturally leads onto facilities-based provision in the way claimed by some NRAs.

5.4   What drives penetration?

As broadband delivery platforms, both DSL and cable have achieved critical mass across many OECD countries. The heterogeneous position with respect to their relative market shares indicates that neither cable nor DSL has a clear competitive advantage over the other; relative take-up has been very much determined by the history of local market developments and regulatory conditions.

As we describe below, our initial study of European broadband statistics up to end-2002 and mid-2003 produced compelling empirical evidence that competition between DSL, cable and other platforms is a driver of broadband penetration. We have examined recently available new data up to mid-2004, and found substantially the same results. By contrast, we found no corresponding evidence from data up to mid-2003 that access-based entry has stimulated penetration, although there are some country-specific examples of LLU apparently encouraging broadband take-up. Revisiting the data from 2004, we again found no evidence that bitstream or resale entry stimulates broadband penetration. However, there is some evidence that LLU might complement facilities-based provision.

5.4.1   Platform competition and penetration

The hypothesis that the existence of multiple delivery platforms for broadband in a country stimulates competition and therefore drives broadband penetration is widely stated in industry research. For example, in its analysis of the drivers of broadband take-up, Point Topic identifies competition between DSL and cable providers as *"making a major contribution"* to broadband take-up. It argues that cable both stimulates take-up in its own right and acts as an important stimulus for DSL rollout by incumbent telecom operators, for example in Belgium.[180] This is also reflected in the statements of many domestic regulators and international institutions, as described in section 5.1.2.

To test the validity of this hypothesis, we looked at a panel of data on total broadband penetration per household and the relative shares of DSL and other platforms (including cable, fibre and other) for 18 Western European and North American countries at end-2002, using data from Informa's World Broadband Database. Analysis of this data supports the hypothesis that platform competition is a driver of broadband penetration:

□ We plotted total broadband connections / households against non-DSL market share (which is mainly cable, except in Italy and Sweden, where fibre is also significant). We found that high levels of broadband penetration are generally associated with a relatively even split between DSL and non-DSL subscribers: the countries with the eight highest penetration rates all had

---

[180]Point Topic (April 2003b), page 4.

Figure 12: Broadband penetration & platform competition, end-2002

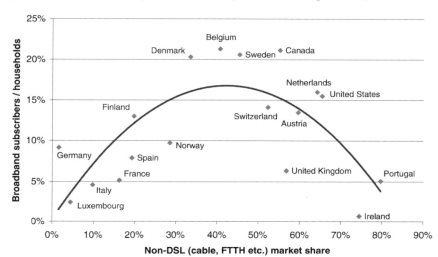

Source: Informa (2003) data

non-DSL market shares of between 33% and 65%. Countries with low penetration rates typically have market shares much more heavily skewed to either DSL or non-DSL platforms. This is illustrated by the hump-shaped relationship in Figure 12.

□ An alternative approach is to look at the correlation between broadband penetration and the difference in market share between DSL and non-DSL platforms, which may be considered a proxy for platform competition. Where this difference is small, there are similar-sized DSL and non-DSL subscribers bases. We observe a strongly statistically significant, negative linear relationship between the two, indicating that penetration tends to increase as the difference between platform market shares diminishes. The rank correlation between the two variables for the 18 countries is –0.7[181], which again supports the hypothesis.

Ideally, a next step would be to undertake a wider econometric survey of the drivers of broadband penetration across OECD countries, looking at the role of platform competition alongside other potential drivers, such as price, IT readiness, urbanisation and time since launch. Such analyses have been attempted prior to 2004, for example by Bauer (2003), but have not produced meaningful results.[182] The basic obstacle is the lack of sufficient time series data

---

[181] A correlation of –0.7 is strongly statistically significant in relation to the available sample. NB. –1.0 would indicate a perfect negative correlation and 0.0 would indicate no correlation.

[182] Bauer (2003) used multiple regression models to attempt to explain variations in broadband diffusion across 30 OECD countries at end-2001, but "the results are not very robust."

available, owing to the early state of development of the market. We investigated the scope for undertaking a wider analysis using the latest available data up to end-2002, but concluded that we could not obtain statistically meaningful results.

Following the release of our initial report, Distaso, Lupi and Manenti (September 2004) attempted an econometric analysis of 14 European broadband markets using newly published data. This is the first such study to our knowledge that has produced statistically significant results, although care must still be taken in interpreting the results given the early state of the adoption process in many of the states included in their analysis. Consistent with our own findings, they observed "that while inter-platform competition drives broadband adoption, competition in the market for DSL services does not play a significant role."[183]

The many examples of countries where *both* cable and DSL have 'substantial' market shares include: Austria, Belgium, Canada, Denmark, the Netherlands, South Korea, Sweden, the United Kingdom and the United States. These countries are generally the world leaders in terms of broadband penetration. Using end-2002 data, the United Kingdom appears to stand out as an exception, having an unusually low penetration level given the small gap between DSL and cable broadband shares. However, this may in part be attributed to relatively late roll-out of DSL in the United Kingdom relative to the other countries; there is also evidence that the UK broadband market is catching up – growth rates are amongst the fastest in the world at present (see Figure 13 and case study in Annex I).

Data on broadband take-up supplied by NRAs to the EU Commission for the six months from January to July 2003 provides further evidence that platform competition is a driver of penetration. As Figure 13 illustrates, it is possible to divide the 15 EU states into three groups during this period:

1. 'Lead performers'. The six fastest growing EU markets saw increases in penetration of 4% or more of households. All of these countries have relatively high levels of platform competition (neither DSL nor cable have more than 70% of the market). This includes the United Kingdom, which has apparently overtaken Germany and Spain in terms of penetration during this period.
2. 'Other growth areas' – This group of six countries had more modest growth, increasing household penetration by 2.0–3.3%. The level of competition across platforms varies widely across this group, but all have DSL shares of 74% or higher.
3. 'Laggards' – Three markets saw negligible growth in broadband connections. Amongst these, Greece and Ireland are still at the very earliest stages of service deployment. Portugal's poor performance is more surprising, given penetration is above 5%; one possible explanation is the lack of competitive

---

[183] Distaso, Lupi & Manenti (September 2004).

Figure 13: Platform competition and new broadband additions, Jan–Jun 2003

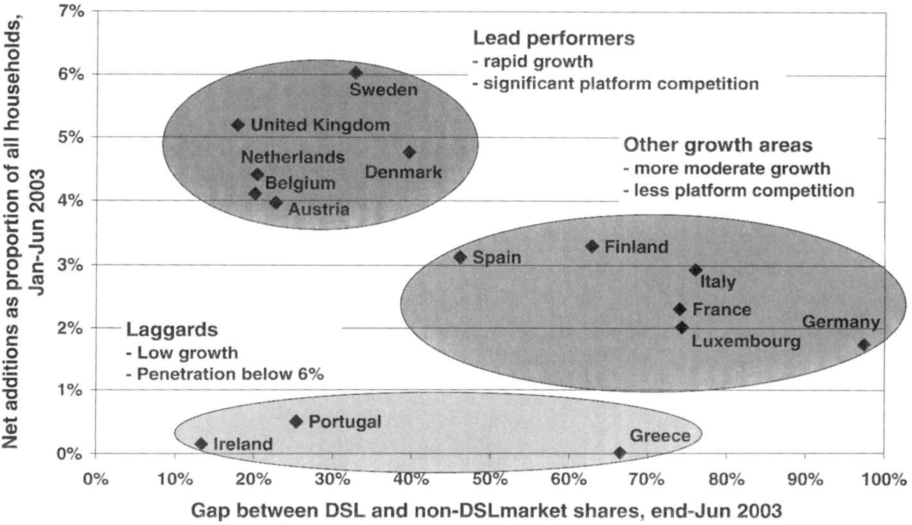

Source: European Commission (September 2003) data

pressure on incumbent Portugal Telecom, which owns both the main cable and DSL platforms.

Clearly platform competition is only one of a number of factors behind this disparate growth performance. Nevertheless, the evidence that it is a significant driver of penetration is compelling.

5.4.2 Access products and penetration

Whereas the hypothesis that platform competition is a key driver of broadband penetration is widely acknowledged, the potential contribution of access-based entry is much more controversial. Advocates of greater regulatory intervention in broadband often put significant emphasis on the potential contribution that increased access-based entry could make to overall broadband take-up, through competition. For example, the ECTA advocates *"an appropriate range of DSL wholesale and cost-orientated interconnection products to meet all aspects of demand for DSL services"* as a way of enhanced competition and thus the development of *"Broadband Europe"*.[184] However, our empirical analysis of end-2002 data on broadband provides no evidence of a relationship between broadband penetration and take-up of access products.

---

[184]See, for example: ECTA news release (Nov 2002).

Figure 14: Broadband penetration and non-incubement DSL access, end-2002

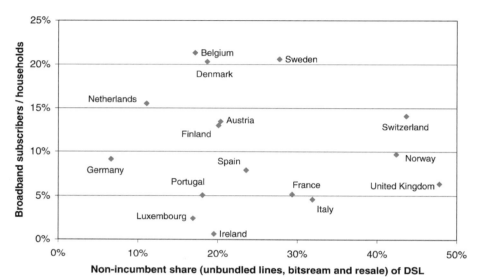

Source: Informa (2003) data

To test the validity of the hypothesis that take-up of access products may be a driver of penetration, we looked at a panel of data on broadband penetration and the relative shares of incumbent and other operators using access products over DSL for 16 European countries[185], using data from Informa's World Broadband Database. We then undertook a number of tests to investigate whether there is a relationship between broadband penetration and take-up of access products in general and/or specific categories of access products.

In the following figures, we plot broadband penetration in the sample countries at end-2002 against:

☐ non-incumbent access of all types, as a proportion of all DSL (see Figure 14);

☐ bitstream and end-to-end resale as a proportion of all broadband subscribers (see Figure 15); and

☐ LLU and line sharing as a proportion of all broadband subscribers (see Figure 16).

As can be seen in all cases, the available data provides no evidence of a systematic relationship between take-up of any form of access products and greater broadband penetration. Performing a rank correlation analysis confirms this conclusion. Table 12 reports the rank correlations between both DSL

---

[185]EU 15 (except Greece) plus Norway and Switzerland.

Figure 15: Broadband penetration against bitstream & resale take-up, end-2002

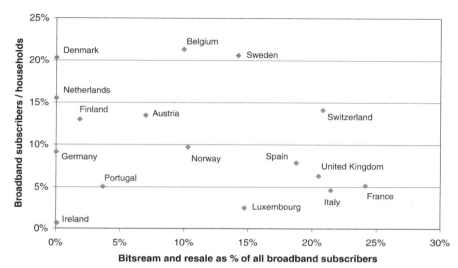

Source: Informa (2003) data

Figure 16: Broadband penetration and LLU / line sharing, end-2002

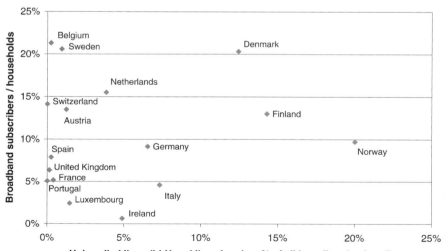

Source: Informa (2003) data

Table 12: Rank correlations between DSL/Broadband penetration and measures of access take-up, end-2002

Sample of 16 European states, end-2002 data	Rank of DSL penetration	Rank of broadband penetration
Rank of LLU subscribers (as share of DSL)	0.18	0.02
Rank of LLU subscribers (as share of all broadband)	0.25	-0.04
Rank of resale/bitstream subscribers (as share of DSL)	-0.25	-0.15
Rank of resale/bitstream subscribers (as share of all broadband)	-0.27	-0.29
Rank of all access subscribers (as share of DSL)	-0.07	-0.08
Rank of all access subscribers (as share of all broadband)	0.07	-0.14

Source: Informa (2003) data

penetration and broadband penetration, on the one hand, and various measures of access product take-up, on the other. The rank correlations for LLU are generally mildly positive (implying LLU in Europe may encourage penetration), while those for resale/bitstream are negative (implying they actually set back penetration). However, the very small correlations in all cases imply that there is no strong systematic relationship. These results contrast markedly with the evidence of a strong correlation between platform competition and broadband penetration, identified in the previous subsection.

In updating this book, we repeated these tests using data from July 2004, with similar results. As we discuss below, the hypothesis that LLU can have a positive impact on broadband take-up cannot be rejected. However, there is still no evidence of any positive relationship between take-up of resale and/or bitstream and overall broadband penetration.

Given both the early state of development of the broadband market and the limited sample of data available for this analysis, care should be taken in drawing too strong a conclusion from this analysis of access products. In particular, the analysis in relation to LLU take-up and penetration may not be particularly robust, given that take-up of LLU is generally low across EU states. The conclusion that there is no significant relationship between resale/bitstream take-up and penetration should be more robust given the much higher take-up of these products.

5.4.3 What is the role of LLU?

Although the cross-country empirical evidence (using end-2002 data) that LLU enhances broadband penetration is not significant, there are some country-specific examples of companies using LLU alongside facilities-based provision in ways that appear to have increased penetration. For example[186], fibre operators B2 (Sweden) and FastWeb (Italy) use DSL over LLU to gain access to customers located close to their local networks but not (yet) cost effective to connect directly. Similarly, Hanaro in South Korea has its own cable and DSL networks, but also uses DSL over LLU from incumbent KT. In addition, some other companies, such as HanseNet (Hamburg) and Bulldog (London) use LLU as a last mile solution between customers and their own high-specification fibre networks, enabling them to offer innovative services.

In these cases, the availability of LLU does appear to have enhanced the business cases of alternative infrastructure providers. Other forms of access products (other than line sharing) could not be used in this way, as they do not provide sufficient scope for adding value-added services that are distinct from local incumbent offerings. Nevertheless, consumers may benefit even more if these companies eventually migrate customers to a fully alternative network. If access prices are set too low, this is very unlikely to happen; rather such companies will continue to use LLU as a substitute to further infrastructure roll-out.

New data released since our initial report appears to support the hypothesis that LLU alongside facilities-based provision can stimulate broadband penetration, especially in countries where platform competition has not taken hold. The econometric analysis by Distaso, Lupi and Manenti (September 2004), which found that platform competition was a key driver of penetration, observed that "lower unbundling prices stimulate broadband."[187] Further, data for the EU-15 countries for July 2004 shown in Figure 17 indicates a positive relationship between broadband penetration and take-up of non-DSL platforms *plus* LLU (including shared lines). Treating LLU and line sharing as types of facilities-based competition helps to explain, in particular, the relatively strong performances of France and Italy in broadband take-up over the year to July 2004. By contrast, if bitstream and resale data are also incorporated alongside non-DSL and LLU, the relationship is much weaker.

Given that LLU can apparently bring higher penetration, especially where platform competition is developing, the low take-up of such products has, unsurprisingly, been identified as a potential cause for concern by some industry observers. There appear to be a number of reasons why take-up of LLU for broadband to date has been concentrated in just a few EU Member States:

---

[186]We explore some of these examples in more detail in the entrant case studies in Annex II.

[187]Distaso, Lupi & Manenti (September 2004).

Figure 17: Broadband penetration and facilities-based competition (including LLU and line sharing), July 2004

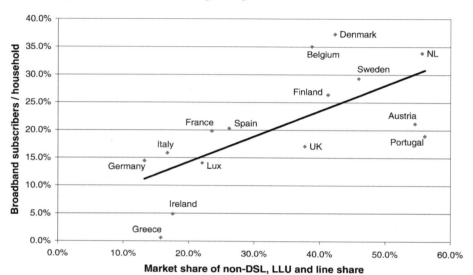

Source: EC 10th Implementation Report (2004) data

□ In a few countries (Germany, Denmark and Italy), a few particularly dynamic entrants using LLU may be largely responsible for driving up local LLU take-up.

□ In some countries, access-based entry strategies are limited, as no resale or bitstream access is available (Germany), or else it is difficult to obtain (Finland).

□ Two countries – Denmark and Italy – appear to have particularly low LLU access prices compared with the EU average (see Table 4).

□ In many other EU states, availability of bitstream and wholesale access at relatively low regulated prices may be crowding out LLU. Notably, in France and the United Kingdom, which in March 2003 had the highest take-up levels of bitstream access and resale (34% and 49% of DSL lines in the two countries respectively) and very little LLU take-up, the price increment in the monthly charge for the main wholesale products over full LLU was small.[188]

There are good reasons why availability of cheap regulated resale and bitstream access may tend to crowd out LLU. Such services:

---

[188] As of mid-2003, France Telecom charged 15.5 euros per month for its IP/ADSL512 wholesale access product and 10.5 euros for an unbundled line. BT charged 21.5 euros per month for its IPStream Home wholesale access product and 15.08 euros for full LLU. This premium appears small given the additional cost of facilities investment faced by entrant using LLU relative to those using wholesale access.

Figure 18: Take-up of LLU / line sharing versus bitstream / resale

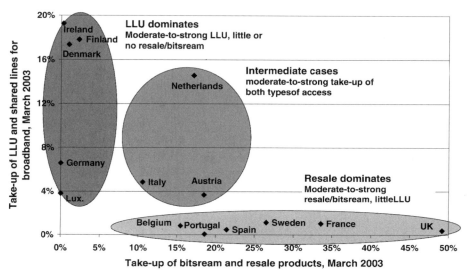

Note: All data reported as proportion of total national DSL subscribers.
Source: ECTA DSL Scorecard (March 2003) data

☐ provide commercial flexibility as operations can be scaled up or down in response to changing demand;
☐ do not lead to a commitment to any particular technology or standard;
☐ make fewer demands for capital, avoiding equipment and one-off installation costs; and
☐ avoid the need to gain access to local exchanges and collocate equipment.

Developing an empirical test to identify if there is such a crowding out effect is difficult, given the limited data available. However, a simple chart (Figure 18) comparing take-up of LLU/line sharing and resale/bitstream across 14 EU countries provides possible evidence of this effect. As of March 2003, there were only three countries where there is significant take-up of both levels of access products. In six countries, there is high use of resale/bitstream and negligible LLU take-up; these are all countries where resale/bitstream has for some time been available at relatively advantageous terms, which may have severely weakened the business case for LLU entry. There are five countries with relatively strong LLU take-up but negligible resale/bitstream: Denmark, Ireland, Finland, Germany and Luxembourg. These are generally countries where resale/bitstream services are unavailable or difficult to obtain, meaning that the business case for LLU entry has not so far been weakened by the availability of cheap resale/bitstream access.

Note that this is a dynamic situation, and that take-up levels can be expected to respond to changes in price differentials between access products. For example, since the above analysis was undertaken, there has been a big jump in take-up of line sharing in France, from 60,274 in July 2003 to 717,654 in July 2004.[189] At the beginning of this period, France had amongst the lowest access prices for line sharing in the EU, although this cost advantage has since been eroded by reduction elsewhere.

The forgoing discussion concerns the incremental effect of LLU on penetration rates. However, penetration rates do not serve as perfect proxy for consumer welfare. While welfare may rise in the short run due to the effects of LLU, dynamic efficiency considerations relating to investment incentives and the efficient allocation of resources could offset those gains.

---

[189]European Commission (2003) and (2004).

6 Appropriate policies for broadband regulation

What is the appropriate way forward for policy towards broadband? Our analysis so far has identified many potential problems with current policy, some carried over from 1998 EU regulatory framework, but many unfortunately present still in the New Regulatory Framework (NRF). In section 6.1, we briefly recap on what the main features on the current regulatory framework are and, in section 6.2, summarise its main problems. Broadly, this policy framework leads to a situation where incentives to invest in infrastructure (both in new platforms and using unbundled local loops) are suboptimal. In section 6.4, we lay out a road map for how policy could be reformed (largely within the existing powers of the European Commission) to provide a coherent approach that provides appropriate incentives for investment, promotes facilities-based competition and better achieves the public interest.

6.1 Overview of the regulatory regime in the EU

6.1.1 The New Regulatory Framework

The recently adopted NRF for telecommunication is intended to provide a greater degree of consistency between the decisions of NRAs and, where possible, to replace regulation with competition law. The key procedures are as follows:

☐ Article 15 of the Framework Directive requires the Commission (after consultation with the public and the NRAs) to adopt a recommendation on relevant product and service markets. These are markets (defined by the Commission based on competition law principles[190]) in which there may be competition problems that cannot be corrected by competition law and so require regulation. The Commission has already issued its recommendations on market definition[191], but there is a requirement that this is regularly reviewed.

☐ NRAs must define relevant markets taking account of national circumstances, but giving "utmost account"[192] to the recommendations and guidelines on relevant markets issued by the Commission. At the time of writing most NRAs are in the process of issuing their own recommendations.

☐ There is a procedure that NRAs must follow to deviate from the Commission's recommendations on relevant markets. Ultimately, the Commission has the

---

[190] There is a minor difference between market definition according to the principles of the NRF and traditional competition law analysis, in that the Framework Directive explicitly requires the Commission to take a forward-looking approach to market definition.

[191] Recommendation on relevant product and service markets, European Commission (February 2003b).

[192] Framework Directive, European Parliament and Council (2002), Article 15(3).

power to refuse requests from NRAs to extend the list of relevant markets (subject to issuing a detailed and objective analysis justifying this).[193]

☐ Remedies should only be applied to dominant[194] players (in the sense of competition law) within these relevant markets.[195] Where a market is effectively competitive, regulatory obligations should not be imposed (and existing obligations should be withdrawn).[196] There must be regular market reviews by NRAs to take account of changing competitive conditions.

☐ There is a general requirement that the remedies adopted by NRAs are proportionate to the competition problem that they are trying to remedy.[197] NRAs should seek to agree on the types of instruments and remedies best suited to address particular types of situations in the marketplace.[198] In particular, there is a general requirement that retail-level remedies should only be used where there is a competition problem that cannot be remedied through wholesale access measures.[199]

Access to unbundled local loops is one of the few services identified explicitly in the Framework Directive[200] for necessary inclusion in the initial list of relevant markets, despite this approach clearly not being platform or technology neutral. This provision carries over local loop unbundling measures from the previous regulatory framework that were enacted in 2000 through the Unbundling Regulation[201]. This required unbundled access to both full and shared local loops on transparent, fair and non-discriminatory terms and with cost-oriented prices.

Under the NRF, the Commission's Recommendation on relevant markets identifies two markets related to broadband services:

☐ wholesale unbundled access (including shared access) to metallic loops and sub-loops for the purpose of providing broadband and voice services; and
☐ wholesale broadband access.

The Recommendation explains that wholesale broadband access *"covers 'bit-stream' access that permits the transmission of broadband data in both directions and other wholesale access provided over other infrastructures, if and when they offer facilities equivalent to bit-stream access.)"* By "wholesale broadband access", the Commission means bitstream services over PSTN

---

[193] Framework Directive, European Parliament and Council (2002), Article 7(4).

[194] Under the new framework, "significant market power", the trigger for regulatory obligations is redefined to be equivalent to dominance under competition law.

[195] Framework Directive, European Parliament and Council (2002), Article 16(4).

[196] Framework Directive, European Parliament and Council (2002), Article 16(3).

[197] Framework Directive, European Parliament and Council (2002), Article 8(1).

[198] Framework Directive, European Parliament and Council (2002), Article 7(2).

[199] Universal Service Directive, European Parliament and Council (2002), Article 17(1).

[200] Framework Directive, European Parliament and Council (2002), Annex I.

[201] Regulation No. 2887/2000 on unbundled access to the local loop.

infrastructure in the first instance, but the Commission *"allows NRAs to take account of alternative infrastructures when and if they offer facilities equivalent to bitstream services".*[202] Therefore, even with the NRF, there is still asymmetric treatment of different delivery platforms as DSL over PSTN infrastructure is treated differently to cable and other infrastructure; only DSL is subject to specific access obligations. Further, the potential clearly exists for such obligations to be extended to new platforms or to require existing platforms to offer new access services:

☐ The Dutch NRA, OPTA, is reported to be considering applying bitstream regulation to cable networks;[203]
☐ In Canada, open access to cable networks for ISPs has been required since 1999; although legal challenges have delayed implementation, some voluntary agreements are in place;[204]
☐ Providers may offer differentiated grades of service over time and there may be demands for increasingly differentiated bitstream services to support these.

6.1.2 NRA's positions

Current policies of NRAs are primarily shaped by the former 1998 regulatory framework, as the NRF has only just been adopted. All Member States require cost-based LLU and line sharing as a result of the 2000 Unbundling Regulation, but NRAs have considerable discretion over the terms and conditions. Bitstream access and wholesale end-to-end access (for resellers) were not required by the Unbundling Regulation, though are now included in the "wholesale broadband access" market defined in the Recommendation on relevant markets and so are an area where NRA's can regulate. Nevertheless, bitstream access is now available in most EU countries and others are considering introduction. The basis for pricing bitstream access varies substantially from country to country, as shown in Table 5.

Although not all NRAs have implemented bitstream access to date, this Recommendation from the Commission is likely to encourage them to do so. In many Member States, there is already a hierarchy of access regulation, i.e. line sharing and full LLU, bitstream access and wholesale end-to-end products for resale. Most NRAs are currently undertaking market analysis to identify relevant markets susceptible to ex ante regulation. Depending on the findings of these exercises, the current position is likely to change. The fact that the Commission's Recommendation on market definition distinguishes wholesale broadband access (i.e. bitstream access) and unbundled wholesale access (i.e.

---

[202] Explanatory Memorandum of the Recommendation on relevant markets, European Commission (February 2003b), page 24.
[203] Idate (2002).
[204] FCC (October 2003), page 13.

LLU and line sharing) is likely to lead to more NRAs putting in place bitstream access requirements.

Since the Unbundling Regulation of 2000, LLU on both fully unbundled and shared terms is now a reality across the EU. Pricing of unbundled local loops is cost-based, though the pricing of these network services varies significantly across Member States. Cost-based pricing uses forward-looking LRIC, effectively pursuing an objective of efficient bypass (i.e. encouraging facilities-based entry only where this is cheaper than an artificial efficient incumbent, costing this on a forwarding looking MEA basis). These local loop unbundling obligations have been carried over into the initial list of relevant markets susceptible to ex-ante regulation recommended by the Commission.

At present, there is no presumption of non-intervention when new infrastructure is built or services are offered. NRAs can try to subject new services to access requirements, though the NRF puts some hurdles in the way of them doing so (the Article 7 procedures). They first need to convince the Commission that there is an appropriate relevant market that is susceptible to ex ante regulation.

6.2   Potential flaws in the existing regime

Although the existing regulatory regime has an explicit objective of encouraging competition through infrastructure investment and innovation, this is not matched by the implementation of policy. Once LLU is in place, additional forms of access regulation add little.

6.2.1   Tension between the implementation and objectives of policy

Both the Commission and NRAs are on record as being in favour of encouraging facilities-based competition. Indeed, Article 8(2)c of the Framework Directive requires NRAs to promote competition by *"encouraging efficient investment in infrastructure, and promoting innovation"*. This rightly reflects the main benefits of facilities-based competition:

☐ facilities-based competition has a different competitive dynamic to access-based competition, as the marginal costs of adding customers are lower and, therefore, the incentives to expand greater. Facilities-based competition is tougher than access-based competition. Cross-country comparisons clearly demonstrate that facilities-based competition leads to greater penetration of broadband whereas there is no evidence that access-based competition promotes penetration;

☐ facilities-based competition exposes the entire value chain to competitive discipline, encouraging internal efficiency amongst providers and reducing cost;

☐ facilities-based competition generates choice for customers over service features that access-based competition does not;

☐ facilities-based competition tests new technologies and techniques, allowing market selection of the most efficient and least cost approaches; and

☐ new theories of economic growth suggest that technological diversity has economy-wide external productive benefits, as new technologies becoming jumping off points for the developing of further new technologies, within the sector and elsewhere.

Tougher competition, greater cost reduction pressure, enhanced choice and greater take-up all generate significant consumer surplus. Estimates of the surplus enjoyed by consumers from introduction of broadband services suggest that these benefits are very considerable.

However, as we have seen there is a tension between this stated objective and the implementation of policy, which generally does not give sufficient incentive for infrastructure-based provision. If we look at the Commission's general policy statements, they explicitly acknowledge the importance of infrastructure investment in achieving platform competition and the need to be careful that regulation does not undermine the incentive to invest:

> "Competing network infrastructures are essential for achieving sustainable competition in networks and services in the long term. When there is effective competition, the new framework requires ex-ante regulatory obligations to be lifted. In the meantime however, those undertakings that were privileged to install infrastructure facilities under special or exclusive rights continue to benefit from those earlier investments – in particular those relating to long-lived facilities in the local access network. Granting others access to these facilities in a way that levels the playing field but does not remove incentives for new infrastructure investment ensures that users enjoy choice and competition during the transition to a fully competitive market. Investment in new and competing infrastructure will bring forward the day when such transitional access obligations can be relaxed."[205]

However, at the same time, the Commission sees access to the local loop as critical to delivering broadband services in the short term:

> "At the current time, upgraded cable systems are not sufficiently widely developed or deployed although the situation might change in some parts of the Community over the timeframe of the current Recommendation. Consequently the only reasonable widespread means of supplying the end user market is over the local access network loops of the PSTN which have been enhanced to provide broadband access services."[206]

---

[205]Explanatory Memorandum of the Recommendation on relevant markets, European Commission (February 2003b), page 3.

[206]Explanatory Memorandum of the Recommendation on relevant markets, European Commission (February 2003b), page 24.

Therefore, the Commission apparently sees granting access to existing local loops as pro-competitive providing it does not undermine the incentives to invest in alternative infrastructure and so delay platform competition.

The difficulty with this position is that it assumes it is possible to pursue an access policy that does not undermine investment incentives. As we have seen in section 5.3.3, an access policy based on the notion of efficient bypass is too static, does not take account of costs related to risk-bearing and flexibility, and fails to take account of the social benefits of infrastructure competition. This has adverse effects not only on entrants, who may be deterred from investing in infrastructure (be this a new platform or services based on LLU), but also on incumbents who will take account of the impact of access regulation when investing and innovating.

NRAs have taken a mixed position on the benefits of facilities-based competition relative to access-based competition. Although many NRAs have publicly stated positions that are positive towards facilities-based competition, individual decisions rarely support this position, being based much more on a static notion of access pricing that encourages efficient bypass.

If we take Oftel as an example, we observe that it took a strongly favourable policy position in favour of infrastructure competition during the 1990s, but that this has subsequently been diluted into one more favourable towards access-based competition. For example, in 1996, Oftel said:

> "Although competition from and between service providers can provide increased choice to consumers, this is not an adequate substitute for competition between networks. Only competition between networks can deliver competition in the supply of network services, which are necessary input into basic retail and enhanced services for consumers. Without network competition, even vigorous competition between service providers will not prevent customers from being disadvantaged by inefficient and/or expensive provision of such network services."[207]

In contrast, the 2002 Oftel Management Plan re-emphasises access-based competition:

> "In the last few years, development of infrastructure competition has slowed down as the cable companies finish their build rates and the mobile industry achieves full national coverage. At the same time there has been greater demand from service providers for access to BT's network, particularly in relation to unmetered internet access and to broadband services. Oftel's response has been to use its discretion, both in granting access to the network and also in setting the terms and conditions on which access is to be made available. . ."[208]

---

[207] Oftel (1996), Chapter 2: paragraph 2.7.
[208] Oftel (April 2002), Chapter 1: paragraph 1.11.

Oftel goes on to claim that there is no conflict between access regulation and encouraging infrastructure competition:

> "The greater emphasis on developing access to networks, both by other network providers and particularly by service providers in recent years, does not reflect a policy change away from infrastructure competition. Oftel's goal is to have competition at all levels in provision of wholesale and retail services. The regulator cannot predict, nor can it create, investment in infrastructure amongst aspiring entrants. Oftel sets the rules consistent with its overall strategy and in response to the needs of new entrants and overall impact on the market. . . ."[209]

However, as we have seen in section 5.3.5, there is an inherent conflict between access regulation and giving the appropriate incentives for the development of infrastructure-based competition; access regulation based only on the static notion of efficient bypass (which the current LRIC framework is) delivers insufficient incentive to invest in infrastructure. Therefore, despite general policy statements favourable to infrastructure investment, Oftel's detailed decisions do not deliver on this objective.

Further, Oftel has made statements to suggest that it might respond to tighter capital markets by encouraging *more* access-based entry to make up for a lack of infrastructure-based entry:

☐ Companies generally had less funds to invest in infrastructure, so there was greater pressure on Oftel to promote service competition by ensuring appropriate wholesale access to the incumbent's network. At the same time it was important for Oftel to ensure that there were still incentives for companies to invest at the network level, and to keep this area open to future competition.[210]

☐ In parallel with actions to promote competition, there was significant pressure from alternative providers for Oftel to intervene to enable access to the market on a 'buy' rather than 'build' basis, because of the lack of capital funds available to develop infrastructure.[211]

This is a flawed response; it is not possible to encourage more access-based entry without at the same time undermining infrastructure investment incentives. There is a trade-off that must be struck.

Although other regulators (such as RegTP) have adopted a more positive public position on infrastructure investment, it is still the case that all have an approach to access pricing that is very deeply grounded in the static view of access pricing as promoting efficient bypass. This is no longer the key issue for the future development of the telecommunications sector, as innovation and the

---

[209] Oftel (April 2002), Chapter 1: paragraph 1.13.
[210] Oftel (May 2003), Chapter 2: page 9.
[211] Oftel (May 2003), Chapter 2: page 10.

development of competing infrastructures are critical for advanced services. If public policy statements on encouraging the development of infrastructure competition are to be put in place, these objectives need to be reflected in the detailed implementation of policy and, in particular, the methodology for setting access prices.

6.2.2   The incremental impact of bitstream access with LLU in place

The Commission argues that wholesale unbundled access (i.e. LLU) and wholesale broadband access (i.e. bitstream access) constitute distinct wholesale markets. This is a key step in the Commission's conclusion that both forms of regulation are needed. The Commission's argument is that:

☐ LLU is a poor substitute for bitstream access for an alternative provider as using unbundled local loops requires complementary network elements. In the Commission's words: *"[f]rom a demand perspective a wholesale provider using wholesale broadband access will only consider unbundled local loops a substitute if the wholesale broadband access operator has all the other network elements needed to self-provide an equivalent service. The supply substitution possibilities depend on the same condition."*[212]
☐ Bitstream access is a poor substitute for unbundled access to the local loop. A broadband provider making use of unbundled local loops would find it difficult to switch to using a bitstream service, as the other network elements (be they self-provided or bought) it would need would be different, requiring the provider's entire network to be reconfigured (the Commission refers to this as *"synchronous deployment of technology"*). The Commission concludes that *"[a]n operator using unbundled local loops will not normally consider another form of wholesale broadband access service to be a substitute even if the service provided by the broadband service provider allowed the supply of all the same services that were provided over the unbundled loops."*[213]

Both evidence and *a priori* considerations suggest that this conclusion about market definition is incorrect. In particular, the Commission's two arguments above effectively reduce to the assertion that bitstream access and unbundled loops are not substitutes as providers require additional inputs and these inputs are very different in the two cases. However, this argument does not show that these two wholesale offerings cannot be substitutes for providers. These other inputs such as backhaul networking and providing DSLAMs are not subject to strong scale economies, can often be purchased on the open market (in the case of backhaul) or otherwise self-provided. Put simply, bitstream access is simply an unbundled local loop bundled together with a range of other largely replicable (and competitively supplied) inputs. Providers will make rational judgments between using unbundled loops and using bitstream services depending on the

---

[212] Oftel (May 2003), Chapter 2: page 10.
[213] Oftel (May 2003), Chapter 2: page 10.

costs of each access service, the costs of the other inputs required to offer a retail service (whether self-provided or bought in) and the risk and flexibility associated with each option. Changing the relative prices of bitstream access and unbundled loops will change the terms of this trade-off.

We can observe providers using a mixed deployment strategy, suggesting that there is a choice between using different access services. For example, in the United Kingdom, Bulldog offers a variety of differentiated DSL services with downstream bandwidths of up to 8 mbps in areas where it installs its own equipment, but resells BT's standard DSL service in other geographical areas. As we have already discussed in Section 5.3.2, reselling services is unlikely to make a significant contribution in terms of gross margins, as reselling is a contestable business. However, Bulldog may gain some benefit in terms of raising brand awareness and scale economies in marketing.

In the case of the business market, there may be limited concerns about the ability of facility-based entrants to contest certain niche business markets where customers have geographically fragmented demand or data networking. Clearly the issue of replicability in such cases is less important for DSLAMs than for the local loop, so there is less to be gained from adding bitstream access given the presence of LLU than from introducing LLU in the first place.

Entrants naturally tend to use whatever form of access provided is most attractive, which depends both on margins and on the commercial flexibility different access services provide. For example, in the United Kingdom to date, there has been much greater use of bitstream access than fully unbundled local loops, as regulated access prices favour this form of entry. If we look across the EU, we find preferential take-up of bitstream services where these are cheapest (see Section 5.4.3). This suggests that various forms of access are substitutes from the perspective of entrants, especially at the point of initial entry.

The Commission's approach to wholesale market definition does not seem to derive, as it should, from a proper consideration of retail level substitution behaviour by consumers. In particular, taking the Commission's argument that bitstream and unbundled access are in different markets because they require different complementary inputs, this argument, if correct, would apply even more strongly across different platforms. Therefore, we could have a hypothetical situation in which there were many competing platforms, offering highly substitutable services at the retail level, but in which any access services offered would, by the Commission's logic, constitute distinct markets, despite no platform operator having market power at either the retail or wholesale level. This is clearly an incorrect conclusion.

Failure to acknowledge the extent to which different wholesale access services are indeed substitutes for providers also leads to the mistaken conclusion that there are significant incremental benefits from requiring many types of regulated access in parallel. In particular, a consequence of the Commission's position on market definition is that it believes there to be a significant benefit from providing bitstream access in addition to local loop unbundling. However:

□ If the rationale for granting access is that incumbent operators have market power over some relevant time horizon in the larger broadband market deriving from control of the local loop, then these concerns can be addressed through local loop unbundling (with line sharing arrangements to mitigate any concerns about customer inertia arising from the need to switch over voice services along with broadband). Access would have then been provided to the non-replicable assets controlled by the incumbent (i.e. the local loop) and there would be little additional benefit from providing access to largely replicable assets (i.e. DSLAMs, subject to the concerns about niche business markets identified above, and cable modems) through a bitstream service;

□ It has been argued that offering many parallel forms of access may encourage entry and ultimately facilitate infrastructure investment to the extent that entrants subsequently switch over from access-based services to building their own infrastructure. Therefore, according to this view, we should see parallel forms of access as complements, rather than substitutes; for example, wholesale end-to-end access for resellers may provide a toe-hold for new entry and ultimately lead to infrastructure investment. Although this argument has been made repeatedly (both by the Commission and NRAs), there is little to commend it, as we have already seen in Section 3.1. As a matter of logic, making one form of access cheaper should simply encourage greater use of that form of access, less use of other forms of access, and less infrastructure investment. U.S. experience shows exactly this substitution effect, with cheap line sharing undermining the case for alternative infrastructure investment and no signs of early entrants making investments in infrastructure having established a toe-hold position using access services.

□ Against these benefits, the costs of having parallel forms of access regulation should be taken into account. Regulation is necessarily imperfect and access prices are set with imperfect information about costs. Given the inevitable uncertainty in setting access prices, this reduces investment incentives both for entrants and incumbents, as discussed in section 3.1. Parallel forms of access regulation compound this risk, as setting any one access price too low is sufficient to harm investment incentives, regardless of the level of other access prices.

□ It is not that case that parallel layers of access regulation can be left in place 'just in case' some activity other than the local loop proves difficult to replicate; even with access prices set using an appropriate methodology, noise and limited information in the regulatory process will necessary lead to depressed investment incentives. If a specific form of access regulation is not necessary because assets and activities are replicable by entrants or because there are other forms of regulated access to non-replicable assets or activities already in place, then the only way to preserve investment incentives is not to regulate.

Overall, this suggests that a cautious approach to bitstream access pricing is needed at the very least.

6.2.3 Poor roll-out incentives

Widespread perceptions that broadband roll-out has been slow can be traced back in part to poor incentives for infrastructure investment. We are seeing investment in alternative infrastructure where local conditions are favourable (e.g. fibre in Italy) or where there are subsidies (e.g. Sweden) or both. Therefore, we are currently at a cusp: it is not that competitive infrastructure is not feasible; it is that the returns are uncertain and in part depressed by regulatory distortions. Moves by NRAs towards favouring access over infrastructure competition, on the grounds that the investment climate for telecom infrastructure is currently unfavourable, do not appear justified as there are notable cases of investment in new cable and fibre networks with uncertain paybacks. By lowering their expected returns, mandatory access undermines investment in these competing platforms.

Both DSL roll-out and cable upgrading need significant resources; there is an entire sequence of future investment decisions facing providers about capacity and coverage. Incentives to invest in expansion of existing platforms are being depressed by:

☐ threat of access requirements on new services (e.g. video over DSL);
☐ threats of extension of access regulation (e.g. bitstream access where not already present, for example on cable or fibre, or for differentiated DSL services), rather than rolling back regulation were competition is effective;
☐ regulatory risks arising from inefficiently low access prices focussing primarily on static efficiency objectives (efficient bypass), rather than taking account of the dynamic benefits of infrastructure based competition;
☐ the presence of parallel layers of access regulation, as setting just one access price too low is sufficient to distort infrastructure investment incentives; and
☐ risk of some form of service obligation being imposed without a compensating subsidy.

There are technologies such as fixed wireless access and developments of WiFi that have great potential to provide mass-market BB services within the near future. The incentives to provide such new services are being undermined by current policy. Not only does an investor in infrastructure face the risk of potential extension of regulation, but also there are attractive alternative ways of entering the market based on bitstream access and reselling services.

6.2.4 The bias against infrastructure investment

New entrants choices are strongly skewed towards using access services rather than investing, as it provides a low risk way to enter the market. Take-up of new services (such as broadband) is difficult to forecast and technological developments uncertain (potentially leading to first mover disadvantages to the extent that investments are sunk and technology moves on). The flexibility benefits of being able to avoid committing technology choices and scale services easily in response to customer take-up strongly favour access services over infrastructure investment, even though the later gives control over service features. In new markets, there may be first mover advantages at the retail level, but infrastructure investment is probably not necessary to achieve these; access-based entry is sufficient.

There are strong grounds to believe that current access pricing methodologies lead to regulated access prices that are too low relative to the social optimum:

☐ Current access regulation is strongly grounded in the notion of efficient bypass, i.e. ensuring that facilities-based entry occurs only where it provides a service cheaper than an efficient entrant (the later generally calculated on a MEA basis). This approach is much too static, as it fails to consider any of external benefits of facilities-based competition to society at large.
☐ In addition, access pricing methodologies do not take account of the flexibility benefits of access services, that both give considerable benefits to users of access services and impose additional resource costs on access providers. In effect, access-based entrants receive commercially valuable options to expand and contract their business (and even to exit the market), which they do not pay for. These benefits are greater, and so the distortions larger, for access regulation applying to a greater proportion of the value chain, i.e. resale access as compared with LLU.

Parallel layers of access regulation (e.g. wholesale products for resellers, bitstream access, line sharing, full LLU) again compound the risk of biasing entry decision in favour of using access rather than investing in infrastructure. Getting any *one* of these many parallel access prices too low simply causes entrants to herd into using one particular access service, depending on where margins are greatest.

Substitution between different forms of entry creates the potential for self-justification by regulators. Poor take-up of LLU appears to derive primarily from excessively attractive terms for bitstream access and resale. Where this occurs, poor take-up of LLU should not suggest that there is an intrinsic competitive problem with entry based on LLU, thereby justifying bitstream regulation at low access prices. It is rather that cheap resale and bitstream access is likely to have crowded out the use of unbundled loops, and making the terms of such access less attractive could address the problem.

6.2.5   Unsustainable business models and regulatory inertia

Business models for entrants are strongly shaped by regulation. U.S. experience with the bankruptcy of many CLECs in 2000 and 2001 shows the fragility of business models based on regulatory arbitrage, as the FCC Chairman has acknowledged:

> "[t]he regulatory arbitrage bubble expands ever more perilously with each regulatory variable and is sure to eventually pop, like dot coms of old, if government policy does not diligently steer the balloon to stable ground"[214]

In contrast, facilities-based entry is more robust to changes in regulatory policy. Even if an infrastructure-based provider goes bust, its network will live on and can be used by others.

Any change in access policy would create winners and losers. In particular, a move towards a system that encouraged greater infrastructure investment would hit access-based entrants, particularly resellers with narrow margins. This is a self-reinforcing problem: it creates substantial regulatory inertia, as NRAs are unable to change access pricing or policy for fear of opposition from adversely affected interest groups, even if such changes might be in the general public interest. For example, if access regulation leads to inefficient entry, this situation is very difficult for an NRA to reverse, owing to the adverse commercial impact on the entrant. Access pricing setting is imperfect and noisy; it needs to take a precautionary approach to avoid encouraging inefficient entry and discouraging infrastructure investment.

6.3   Subsidies and USO requirements

State resources are already flowing into broadband provision, though in an un-focussed and distorting way. State-funded and controlled infrastructure projects (often undertaken by local government in an uncoordinated way) bias technology choices, undermine investment incentives, and are very unlikely to provide the least cost means of deploying services. For example, the government of Ireland has threatened to build its own fibre network should *eircom* not reduce its LLU rates. Concerns about possible service obligations and missing out on future subsidies create substantial investment risks, decreasing incentives for infrastructure investment in a similar manner to regulatory risks. While the objectives of such initiatives may themselves be laudable, any policies that do not take into account the potential distortion of investment incentives for private operators may ultimately do more harm than good.

It is beyond the scope of this study to consider whether there is an economic case for specific subsidies and/or service obligations in relation to broadband. Rather, we seek to highlight some of the potential competitive distortions which could emerge as a result of particular subsidies and service obligations, and discuss which possible policy principles could be adopted to minimise such problems.

---

[214]FCC (February 2003b).

Some policy statements by EU Member States in recent years could be read as suggesting that policymakers see broadband as a service of such great social and economic importance that it should be subject to a universal service obligation of some type. There is no imminent prospect of such a development within EU law. Nevertheless, the Universal Service Directive in relation to the provision of access at a fixed location states that:

> "The connection provided shall be capable of allowing end-users to make and receive local, national and international telephone calls, facsimile communications and **data communications, at data rates that are sufficient to permit functional Internet access, taking into account prevailing technologies used by the majority of subscribers and technological feasibility**"[215] [emphasis added]

Elsewhere, in the directive, functional Internet access is described as a data rate of about 56 kbps, with flexibility for member states to identify lower rates depending on local circumstances, i.e. narrowband only. Nevertheless, the emphasis on "prevailing technologies", "majority of subscribers" and "technological feasibility" leaves open the possibility that future interpretations of the directive could define functional internal access in terms of broadband speeds and always-on capability.

Whilst the economic importance of broadband provision is widely recognised (see section 2.1), the situation is very different from the history of voice telephony. When USOs were first imposed, telephony services were provided by state-owned monopoly PTOs and funded by cross-subsidies between customer groups. In contrast, broadband is *already* provided by competing operators and any obligations that enforce provision (be this a USO or coverage obligations of some sort) need to preserve the competitive dynamic already in play.

There are already many examples of direct intervention by EU Member State in broadband provision. These initiatives may have a number of different objectives, including, for example: more widespread access to broadband services; reducing the cost of broadband for businesses and consumers; and promoting 'higher quality' broadband services. While these underlying objectives appear worthy, the specific methods being used to achieve them often raise concerns. Specifically, they often show state resources being used to pick a particular technology or a particular provider or both, rather than meeting an explicit service obligation in a competitively and technologically neutral manner.

Examples of countries that have introduced such initiatives illustrate some of the potential pitfalls:

☐ *Sweden.* With a programme worth around 1 billion euros to develop broadband networks at the local, municipal and national levels, Sweden has the

---

[215]Universal Service Directive, European Parliament and Council (2002), Article 4(2).

most developed system of broadband subsidies in the EU. It is often portrayed as a success story, owing to the low prices and competitive nature of the market for broadband services (see case study in Annex I). Indeed, the roll-out of municipal-sponsored fibre networks has assisted the emergence of FTTH operator B2, which has been influential in driving price and product competition (see case study in Annex II). However, the programme has also created significant concerns about competitive neutrality and contravention of EU State Aid rules, especially given the desire of some municipals to build and run their own networks.[216] Notably, the bandwidth requirement for local access has now been reduced from the original threshold of 2 mbps so that upgrading of existing DSL and cable networks would be eligible for subsidies, after public tender, as well as fibre.

☐ *Netherlands.* Influenced in part by early developments in Sweden, the government's Broadband Expert Group has set out an ambitious plan for the roll-out of a national FTTH network by 2015, costing about 2 billion euros. Apparently, the Group has indicated that it views the network as a 'natural monopoly' but it has not provided any recommendations as to how to address the competitive implications of this.[217] Given that the Netherlands already has a highly competitive broadband service market, with cable and DSL providers investing heavily to upgrade their networks to provide data services at increasingly higher speeds, it is unclear what benefits, if any, such heavy public spending will bring (see case study in Annex I). This initiative is likely to be bitterly opposed by the country's cable and DSL operators, whose own incentives for further upgrades could be killed by such a project.

☐ *Ireland.* Notwithstanding the country's record to date in broadband roll-out, the Irish government has lofty ambitions with regard to broadband penetration and average data speeds relative to other OECD states (see case study in Annex I). A key element in its ambitions is the construction by local authorities of metropolitan fibre rings, available on *"an open access basis"* to local operators. However, the emphasis on supply of public infrastructure construction rather than public demand may well have set back broadband penetration, especially in the medium term. For private operators, it has created incentives for them to delay their own roll-out plans, owing to both the potential to 'piggy-back' on state funding and uncertainty over the extent to which the government may itself re-enter the telecoms market.

A further potential source of uncertainty for private operators is the activities of local governments and regional development agencies. Many such bodies, especially those in deprived regions, have targeted broadband access as a key way of differentiating their regions from others, and thus attracting inward investment. This has prompted local intervention on both the supply (building or sponsoring infrastructure provision) and demand (subsidising consumer

---

[216]Cullen International (2002), page 17.

[217]Paul Budde Communications (2003), page 2.

purchases of broadband services) sides. Meanwhile, other such bodies have proposed to develop their own commercial services as spin offs from public initiatives. For example, in London, Westminster Council is proposing to roll out a WiFi 802.22b network, the pilot phase of which will cover the Soho area by mid-2004. The immediate focus of the service is to improve communication between council workers, but council officials also envisage this as a commercial opportunity, providing data and voice over IP services to local residents, businesses and visitors in competition with broadband providers and mobile phone services.[218]

Intervention and/or the threat of intervention on the supply side of the broadband market is much more likely to lead to competitive distortions than demand stimulation. It creates uncertainty for businesses about the potential competitive landscape in terms of both firms and technologies. Moreover, there is a particular risk that government decisions will be determined by their view of how they would like to see the market develop rather than sound commercial judgement. Many such initiatives to date appear to place great emphasis on connection speeds, which has led to an apparent bias towards technologies that deliver higher bandwidth (usually fibre and, to a less extent, WiFi), even though these may not be the most cost-effective solutions and there is often little evidence to suggest there is presently much demand for such additional speeds.

Overall, this situation is causing two major uncertainties:

1. that infrastructure-based providers of broadband services might be subject to service obligations – with respect to both universal coverage and available connection speeds – at some point in the future; and
2. that there might be subsidies available for broadband infrastructure provision at some future date.

Both forms of uncertainty create great value to 'waiting and seeing' what might happen. For example, those early to market might be subject to harsher obligations or miss out on subsidies. This both disincentivises entry and also tips the balance strongly in favour of access-based entry, rather than building infrastructure.

6.4   Appropriate policy for broadband

6.4.1   Bitstream access adds little given LLU

There are already plenty of examples of multiple infrastructure platforms coexisting in sustainable competition. Therefore, it is not the case that broadband is a natural monopoly. This has been demonstrated by market outcomes; urban and suburban areas already sustain competing platforms despite regulatory biases

---

[218]newswireless.net (April 2003).

against such an outcome. There are interesting new technologies (particular fixed wireless and developments of WiFi) waiting for the right conditions for entry and under constant review by existing players in related markets. 3G provides a potential substitute to fixed broadband services for some users.

If there are areas that are costly to serve because of demographical or geographical factors and so cannot sustain multiple operators, then market power resulting from control of the local loop by the incumbent operator can be addressed using local loop unbundling. This should be a largely sufficient remedy to address market power arising in such cases.

Therefore, the case for multiple layers of regulated access at various levels of the value chain given the risks relative to the benefits is weak. In a hypothetical situation where DSL over existing local loops is the only feasible platform for a particular customer segment in a particular location, LLU should largely be a sufficient remedy to control market power due to lack of substitutes to the local loop. One could imagine a hypothetical worst case in which there were question marks whether some other aspects of the service might be subject to scale economies at low demand (e.g. due to indivisibilities in DSLAM capacity). However, even in this case it is important to be cautious in using additional forms of access to address specific, geographically limited problems in fringe areas when there are possible adverse effects on the incentives for facilities-based provision generally.

Opening access to assets or activities that are largely replicable by entrants runs considerable risks when there are systematic distortions built into access pricing methodologies. Arguments that multiple forms of access encourage entrants who eventually switch over to infrastructure investment are contradicted by the evidence; cheap access causes a dependency culture.

6.4.2   A more dynamic view of access pricing is need

To promote facilities-based competition, a different approach to access regulation is needed with a more rational basis for access pricing:

☐ Even if a specific form of access regulation were justified, the current methodology sets access prices that are too low relative to the public interest. Access prices should be based on the actual costs of meeting access obligations, including the flexibility benefits provided for access users and the corresponding resource costs these impose on providers. The greater the proportion of the value chain exposed to regulated access requirements, the greater the uplift required to reflect the costs of providing flexibility options will need to be. An alternative (or additional) approach could be to require those using regulated access to commit to take these services for a minimum period (which would have to be comparable to the economic life of the assets involved in providing the service to them), thereby reducing the flexibility benefits that entrants currently obtain for free and which distort their choices.

□ Additionally, access pricing should be set to take account of the external benefits of infrastructure competition relative to access-based competition. Infrastructure competition is generally acknowledged to generate significant benefits that cannot be achieved from access-based competition and is feasible. Access prices should be set in the general public interest, which should include giving weight to realising these general benefits of infrastructure competition.

It is entirely possible to address the first problem within the confines of the existing EU regulatory framework, as this is primarily a question about what cost-based access means in practice. Mandated access transfers commercial risks associated with demand and technological uncertainty from the access seeker to the access provider. These costs need to be priced into access.

Although pricing the costs of risk and flexibility appears to be rather subjective, in that it depends on beliefs about possible developments in market conditions, this is not an argument for ignoring these costs in regulated access prices. It is already the case that many aspects of regulatory cost measurement are approximations and best guesses. The fact that option values might also be approximations and best guesses is not reason to treat the costs of providing flexibility as if they were zero, as NRAs currently do; this amounts to a policy of being 'exactly wrong', rather than trying to be approximately correct. Clearly it is the case that many real world markets are able to price risk and flexibility. For example, in the commercial property market, short leases trade at a premium over long leases, reflecting the additional costs to the landlord of providing flexibility to the tenant. Financial markets provide many examples of efficient pricing of risk, with markets aggregating participants' expectations about future outcomes to produce a consensus view.

Broadly, there are two means of including option values in access prices. The first is to try to approximate option values, either using theoretical models, and/or benchmarking with other sectors in which there are sunk investment decisions made to conditions of uncertainty. This is difficult, but not impossible. Although many inputs to the process will need to be assessed and are subject to argument amongst access seekers, access providers and regulators, this is no different from the current situation with LRIC-based costing.

The second approach is to leave it to the market to price the costs of flexibility. For example, if access rights entailed a long-term commitment to take (and pay for) the access service, rather than providing a short term right, they would provide a much more certain investment environment for the provider. This would better approximate a level-playing field for entrants choosing between different modes of entry; it would no longer be the case that one mode of entry would be very much riskier than another mode of entry. There would be no reason why long-term access rights could not be repackaged and resold as short-term access rights, which would trade at a premium over long term rights. The aeroplane leasing market provides a good example of such arrangements.

Taking account of the benefits of facilities-based competition relative to access-based competition provides a rationale for a further uplift of access prices. However, although the principle of encouraging investment and innovation is enshrined in the Framework Directive, it might be more difficult to take account of this policy objective within the confines of pure cost-based access pricing. Nevertheless, at the very least it might be possible for NRAs and the Commission to take a precautionary approach to the setting of access prices, taking care that where costs are uncertain or unknown, regard is given to the risk of undermining the incentives for facilities-based investment.

6.4.3 Forbearance of regulation of new services and platforms

There needs to be greater commitment from regulators not to subject new services and platforms to access regulation. The current highly discretionary approach of NRAs does not allow this. This is an area where the Commission has an important role, it is has powers under Article 7 of the Framework Directive to deny NRAs' requests to define new markets and extend their powers. The Commission could issue guidance on services it would not expect to be subject to regulatory requirements. For example, it could set out those areas where it would expect to deny NRAs' attempts to extend regulation unless there were compelling special circumstances. This would favour a rules-based, rather than discretionary approach and so promote much greater certainty in investment decision making.

Potential developments with regard to extending bitstream access to new platforms and new services on existing platforms provide a good example of the urgent need for regulatory certainty. The current regulatory framework clearly anticipates the potential need to extend bitstream access to platforms other than DSL and some NRAs are considering such moves. Existing operators providing bitstream access could be subject to additional requirements to offer many differentiated forms of bitstream access. These potential extensions of regulation undermine incentives for both innovation by incumbents and new facilities-based entry.

6.4.4 Technological and platform neutrality

Asymmetric access obligations applying to particular platforms distort competition, reducing roll-out incentives for those platforms affected. Broadband delivery platforms operate in the same market; convergence means that they all have the potential to deliver similar, closely substitutable services. Therefore, there is no rationale for imposing technology-specific or platform-specific obligations.

It is inappropriate to apply access obligations to a particular platform (e.g. DSL) simply because it is more widespread than other platforms. To the extent to which there are different competitive conditions in different geographical areas, then there may be a case for identifying a variety of sub-national markets for broadband that need different treatment.

As competition between platforms develops, it would be quite wrong to extend the obligations faced by one platform to other platforms offering substitutable retail services, be this cable, fibre or even 3G. Rather than extending regulation to maintain equal treatment as platform competition develops, such a situation would suggest winding back regulation wherever platform competition is effective.

6.4.5   Clarity over subsidies and obligations

In the event that subsidies were introduced in return for universal service, it would be necessary to ensure that they operated in a competitively and technologically neutral manner. For example, a 2003 report by Analysys for the Scottish Executive on broadband deployment for business concluded that:

> "To ensure that Scotland is best placed to take advantage of the next generation of broadband technologies . . . the Executive should not seek to pick a 'winning' technology, but instead focus on requirements common to all technologies."[219]

The policy environment should also seek to avoid creating unnecessarily uncertainty about future subsidies that might delay infrastructure investment and ultimately broadband roll-out. There should be clarity from NRAs and the Commission that:

☐ Cross-subsidies between different services (i.e. as with the access deficit for voice telephony) or classes of user (e.g. geographical averaging) are not an appropriate way to fund a USO as they distort current and emerging competition. For example, Cave says that:

> "A further feature of retail tariffing which was once thought necessarily to carry implications for access pricing is the requirement of a geographically averaged tariff, based upon a universal service obligation. However, it is now recognised that a situation of this kind is best resolved via a universal service fund, which makes it possible to share the burden of subsidising loss-making customers among telecommunications operators."[220]

☐ Obligations and subsidies go hand in hand and that one would not occur without the other. Imposing a USO without matching subsidies (from the public purse or through the publicly sanctioned right to apply higher charges to some customer groups) would be similar to imposing a tax on the business affected. However, compliance with State Aid rules require that these

---

[219]Analysys (2003), page 4.
[220]Cave (2002), page 49.

subsidies are proportionate, i.e. no larger than necessary to compensate for the obligation.

☐ Any policy change applied in the future would not be applied in a way that penalised those who had *already* made investments in infrastructure. Moreover, it would not be appropriate to impose an obligation on a company that might have significant market power in one market (e.g. narrowband PSTN) to subsidise activities in another market (e.g. broadband), especially if the second market is competitive.

☐ Obligations to provide a service in a particular area (be this universal service or 'hotspot' provision) should be met in the least cost manner. Allocation of a USO through a competitive process (e.g. USO auction or tender process) would be one way to achieve this.

If there are particular customer groups that are uneconomic to serve, but which social concerns suggest should be served, this strongly suggests defining a clear USO, rather than piecemeal government-sponsored infrastructure projects. Potential providers could then compete to meet the USO in the least cost manner.

Uncertainty over possible obligations to serve uneconomic customers decreases a carrier's incentive to invest. To the extent that such obligations would naturally apply to infrastructure investors rather than access-based operators, such uncertainties bias entrants in favour of using access rather than investing. Any USO (or similar obligations) needs to go hand in hand with compensation for the loss that follows from serving such customers.

There is an important interaction between regulation on the one hand, and USOs and subsidies on the other. To the extent that there are specific customer groups who are costly to serve and which cannot sustain competing platforms, access regulation cannot be used successfully to induce provision to these customers. By definition, access regulation would only lead to provision by an access-based entrant if access were priced such that the access provider would make a loss. Therefore, the access provider would choose not to roll out infrastructure in these areas. If access regulation is used as a backdoor means of trying to force roll out, it will ultimately fail, as it is the wrong instrument to address the problem. In contrast, an appropriately funded USO benefits competition, as it increases the feasible number of players in the market.

6.5 The role of the European Commission

The Commission has a pivotal role in implementing any change in approach. Through the Article 7 procedure, the Commission can limit NRAs' ability to define new relevant markets susceptible to ex ante regulation and so limit an extension of regulation to new markets. In a similar manner, the Commission can stop NRAs from applying remedies that are not already anticipated by the framework[221]. The Commission could issue guidelines on how it would expect to deal with NRAs requests to add new relevant markets or new remedies, thereby providing a much more predictable regulatory environment for new services and platforms.

Many of the problems we have identified arise from the existing access regime applied to existing services. Under the NRF, NRAs are under an obligation that any remedies they impose are proportionate to the identified competition problem they seek to address. In the case of broadband, we would dispute that there is evidence of any serious durable competition problems; to the extent that there are issues about transitional market power from control of the local loop, these can be addressed easily by LLU. Even in the worst possible case of there being competition problems due incumbent control of the local loop, having many parallel forms of access set at inefficiently low prices is clearly not proportionate, as simple LLU with rationally set access prices would be less intrusive and superior for the public interest.

The proportionality provision in the NRF is an important ground for operators to challenge NRAs' decisions. Nevertheless, this is not just a matter for individual operators; the Commission could, if it saw fit, issue guidance on what remedies it saw as being proportionate to address particular competition problems. Such guidance, although not binding, would have an impact on the potential decisions of Courts in Member States, and hence indirectly shape the remedies imposed on NRAs. Therefore, there is a natural route for the Commission to address the concerns we raise here. For example, it would entirely possible for the Commission to consider the question of risk and flexibility in access prices by issuing guidelines that it made clear that cost-based access pricing should include the resource costs of the flexibility options provided by regulated access.

At present, the Recommendation on relevant markets distinguishes bitstream access and LLU, with the effect that regulation of bitstream access is considered necessary over and above LLU. The Commission is required by the Framework Directive to review this decision at regular intervals. Therefore, it would be entirely possible for the Commission to consider this question again in detail. The argumentation in the Explanatory Memorandum accompanying the current Recommendation does not prove the need for regulated bitstream access. As we have seen, in fact there are many dangers from mandating resale and bitstream access given current access pricing methodologies. Mandated bitstream access risks generally undermining incentives for facilities-based investment to address rather limited concerns about the inability of entrants to replicate assets such as DSLAMs where demand is thin. Mandated resale access brings no benefits at all.

---

[221]Remedies for wholesale services are listed in the Access Directive and those for retail services in the Universal Service Directive, European Parliament and Council (2002).

7 Conclusion

Public policy should recognise the difference between broadband and traditional voice telephony services

Broadband is a new market which will play a major role in the development and competitiveness of EU economies over the next decade. Its importance is well understood by governments and other commentators alike.

However, public policy towards broadband appears to have been unduly influenced by traditional approaches to the regulation of voice telephony services in the era before cable telephony. This is almost certainly a mistake, as broadband is very different to plain old telephony. Broadband offers a variety of services, including high-speed data connectivity, voice telephony, broadcast television and video on demand; further innovative applications are likely to emerge. New innovations have the potential to bring massive benefits to consumers and an innovation-friendly policy environment is essential. Voice telephony regulation was about lower prices for a service with defined and unchanging characteristics; the new world should be about enabling new services and doing the previously impossible.

The competitive landscape is also different for broadband. There are many possible delivery technologies, including DSL, cable, FTTH, WiFi, mobile and satellite platforms. The type of delivery platform makes little difference to customers' experiences. They provide closely substitutable services that compete head-to-head and so lie in the same relevant retail market.

At present it is unclear which technologies will ultimately succeed and there is a possibility of sudden dislocating change in the marketplace. Once adoption of a technology in sufficient volume is anticipated, equipment costs fall as manufacturers compete for the new market created; on-going learning-by-doing reduces both equipment manufacturing and deployment costs, further accelerating take-up. This is already happening with 3G as rollout starts. Other technologies, such as the 'new mobile' platforms, are at a cusp, where a favourable shock could lead to broad adoption alongside other platforms. Innovation is a key component of competition in broadband, reducing cost and providing enhanced functionality.

Competition between platforms already exists. There is already competition between DSL, cable and FTTH in many EU countries, such as Belgium, Denmark, the Netherlands and Sweden. Although DSL and cable provision have benefited from being able to use networks originally rolled out for other purposes, wireless technologies have great potential, not just for fully mobile access, but also for nomadic and fixed access. Existing wireless LAN standards are already being used for wide-area broadband provision. There are developments of this technology that have the potential to provide a cost-effective high-bandwidth mobile service within existing spectrum allocations. There are also many potential providers of such services, including fixed line telcos, MNOs, equipment manufacturers and entirely new entrants.

Even given the current size of the retail market, broadband infrastructure is clearly not a natural monopoly; it can support multiple players competing effectively. As demonstrated by cable and DSL, competition can be vigorous with just two platforms, as there are strong incentives to win and retain customers. As broadband demand grows, the number of sustainable competing infrastructures will increase.

Effective competition has developed despite capital scarcity following the bursting of the telecoms and technology bubble. Therefore, renewed emphasis on access regulation by NRAs cannot be justified simply on the grounds that short-term capital market conditions have limited infrastructure-based entry. Broadband provision has much more in common with mobile telephony, where platform competition has worked, than with narrowband voice telephony.

Facilities-based competition, not access-based entry, delivers broadband take-up

Facilities-based competition leads to competition over more aspects of a service than access-based competition, and is self-sustaining. Where broadband provision depends on regulated access services, it is the regulator and the incumbent who ultimately determine the characteristics of the service provided to customers, including its pricing, rather than these characteristics emerging through the process of competition. In contrast, facilities-based competition brings real choice to customers. Much greater differentiation of services is possible through investment in infrastructure (shown by the variety of different speeds of broadband service now available) and can drive penetration, meeting the various needs of different customer groups.

Competition between platforms produces many benefits that even the most enlightened and optimally designed regulation cannot, including:

□ pressure to minimise costs applying to a larger part of the value chain;
□ increased diversity of choice for customers;
□ enhanced pricing and service innovation, as platform operators compete to attract customers to fill network capacity already in place;
□ Darwinian selection of efficient technologies and techniques; and
□ economy-wide knowledge spillovers.

Looking across OECD countries, our analysis of broadband data shows evidence that it is competition between platforms, rather than access-based entry, that speeds up the take-up of broadband:

□ Where the broadband market is served by competing platforms, penetration tends to be higher where DSL and non-DSL platforms have more similar shares. Where market shares are skewed towards one particular platform, penetration tends to be lower.

□ In contrast, there is no such relationship between the take-up of simple access services, such as bitstream and resale, by entrants and greater broadband penetration.

It has been argued (for example, by some NRAs) that access-based entry can be complementary to facilities-based entry, either because access-based entrants will ultimately build their own facilities or because such provision can be used as an adjunct to extend the coverage of an infrastructure-based entry strategy. There is little reason to expect this to be the case, as cheap access reduces the relative benefit of infrastructure investment compared with access-based entry and maintains this differential incentive.

A facilities-based provider serving the residential mass market is unlikely to gain significant benefit from extending the reach of such services using regulated bitstream access or resale, other than modest scale economies in marketing. Provision based on regulated bitstream access or resale is easily replicable by competitors and so margins on such business will be thin. In addition, such a facilities-based provider would have the problem of undermining the distinctiveness of its mass-market retail offer by providing access-based services (which would be largely undifferentiated from those of its competitors) alongside services based on its own infrastructure. These conclusions may not apply universally to the business market; it may be difficult for a facilities-based entrant to compete for corporate entities with geographically fragmented demand without access to bitstream services outside main urban areas.

The use of LLU may in some cases be complementary to infrastructure-based provision strategies. For example, FTTH players may use LLU to extend the reach of their fibre network. However, there are as yet no examples of a provider initially using LLU and then migrating to a platform-based strategy. Even if LLU is used to extend the reach of other platforms, it is still important that access prices are set appropriately.

U.S. experience demonstrates that very cheap access to local loops largely eliminates incentives to build alternative platforms. Entrants using cheap unbundled local loops have no reason to switch to a platform-based strategy. Although cheap access has encouraged many entrants into the U.S. market, it has not delivered sustainable competition. Rather, by eroding margins and raising customer acquisition costs, cheap access has lead to entrants' business cases being highly leveraged and fragile.

There are interactions between different forms of access. The availability of regulated bitstream and, in particular, resale access has the potential to undermine incentives to use local loops, especially given the deficiencies of existing access pricing methods. Rather than deploying LLU, entrants have the option of using other forms of access requiring less investment, which may be attractive as they require no commitment to a particular scale of operation or technology. Thus, depending on their relative terms and conditions, the availability of parallel tiers of access services can crowd out entry based on unbundled local loops or competing platforms.

As of July 2004, bitstream and resale together accounted for 4.6 million of the EU15's 28.7m broadband lines, more than double the number of LLU and shared lines. It is unsurprising that most DSL-based entry into broadband provision has followed routes that minimise facilities investment. Bitstream and resale entry provide great commercial flexibility and eliminate many risks at current regulated terms, by:

☐ not committing an entrant to remain in the market, as there are few sunk investment costs;
☐ allowing entrants to scale up or down their operations rapidly in response to changing demand from customers;
☐ not tying the entrant to any particular technology or standard; and
☐ giving the entrant the option to make an infrastructure investment once technology choices are mature and likely consumer demands known.

In contrast, all the risks associated with stranded assets (which arise from many sources, including both demand shocks and technology changes) fall entirely on the access provider.

These flexibility options are valuable to the entrant. Although providing them is costly to the incumbent, regulation grants them free of charge to the entrant. In other industries, contractual arrangements that provide enhanced commercial flexibility and reduce risk are of greater value to the user, cost more to provide and are priced to reflect this. For example, a short-term lease on a commercial property trades at a large premium over a long term lease, despite the commercial property rental market being highly competitive; this reflects the additional costs that the landlord faces from providing flexibility to the tenant. Mandating that short-term leases trade at the same price as long-term leases would grossly distort competition, yet, by analogy, this is largely what current telecoms regulation does.

Broadband provision based on bitstream access offers little opportunity for substantial differentiation of services and resale offers virtually none. They are easily replicable, and, therefore, can be easily contested. By themselves, they deliver limited benefits to customers in terms of true choice, service innovation or significant reduction in costs, as providers are largely unable to differentiate the characteristics or to control the majority of costs of their services.

Moreover, access-based entrants are often highly leveraged or under-financed. Even small adverse shocks can make players unviable given the high level of customer acquisition costs. Cheap access can lead to inefficient 'froth', with much entry and exit. The unsustainability of access-based entry creates regulatory inertia. Once access is granted, especially if access charges are inefficiently low, regulators naturally find it difficult to remove such concessions, owing to the adverse impact on entrants whose business cases may depend on inefficiently low access prices.

Public policy could do more to promote infrastructure competition

Many NRAs and the European Commission itself are on record as claiming the development of infrastructure competition as an objective of public policy. However, there is an inconsistency between these policy objectives and current practice, especially in terms of the setting of access prices. Access regulation is more interventionist than necessary to level any advantage that incumbent PSTN operators might have from control of the local loop.

There is a considerable danger from access regulation being applied uncritically to broadband. Access pricing methodologies developed for narrowband voice telephony have focussed almost exclusively on efficient bypass (i.e. providing an incentive for an alternative provider to use its own facilities *only* where it is cheaper than using the incumbent's facilities). The objective of this policy has been largely to minimise end-to-end costs in an entirely static sense and to prevent duplication of network assets that would otherwise lead to loss of economies of scale.

In the case of broadband it is the wrong objective. It is mistaken to disregard the importance of innovation, which both delivers new services and leads to existing services being provided more cheaply. Broadband is an emerging service with a substantial impact on the productivity and organisation of the whole European economy; there is no justification for ignoring the dynamic benefits of competition when designing policy.

Although some EU countries have well-developed cable networks, others do not. However, even without significant existing cable infrastructure, there may be rollout of new cable networks (e.g. ONO and Auna in Spain) or other platforms (e.g. Italy and Sweden). In all EU states, multiple 3G licences have been awarded and services are expected to be generally available in the near future; WiFi and 'new mobile' initiatives are also being launched. This generates both actual and potential competition for DSL providers.

Clearly, concerns may remain about incumbent control of local loops in cases where platform competition is still in its infancy. In such cases, regulation can be targeted at those activities that entrants cannot replicate, namely access to local loops. In those countries where facilities-based competition is thought not currently effective, properly priced regulated access to local loops should be a sufficient remedy to restrict any market power resulting from incumbent control of local loops.

Bitstream access provides regulated access to incumbent operators' activities that are largely replicable by entrants. Given effectively regulated and properly priced access to a local loop and sufficient retail demand, there is no reason why the incumbent should have any significant advantage in the provision of DSLAMs and DSL modems to enable DSL service over that local loop; this activity is not subject to strong scale economies and is demonstrably not a natural monopoly, else we would not observe small-scale providers using unbundled local loops. The incumbent may be more efficient in delivering broadband over the local loop than an entrant or the reverse may be the case; it should be for competition to reward the more efficient operator and provide incentives for the less efficient one to improve.

Fears of incumbent control of local loops undisciplined by alternative platforms may provide a rationale for LLU. However, it is important that access to un-bundled local loops not be priced too low, else it will crowd out investment in competing platforms, including both the development of cable and new delivery platforms. Cheap access can create a vicious circle, preventing the emergence of platform competition that would remove the need for regulation in the first place.

At present, PSTN operators are distinguished by platform-specific regulations on unbundling. However, given actual and emerging competition between plat-forms, this asymmetric approach is increasingly distorting. Where effective competition between platforms exists, access regulation should be rolled back for all platforms, rather than extended to new ones. Harmonisation should lead to less regulation, not more.

Ways forward for policy

We have identified a set of measures that could deliver appropriate investment and innovation incentives and deliver more facilities-based competition. At present, public policy does not fully reflect the social benefits of facilities-based competition relative to access-based competition, especially in regard to access pricing. Five general measures could reduce the potential for access regulation to crowd out facilities-based competition:

☐ rolling back access regulation where platform competition is effective;
☐ avoiding unnecessary parallel tiers of access regulation;
☐ taking a more dynamic and longer-run view of access pricing by considering flexibility and risk in cost-based regulation;
☐ committing not to regulate new services and networks; and
☐ ensuring that any subsidies are transparent and competitively neutral.

The Commission has instruments available by which it could implement these measures. It could resist any attempts by NRAs to increase the scope of regu-lation by applying the Article 7 procedures in the new framework, and, when reviewing the Recommendation on relevant markets, consider whether paral-lel tiers of access regulation generate significant benefits compared with the risks. It could also monitor the proportionality of remedies proposed by NRAs, issuing guidance on appropriate remedies for broadband and encouraging a consistent, rules-based policy; and issue guidance on the incorporation of the costs of risk and flexibility into regulated access prices.

Annex I Country case studies

A Germany

Background

Germany had a broadband penetration rate of just under 10% at end-2002, placing it in the middle rank of EU countries. Three main features distinguish the development of competition in the German broadband market:

- *Very little platform competition.* At end-2002, some 98% of subscribers received broadband via DSL lines owned by the incumbent Deutsche Telekom (DT). Cable broadband accounted for less than 2% of subscribers, reflecting its very limited availability. At least three companies – DT, Tiscali and Strato – have launched broadband satellite services, but these have only a very small subscriber base. Some 12 FWA operators were established in 1999 but they have struggled to win subscribers, and many have failed.
- *Relatively high take-up of unbundled lines.* By end-2002, some 220,000 subscribers (6% of the market) were being supplied with broadband by alternative providers using unbundled lines from DT. Germany has significantly more fully unbundled lines than any other country in Europe. Of these, some 40,000 lines were being operated by HanseNet, a partial facilities-based operator which has captured around one-third of the market in the Hamburg area (see Annex II).
- *No bitstream/wholesale access.* DT is not subject to any bitstream of wholesale access regulation, and there are no alternative providers in Germany using such services.

The very weak penetration of cable broadband is the most surprising feature of the market, given the leading role of cable in supplying television in Germany. Cable passes some 86% of homes[222] and, at end-2002, had over 22 million television subscribers but only 53,000 cable broadband subscribers.[223] This reflects the fact that most existing cable infrastructure features only a one-way path and thus requires substantial upgrade investment to offer broadband.

Analysis

Why has DSL in Germany performed so much more strongly than cable? In most other countries where there is extensive existing cable infrastructure, cable has been very successful in winning broadband market share. For example, in the Netherlands, where cable television is similarly ubiquitous, cable companies

---

[222] OECD (May 2003).
[223] Informa (2003).

Figure 19: German broadband subscribers – Q4 2000 to Q4 2002

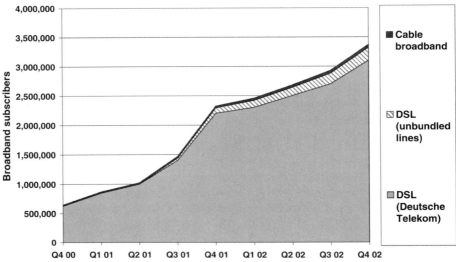

Source: Informa (2003) data

have invested heavily in upgrading cable and been rewarded with a market share exceeding DSL (see Netherlands case study).

There are good reasons why DSL has been so successful in Germany. The average copper loop length is only 1.5-2 km and there was already an unusually large base of customers using ISDN, making the switch to DSL easier.[224] DT has also aggressively pushed DSL take-up, with rapid roll-out from April 1999 and low initial subscription charges (later raised at the behest of the regulator). Relative to incumbents in some other EU countries, the absence of bitstream and wholesale access obligations may also have given DT a greater incentive to accelerate roll-out, given the reduced scope for entrants to 'piggy-back' on its expansion.

However, these factors are by no means sufficient to explain why investment has not been forthcoming to upgrade cable. In fact, the explanation for this appears to lie largely with the peculiar ownership structure of the local cable industry, which has had a detrimental impact on investment incentives.[225]

The German cable market has a unique feature – a separation of licensing and ownership between so-called level 3 (the cable distribution network from the head-end to the customer connection point or 'front door') and level 4 (delivery of the signal from the front door to the wall sockets in the customer's home).

[224]Point Topic (2003a), page 411.
[225]Deutsche Bank Research (2003).

The profusion of owners of level 4 infrastructure – which include hundreds of private craftsmen – has made it very difficult to coordinate infrastructure upgrades which require:

☐ upgrading of cables from the head end to subscriber nodes from co-axial to fibre, to accommodate greater bandwidth; and

☐ replacement of one-way co-axial cables between the nodes, the customer connection points and wall sockets.

Moreover, the historic business model of most Level 3 and 4 operators, which was to act as transporters for television companies rather than having a direct customer relationship themselves, is not very compatible with the development of broadband consumer products.

A further factor considered to be an obstacle to cable broadband development was the ownership, until recently, of level 3 infrastructure by DT. It has been argued that DT has little incentive to develop the sector, owing to the risk it will cannibalise its fixed line business.[226] DT has for some time been trying to sell its cable interests. In May 2000, it sold its cable networks in Bade-Würtemberg to Callahan and those in Hessen to Klesch & Company Limited. This was followed by the sale of its remaining cable businesses to Liberty Media in September 2001. However, this latter sale was blocked by the German Cartel Office in February 2002, which ruled that the deal would give Liberty a dominant position in the supply of end-customers with broadcasting signals. Finally, in January 2003, DT announced the sale of the cable businesses to a private investment consortium.

The Cartel's Office decision to block the Liberty transaction may have set back the prospects of cable competing with DSL. Liberty had proposed significant investment in upgrading cable to carry broadband and telephony services (although the Cartel Office had cast doubt on the viability of its plans). A national campaign would have also have helped to boost general public awareness of cable broadband, thus improving the business case for upgrades by smaller regional operators. Subsequently, the Cartel Office's decision has been widely criticised. For example, the German Monopolies Commission had, in its 14th Regular Report (2002) concluded that the FCO's approach to market definition was too narrow and created undesirable obstacles for the necessary upgrade of the German cable network.[227] The high level of switching between cable and satellite transmissions in North-Rhine Westphalia following price rises in 2002 by cable operator *ish* would appear to support this criticism.[228]

Despite the weak performance of cable, DT has not been without competitive pressures in the market, especially at the regional level. LLU entry has

---

[226]OECD (May 2003).
[227]Netzwettbewerb Durch Regulierung (2001).
[228]teltarif.de (May 2002).

stimulated some facilities-based competition, most obviously from HanseNet. Perhaps partly motivated by this threat, DT has made some notable strides in product innovation, for example launching multi-speed broadband products and a video-over DSL service. Nevertheless, it is likely that both overall broadband penetration and product innovation has suffered from the absence of platform competition.

Outlook

The sale of DT's cable network clears the way for potential substantial investment in cable broadband. For example, DrKW Research *"expect cable operators to begin marketing broadband more successfully going forward."*[229] This would likely have significant benefits in terms of stimulating product and price innovation (DSL as well as cable), and hence faster growth in broadband demand. However, cable investors first face the daunting task of totally restructuring the ownership of the sector. Given cable's large existing customer base, it has the potential to grow its market very quickly, but does have the disadvantage of being late-to-market. Given the heavy investment required, cable development may be very sensitive to any setbacks in the business or regulatory environments.

Another source of potential competition for broadband subscribers is the mobile sector. The four incumbent 2G operators are all rolling out national 3G networks, although two entrant 3G licence holders have exited the market.

In the meantime, operators using LLU will remain the main competitive challenge for DT. One possibility in the next few years is that the regulator will also introduce bitstream access obligations on DT, as has happened in many other EU states. While this would potentially significantly increase the number of providers, it would do nothing to solve the bigger problem of insufficient facilities-based competition. Indeed, if access terms were set too generously they might simply attract speculative entry, in the process driving up customer acquisition costs and weakening the business cases for existing LLU operators and the cable sector.

B   Netherlands

Overview

The Netherlands is amongst the leading EU countries in terms of broadband penetration, with over 14% of households connected at end-2002. Around 65% of subscribers use cable modems, with the remainder using DSL. Platform competition has been facilitated by the near-universal reach of the country's cable network, with around 90% of the population receiving television via

---

[229]DrKW Research (September 2003).

cable. The first broadband services were launched in April 1999 by the country's two largest cable operators, chello (UPC) and Essent. These and other cable companies have invested heavily in upgrading their networks to supply two-way channels necessary to provide broadband internet and telephony access.

Incumbent KPN launched a DSL service in June 2000 and has been playing catch-up versus the cable operators ever since. The regulator also requires KPN to provide access to its local loop to competitors via fully unbundled local lines (since 2000) and bitstream (since September 2002). However, this has had only a limited impact on the market: at end-2002, entrants accounted for only 38,000 lines, just 4% of broadband subscribers.

By January 2003, KPN had rolled out some 85% of the population. As a result, the majority of Dutch households now enjoy a choice between DSL and cable providers. Competition between KPN and the cable operators to win subscribers is intense, as evidenced by:

☐ *Low prices*. Dutch broadband prices are amongst the lowest in Europe, according to a survey by Forrester Research.[230] Although KPN does not face a national competitor, its commitment to offering uniform national pricing means that the pricing strategies adopted by the regional cable company's impose a significant constraint.

☐ *Product innovation*. Since mid-2002, KPN has offered broadband at three different speed and price levels. It has gained significant market share relative to the cable operators (winning 108,000 new subscribers in the second half of 2002 and 118,000 in the first quarter of 2003), success it attributes to: *"the successful launch of ADSL Lite [with a download speed of 256 Kbps] and also due to the increasing number of ISPs offering ADSL from KPN".*[231] The cable operators have been forced to respond by launching their own low-end products. For example, chello introduced 'chello Light' (top speed 300kbps), to complement its existing 'Classic' (1.5 Mbps) and 'Plus' (3 Mbps) products

It is interesting to note that these benefits have been achieved without any major advances in new entrant access to KPN's network.

Outlook

Forecasters project continued strong growth in broadband demand over the next five years. For example, Idate (2002) project that the total subscriber base will grow to around 4.5 million by 2007, up from 1 million at end-2002. However, forecasts for the relative share of DSL and cable vary widely. For example, Idate anticipate that DSL will overtake cable in 2004, whereas Strategy Analytics expect cable to maintain its lead over DSL through 2008.

---

[230] Forrester Research (2003a).
[231] Point Topic (2003a), KPN Telecom.

Figure 20: Dutch Broadband subscribers, Q4 2000 – Q4 2002

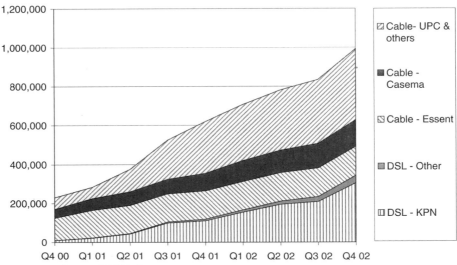

Source: Informa (2003) data

Although KPN and chello have largely completed the upgrading of their networks, new investment by the other cable networks is stalled. Two significant developments threaten to undermine the business case for further investment by existing operators:

☐ *Access regulation.* The Dutch regulator and competition authorities ruled that the cable operators should open up their networks to competing internet and television providers. However, this ruling is vigorously opposed by the cable operators and it is unclear whether it will ever be implemented.

☐ *Fibre roll-out.* The government's Broadband Expert Group has set out an ambitious plan for the roll-out of a national FTTH network by 2015, which will require about 2 billion euros from national and regional government-funded initiatives.[232] Unless these initiatives are revised to take a more platform-neutral approach, existing operators can be expected to oppose them on state-aid grounds.

The high rate of urbanisation in the Netherlands, combined with the extensive roll-out of cable and DSL, means that there is little scope for niche technologies such as FWA and satellite to win market share. However, a further source of platform competition may come from the mobile sector, where all five 2G incumbents have licences to offer 3G services.

---

[232] Paul Budde Communications (June 2003), page 3.

C Ireland

Background

Broadband penetration in Ireland was under 0.5% at end-2002, the second lowest figure in the EU after Greece, and behind many EU accession states (see Figure 21). This performance is surprising given the key role that the ICT sector has played in the transformation of Ireland from one of the least developed EU economies to one of the strongest in the EU.[233] Moreover, there is abundant evidence that Irish businesses and consumers are receptive to new technology. Since the liberalisation of the telecoms sector in 1995, Irish mobile penetration has climbed to over 80% (just below the EU average) from just 4% in 1995, while mobile phone usage is amongst the highest in the EU.[234] Meanwhile, household Internet penetration reached 47.9% in June 2002, significantly above the EU average of 40.4%[235].

DSL services were only launched in Ireland in May 2002, led by the former monopoly PTO eircom, with competitor EsatBT following suit soon afterwards. A third provider, UTV Internet, launched its service in June 2003. eircom had originally planned to launch DSL in October 2001 but were prevented from doing so by the regulator (ComReg, formerly the ODTR) because of a lack of terms for a corresponding wholesale DSL product. Initial take-up of DSL services has been very slow: only 3,850 DSL lines were installed up to June 2003.[236]

As of June 2003, DSL connections were only just ahead of cable broadband with 3,000 and behind fixed wireless services with 5,300 (residential and business lines). However, this relatively even performance disguises the fact that there is really negligible platform competition. Whereas ComReg estimates that 50% of all lines have been enabled for DSL, the geographical reach of both cable and FWA is very limited. For example, ntl, the largest cable company, only provides broadband services in selected areas of Dublin. Meanwhile, Irish Broadband – one of two public WiFi operators and the only one with a residential service – offers broadband services in a few areas in and around Dublin.

Until recently, access prices were arguably high by EU standards, which almost certainly discouraged take-up. eircom reduced the price of its consumer DSL product by 50% in May 2003, to 54.45 euros per month (inc. VAT). EsatBT and UTV Internet's competing products are priced at 49.49 and 47.50 euros respectively. Cable and public WiFi operators have similar subscription charges.

---

[233] The Irish economy grew by 8.3% per annum from 1998-2002, compared to an EU average of 2.4%, and it now has above average per income levels (Eurostat data).

[234] Data from ITU and ComReg.

[235] European Commission (June 2002b).

[236] ComReg (June 2003a), Section 2.1.

In June 2003, ComReg stated that these price movements had resulted in a "marked increase in orders."[237]

Regulatory Environment

ComReg (formerly the ODTR) publicly advocates both facilities-based and service competition. It has promoted facilities-based competition, primarily through the issuing of wireless licences (GSM-1800, 3G and FWA), and service-based competition through the aggressive promotion of carrier pre-selection. Fixed termination rates on voice have, since 1998, been low by EU standards and ComReg have, since then, obliged eircom to offer the same rates for origination and termination. Competition in the fixed market is almost exclusively resale-based and customer use of new entrant infrastructure for direct access services is negligible[238]. OLO market share for CPS services has stabilised at around the 20% mark.

In the run-up to full market liberalisation in 1998, Government policy also favoured infrastructure competition. The second 2G mobile licence was issued in 1996 and the provision of alternative infrastructure was fully liberalised in July 1997 (following which seven different operators deployed, to varying degrees, metropolitan fibre networks in Dublin and elsewhere). eircom was obliged to offer its cable network for sale, with ntl purchasing the former Cablelink network in 1999. eircom itself was privatised later the same year.

Since then, the Government has reassessed its position on infrastructure, with a principal focus on the rollout of broadband networks and the take-up of broadband services. From 1997-2002, the Government provided funds to support what it viewed as strategic network deployment, including the Global Crossing international connectivity project and various regional trunk fibre networks. In all, government funding for such initiatives amounted to 230 million euros over this period.

In a policy document published in the run-up to the last General Election in 2002, the Government set out ambitious aims in relation to the deployment of broadband networks:[239]

☐ *"Government wants to see the widespread availability of open-access, affordable, always-on broadband infrastructure and services for businesses and citizens throughout the State within three years, on the basis of utilisation of a range of existing technologies and broadband speeds appropriate to specific categories of service and customers. We wish to see Ireland within*

---

[237]ComReg (June 2003b).

[238]The EC's (2002c) 8th Implementation Report found no evidence of any customer usage of new entrant facilities for either direct access or for local, national and international calls (see Charts 19-21 in Annex 1 to European Commission's 8th Implementation Report).

[239]Taoiseach (March 2002).

the top decile of OECD countries for broadband connectivity within three years."

☐ *"In the medium term, we expect that broadband speeds of 5mbit/s to the home and substantially higher for business users will be minimum standard within 10-15 years for broadband. We will aim for Ireland to be the first country in Europe to make this level of broadband service widely available for its people."*

The Government's policy document identified the key deficit in broadband network deployment to be at the local access level. However, Phase 1 of the strategy put forward in the policy document was for the construction by local authorities of metropolitan rings in 19 selected towns around the country, funded by public investment and, where possible, by PPP-type arrangements. Investment in metropolitan networks would, by definition, do nothing to solve the identified deficit at the local access level. However, work on the construction of these metropolitan rings has now commenced and the Government, as of June 2003, was tendering for the appointment of a Managed Services Entity (MSE) that will be charged with the operation of this new network, with a remit to manage access "on an open access basis".[240]

Analysis

A number of explanations can be identified for Ireland's unimpressive position in broadband take-up:

1. *Timing.* The late launch of DSL services and high initial prices are significant reasons for the lack of consumer take-up. For example, according to Forrester Research, the cheapest available average monthly charge for a broadband connection in Ireland fell from 57.7 euros in 2001 to 40 euros in 2002, compared to a Western European average of 38.27 euros in 2001 and 30.2 euros in 2002.[241]

2. *Lack of platform competition:* In a number of other EU states, notably Austria, the Netherlands and the United Kingdom, the early launch of broadband services over cable acted as a spur to DSL rollout and broadband take-up generally. However, ntl's early ambitions to compete with eircom foundered due to its aborted investment programme. Investment in its network upgrade began in 1999 but stalled completely in early 2001 as the company ran into financial difficulties. As a result, the planned upgrade of its cable network in Dublin and elsewhere failed to materialise and only isolated pockets within Dublin were upgraded. Likewise, the other major cable player, Chorus, has failed to upgrade its franchise areas to any significant degree.

3. *Regulatory regime favouring access rather than build:* The regulatory regime in recent years has been particularly unfavourable to facilities-based

---

[240] See DCMNR (June 2003).

[241] Forrester Research (2003a).

competition. For example, the decision to set call origination interconnect rates at the same low level as termination rates just as the market was being liberalised effectively removed all incentive for new entrants to establish competing access networks. Almost five years on from full market liberalisation, facilities-based competition in the fixed telephony market is restricted to parts of the business market and, for residential customers, is virtually non-existent. The same lack of vigorous competition is now also a feature of the nascent broadband market.

4. *Lack of clarity in Government policy:* In the lead-up to full liberalisation, the Government pursued a clear policy of network divestment, by obliging eircom to dispose of its cable network and then privatising eircom itself. In a blow to investment incentives, the government has threatened to build a public fibre network to compete against privately owned networks. It is likely that the uncertainty created by the Government's move in this area has had some impact on investment decisions by eircom and others in relation to broadband rollout.

Outlook

The government's objective of being in the top decile of OECD countries by 2005 looks too optimistic. Over the next few years, Ireland will probably be one of the fastest growing broadband markets in the EU, but this is only because it is starting from such a low base. For example, IDC (2003) project that Ireland will experience a compound annual growth rate in broadband connections of 130% from 2002-07, compared to an average 30% across Western Europe. However, even with this level of growth, broadband penetration is only projected to reach 9% in 2007, compared to a West European average of 16%. Furthermore, IDC's forecasts assume strong growth in cable broadband as a competitor to DSL, which may not materialise.

ComReg has expressed public optimistic that the gap with other EU economies can be closed. In a June 2003 presentation, it cited evidence prepared by Norcontel (see Figure 21) that Ireland may be following a similar adoption curve to other EU economies, with take-off in subscriber numbers imminent. However, this ignores the fact that many of the factors that have delayed Irish broadband take-up continue to exist. These primarily relate to the lack of platform competition and a regulatory environment that will not encourage it to emerge:

☐ Without significant competition from facilities-based entrants, most obviously from cable companies, competitive pressures on eircom to extend roll-out and introduce product innovations will be limited.

☐ The regulatory focus on encouraging wholesale access on favourable terms may help to bring prices down, but it creates a strong disincentive for facilities-based competition. In particular, it weakens the incentive for

Figure 21: DSL adoption curve and take-up in Ireland

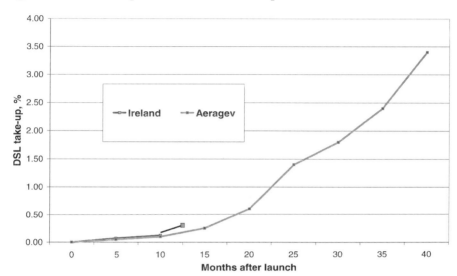

Notes: The benchmark is based on the average growth curves of five top countries, rebased to a common starting point, and plots the growth of DSL in Ireland relative to that curve

Source: Norcontel table cited in: Presentation to Joint Oireachtas Committee on Communications, Marine and Natural Resources, ICT sub-Committee, ComReg, 24 June 2003

network upgrades by the cable companies, who are the most obvious competitive challengers to eircom in the medium-term.

Government initiatives are focused on the development of backbone infrastructure, rather than encouraging demand and the development of local access networks. The new metropolitan rings may ultimately be widely used by new facilities-based entrants, but this is far from certain; in the meantime, such policies have created uncertainty for private investors.

More positively, potential new competition in broadband will come from the mobile sector. The two leading 2G incumbents – O2 and Vodafone – both plan to role out 3G networks, and there is also a new 3G entrant, Hutchison 3G.

D   South Korea

Overview

There were 10 million broadband users in South Korea as of October 2002, a household penetration rate of 70%, the highest level in the world.[242] The

---

[242] MIC (2003a).

number of subscribers is expected to climb to 12 million by end-2003, which is remarkable for a country with a total population of only 48 million.[243] This success story owes much to vigorous competition between DSL and cable operators, as well as strong government support for the sector. Just over 50% of subscribers are served by DSL, with most of the remainder served by cable or fibre LAN services; during 2002, DSL was the fastest growing sector (see Figure 22).

As in the early adoption countries of Europe, broadband in Korea only took off in 1999, but demand has grown significantly faster than elsewhere. The early pace was set by two new entrants: Hanaro, the country's newly licensed second local telephony operator; and Thrunet, a cable company. These two companies were particularly heavily involved in wiring up new apartments, assisted by construction company's enthusiasm to obtain the government's new 'cyber apartment certificates', which certify that buildings are IT ready.[244] By end-1999, these two companies had over 1 million subscribers. Stung by the unexpected success of its new rivals, incumbent operator Korea Telecom (KT) responded with its own aggressive DSL roll-out, which helped grow the market to over 4 million by end-2000.

As of January 2003, KT was the market leader with over five million subscribers, making it the largest provider of DSL service in the world.[245] Hanaro was second with 2.98 million broadband subscribers (April 2003), including 1.63 million cable subscribers and 1.2 million ADSL subscribers.[246] Thrunet had over 1.3 million cable subscribers as of December 2002.[247] Both Korea Telecom and Hanaro have also launched VDSL and wireless LAN service in Korea.

In addition, many apartment complexes are wired up with their own fibre LAN networks. These networks have been enthusiastically endorsed by the Korean Ministry of Communications (MIC), which describes their advantages as follows: *"With a single LAN system, apartment tenants can make calls over the telephone, send and receive faxes, and access the Internet with just a single LAN connection. Apartment LAN services also reduces Internet service costs while also supporting future home networking upgrades. A LAN system supports various kinds of existing and new multimedia services. Since the apartment tenants are connected through a LAN connection, everyone living in the apartment is connected to each other in a network, which allows the tenants to transmit data to each other at speeds that are faster than any Internet connection."*[248]

---

[243] Point Topic (April 2003a).

[244] FinanceAsia.com (April 2002).

[245] Point Topic (April 2003a).

[246] Hanaro Telecom (May 2003), Table 1.

[247] Korea National Computerization Agency & Korea Ministry of Information and Communication (July 2003).

[248] MIC (2003b).

Figure 22: Broadband internet access users by platform, end-2002

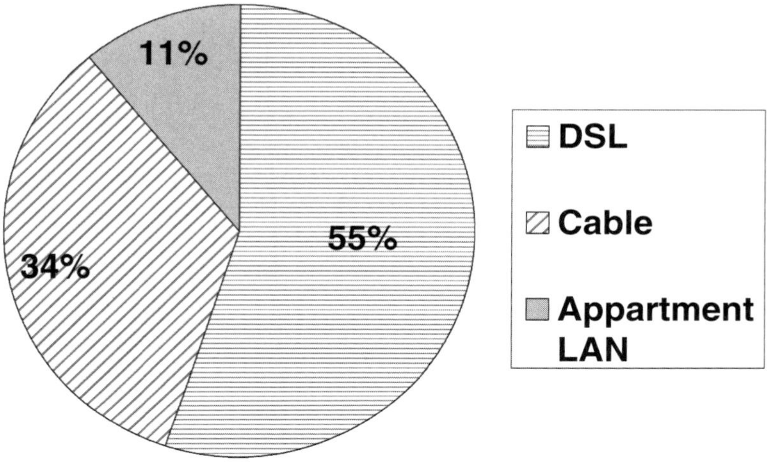

Source: MIC, 2003 Internet White Paper 41

Korean consumers are now demanding advanced broadband services such as VDSL, which offers average Internet connection speeds of 13 Mbps.[249] Korea Telecom initiated a 13 Mbps VDSL in July 2002 and a 20 Mbps VDSL service in December 2002, and had 147,000 VDSL subscribers at end-2002.[250] Hanaro had 81,000 total VDSL subscribers as of April 2003,[251] and is competing "fiercely" with Korea Telecom for new subscribers.[252] An upgraded version of VDSL is projected to be deployed in 2003, offering an average connection speed of 50 Mbps.[253] Korea Telecom launched a wireless broadband service NESPOT in February 2002, and had 112,000 subscribers to the service by the end of 2002.[254] Hanaro also began deployment of a wireless LAN service in South Korea in February 2002.[255]

In addition to vigorous platform competition, a number of other factors have been identified as assisting broadband development:

☐ *A light regulatory regime.* Access obligations were not introduced until January 2001, which meant that (the then state-owned) KT had a greater initial incentive to roll out its DSL network. The MIC enacted subscriber line sharing regulations in January 2001 and introduced full local loop unbundling

---

[249] MIC (2003a).
[250] Point Topic (April 2003a).
[251] Hanaro Telecom (May 2003).
[252] MIC (2003a).
[253] MIC (2003a).
[254] Korea Telecom (2003).
[255] Hanaro Telecom (January 2002).

and a bitstream equivalent product using KT's network in 2002.[256] Subsequently, Hanaro has introduced services over KT's network to complement its own infrastructure.

☐ *Government support for broadband infrastructure and demand.* The Korean government has intervened directly to promote broadband deployment in a variety of ways beyond unbundling. The deployment of the country's broadband infrastructure, including dense backbone fibre networks laid out by KT and the major power utility, was subsidized heavily by the government.[257] In April 2002, the government loaned local ISPs 60 million US dollars as part of an effort to increase the percentage of homes with access to broadband services.[258] South Korea has also undertaken initiatives designed to increase the demand for broadband applications, including eleven e-Government initiatives, which were begun in 2000 and culminated in the launch of South Korea's e-Government website in November 2002.[259]

☐ *Favourable population distribution and infrastructure.* The combination of high population density, prevalence of multi-dwelling units (MDUs), and extensive new residential and other construction has been very favourable to the roll-out of fibre, cable and DSL networks.[260] According to the MIC, more than half of the population live in apartments where VDSL technology's short transmission range is not a critical issue.[261]

☐ *Low consumer prices.* Monthly access charges are only around 24 euros per month, owing to intense platform competition and economies of scale resulting from very large subscriber bases. Installation costs are exceptionally low. A September 2002 report by Enders Analysis observed that ADSL installation fees were just 22 euros, so *"unlike most other countries, there is no barrier to take-up created by a high initial charge."*[262]

☐ *Demand for high-bandwidth applications.* Point Topic site the popularity of online gaming and online stock trading as key drivers of Korean broadband demand, alongside low equipment costs and the network effect generated by the increasing number of broadband users in the country.[263]

A potentially controversial question is the extent to which cultural differences mean Korea is more suited to broadband adoption than say European countries. Enders Analysis argue convincingly that Korea is not as different as might be implied from broadband penetration figures. It points out that internet usage

---

[256]Hanaro Telecom (January 2001). Although Hanaro began as a facilities-based broadband subscriber, it began to offer DSL service over Korea Telecom's last mile network.

[257]Enders Analysis (2002).

[258]Point Topic (April 2003a).

[259]Korea National Computerization Agency & Korea Ministry of Information and Communication (July 2003).

[260]Enders Analysis (2002), page 5.

[261]MIC (2003a).

[262]Enders Analysis (2002), page 6.

[263]Point Topic (April 2003a).

(63-65% in 2003) is lower than in some north European countries. Furthermore, using 2001 data, it found that Korean and UK households spent similar amounts of time on the internet.[264] This suggests that much of Korea's success in broadband penetration is replicable in Europe.

Outlook

The market for broadband services is beginning to reach saturation in South Korea, as evidenced by fall in the growth rate of broadband subscriptions from 103% in 2001 to 35.5% in 2002.[265] Intense price competition has also put pressure on revenues. Thrunet went into administration in March 2003, after spending heavily in its bid to catch up with its rivals. However, it remains a going concern, and may be taken over by Hanaro. Meanwhile, Hanaro's broadband access service revenues fell 5.2% in the first quarter of 2003 despite an increase of 96,000 in broadband subscribers."[266]

With demand for higher bandwidth applications growing, companies are likely to place increasing emphasis on upgrading infrastructure. They will be helped by state backing: the government intends to spend 10 billion US dollars to deploy VDSL or fibre to 80% of the population by 2005.[267] Wireless broadband also appears set to be a key growth area.

E   Sweden

Overview

Sweden, alongside Belgium and Denmark, is the leading EU market for broadband internet services. Penetration was already above 20% at end-2002, amongst the highest rates in the world. There are a number of reasons why broadband has been so successful in Sweden:

☐ *An internet-aware population.* Sweden has long had very high PC penetration (70%) and internet usage levels (over 50% in the 12-79 age bracket)[268], creating huge latent demand for high-speed internet access by the late 1990s. Notably, within two months of the launch of its residential ADSL offer in 1999, Telia had received 140,000 requests for connections.[269]
☐ *Population distribution.* The population distribution is particularly favourable to infrastructure roll-out. Over 60% of households in Sweden live in MDUs, which means that the per user cost of installing fixed infrastructure

---

[264]Enders Analysis (2002), page 6-7.

[265]MIC (2003a)

[266]Hanaro Telecom (May 2003).

[267]Point Topic (April 2003a).

[268]Idate (2002), page 141.

[269]Idate, (2002) page 140.

is relatively low compared to many other countries.[270] Furthermore, 90% of the population live within a 4 km radius of a main distribution frame operated by incumbent Telia, making DSL roll-out easier.

☐ *Government backing.* The national government has targeted high broadband penetration as a key policy goal and launched a variety of initiatives to drive take-up. Local municipalities have been granted generous subsidies to build their own metropolitan fibre networks, either by themselves or jointly with companies. Most prominently, Stokab, a commercial company owned by the City of Stockholm, has rolled out a dark fibre network (with over 50,000 km of fibre), which is available to operators and other organisations.[271]

☐ *Strong platform competition.* There has been aggressive price and product competition amongst broadband providers competing over multiple platforms. This might not have been expected given that incumbent Telia controlled both the national telephony network and the main cable television provider Com Hem. However, the success of FTTH entrant Bredbandsbolaget, which launched services in 1999, in rolling out a low-price, ultra high speed service has forced the pace of both DSL and cable broadband roll-out. Some MDU residents in major cities now enjoy a three-way choice between cable, DSL and fibre for broadband access.

At end-2002, DSL was the leading delivery platform, with 54% of subscribers, followed by fibre (24%) and cable (22%). The early years of broadband competition have seen particularly rapid roll-out of DSL and fibre. By September 2001, Telia's DSL service was available to 70% of the population (150 destinations)[272] and the company has targeted universal access by 2006.[273] B2 has rolled out its network to 51 destinations across the country, although its ambitions have been partly frustrated by the mixed progress which municipalities have made in rolling out fibre networks, to which B2's local networks must interconnect (179 of the country's 289 municipalities have so far build optical MANs, but according to B2, only 30% of these are fit for use[274]). Cable companies, although enjoying an estimated TV penetration rate of over 60%, have lagged behind somewhat in upgrading their networks for two-way communication. For example, as of Q1 2003, UPC had upgraded 61% of its network for broadband internet.[275]

Initial prices for broadband access were exceptionally cheap. B2 launched its offering of up to 10 Mbps at just 22 euros per month in 1999. Although, at this point, its services were not widely available, this pushed rival cable and DSL operators to offer similarly low subscription rates. Such low prices proved

---

[270]The Broadband Home Report (June 2000).
[271]Cullen International (2002).
[272]Point Topic (April 2003a), page 536.
[273]Idate (2002), page 144.
[274]Idate (2002), page 149.
[275]UPC (April 2003).

Figure 23: Swedish Broadband subscribers, Q4 2000 – Q4 2002

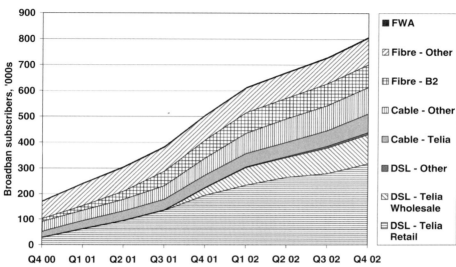

Source: Informa (2003) data

unsustainable and have gradually risen to between 225-475kr (24-51 euros) per month, depending on the operator and type of package. Nevertheless, these prices are still amongst the lowest in the world, as illustrated by the results of the February 2003 Oftel benchmarking study which found that Swedish broadband prices were below those of France, Germany, the United Kingdom and the United States (see Table 14).[276]

As in the Netherlands, platform competition has encouraged product differentiation. As Table 13 shows, consumers can now chose between broadband packages at up to five different speed levels. Notably, the availability of B2's 10 Mbps offer and the innovative services that this makes possible (for example, users are encouraged to host their own web servers) has pushed the DSL and cable operators to respond with their own high speed offers in the 1-2 Mbps range. Meanwhile, in May 2003, B2 introduced a DSL service using unbundled lines from Telia to connect to its fibre network, with speeds "at up to 10 Mbit/s".[277]

Outlook

Sweden is projected to maintain its position as a leader in the European broadband market. For example, Strategy Analytics projects broadband penetration

---

[276]Oftel (June 2003).

[277]www.bredbandsbolaget.se.

Table 13: Selected Swedish broadband packages by speed and price

Company	Platform	Monthly subscription, by speed				
		250 kbps	500-640 kbps	1 Mbps	2 Mbps	10 Mbps
Bredbands-	FTTH	-	-	-	-	320 kr
bolaget (B2)	DSL	-	-	-	399 kr	-
Com Hem	Cable	225 kr	295 kr	350 kr	-	-
Tele2	DSL	-	359 kr	-	-	-
	Cable	-	249 kr	-	-	-
Telia	DSL	299 kr	375 kr	-	475 kr	-
UPC chello	Cable	-	349 kr	399 kr	-	-

Source: Survey of company websites, 30 July 2003 (excludes special offers)

to reach 55% of households by 2008, compared to 40-45% in Germany, France and the United Kingdom.[278] It expects cable to gain market share over the next five years at the expense of DSL and fibre, which appears a plausible projection, given that: (a) the availability of broadband over cable should rise during this period as further progress is made with upgrades; (b) cable offers are generally cheaper than DSL or fibre at the low-end of the market; and (c) Com Hem is now independent of Telia, following its divestment in early 2003 as part of the conditions for EU approval of the Telia-Sonera merger.

Future competition may focus increasingly on product development rather than price. Prices may even rise further as companies switch their focus from building market share to raising ARPUs; notably, senior Telia officials have in the past complained that Swedish broadband prices are much too low.[279] According to Idate, some operators have also cast doubt on the viability of B2's business model, which they suspect has been priced below cost.[280] At the high-end of the market, there will be pressure on Telia and the cable operators to respond further to B2's service. Telia, for example, in March 2003, concluded a deal to buy routers from Riverstone Networks which will allow it to offer Ethernet services over its ATM backbone.[281] At the low-end, operators may face new competition from the mobile sector, where a number of companies are rolling out parallel 3G networks.

One source of uncertainty in the market is the role of government plans to subsidise broadband take-up. There has also been talk of a massive system of state support for individuals to buy broadband, along the lines of the tax subsidy programme launched in 1997 to encourage the purchase of home PCs. On the one hand, the failure so far of many municipalities to develop optical networks

---

[278] Strategy Analytics (January 2003).
[279] Advanced Television (May 2002).
[280] Idate (2002), page 149.
[281] Total Telecom (March 2003).

as envisaged is holding back the spread of new services and, in particular, has significantly weakened B2's business case (see case study in Annex II). On the other, there is concern that the actions of some municipalities have discriminated against private operators and unfairly favoured fibre over other technologies at the local access level, possible in contravention of EU state aid rules. While such initiatives should, generally help to promote broadband, there appears to be a risk that if poorly implemented, they could lead private operators to curtail or delay future network roll-out and upgrades.

F   United Kingdom

Overview

The development of broadband in the United Kingdom to date can be divided into two distinct phases:

☐ *European laggard, 1999-early 2001.* Cable operator ntl launched the first UK broadband offering in April 1999, followed by Telewest in March 2000. However, "in the *absence of a competitive product from BT the initial prices were relatively high and service levels only needed to exceed those of ISDN.*"[282] Although BT eventually launched its first DSL offering in mid-2000, owing to technical problems, lines were not widely available until May 2001.[283] At end-2000, the world's fourth largest economy ranked just 22nd in terms of broadband subscribers.

☐ *Rapid catch-up, mid-2001 onwards.* The launch of retail DSL products by BT and various third parties (via BT's wholesale offer) began a period of intense price competition between broadband providers. This supported a steady increase in penetration during 2001, with growth really taking off from the second quarter of 2002 (see Figure 20). By late 2002, price reductions had transformed the UK broadband market from one of the most expensive in the OECD to one of the cheapest, as observed in Oftel's twice yearly survey of broadband prices (see Table 14). During this period, the United Kingdom has risen to 7th in the world rankings for broadband subscribers.

Price decreases in the UK market can be directly linked to competition between DSL and cable providers. In the months after the launch of BT's DSL service, ntl and Telewest responded with significant price reductions, such that by mid-2001, prices were around 50% of their launch levels and about 35% below those of BT Openworld (see Figure 11). BT responded in March 2003 with a 25% price reduction, which provided the trigger for a series of price cuts by other ISPs using BT's resale service.

---

[282]OECD (October 2001), page 42.

[283]Point Topic (April 2003a).

Outlook

The strong growth experienced by DSL and cable providers throughout 2002 has continued into 2003, with subscribers to both platforms each passing the 1 million mark in the second quarter.[284] This is expected to continue, with forecasters projecting net additions of between 1.5-2 million subscribers per annum, raising total subscribers above 10 million by 2007-08.

With broadband monthly fees already at highly competitive levels, the scope for further reductions appears limited. Competition instead is likely to focus on special offers (especially reduced price connections) and product innovation. Most UK providers still only have one consumer product, whereas providers in the more developed Dutch market typically have three structured by speed and price. The considerable success of ntl's low price 150kbps service (a speed that many consider to be below broadband), introduced in October 2001, suggests that there is potential demand for a variety of products at different speeds.

From 2004, Strategy Analytics expects DSL to overtake cable as the largest platform, primarily owing to its extensive reach (over 90% of the population). Despite its broadband success, cable networks have only been rolled out to 51% of the population. Given the highly urbanised structure of the UK population, there would therefore appear to be significant scope for further cable and/or fibre roll-out in competition with DSL. Further investment will also be required in existing cable networks if they are to overcome capacity problems limiting access speeds in many areas. However, this may depend on an improvement in the financial environment for cable operators. Meanwhile, new entrants may be deterred from investment in new infrastructure by the comparative ease of offering services through regulated access to BT's network and potentially high customer acquisition costs as a result of the profusion of access-based competition at the retail level.

Satellite and FWA services are expected to consolidate their niche positions but are not seen as likely mass market plays over the next five years. A more promising sector may be WiFi, where there are a number of example of localised wide-area networks being rolled out. Another may be 3G mobile, where five operators (including the four incumbent 2G operators) are rolling out networks and new entrant Hutchison launched in early 2003. However, 3G data services at broadband-equivalent speeds are unlikely to be available for several years.

G   United States

Analysis

The two main platforms over which broadband Internet service is provided in the United States are cable and DSL. The cable companies have long enjoyed a significant market share lead over incumbent local exchange companies

---

[284]Oftel (May 2003b).

Figure 24: UK Broadband subscribers, Q4 2000 – Q4 2002

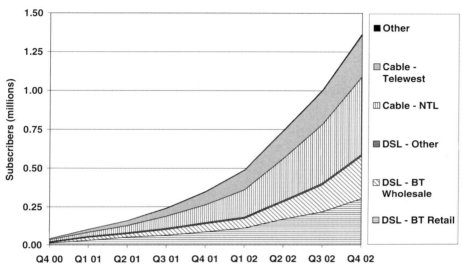

Source: Informa (2003) data

Table 14: Relative broadband prices for selected OECD countries

	October 2000		February 2003	
	Price level £/month	Price Index	Price level £/month	Price index
France	37	92	37	104
Germany	31	78	31	124
Sweden	na	na	20	80
United Kingdom	40	100	25	100
United States	32	79	31	123

Source: Oftel (January 2001) and Oftel (June 2003) – based on the average of the two cheapest DSL or cable offerings in each country

(ILECs) providing DSL (see Figure 25). From end-2000 to the first quarter of 2003, cable increased its share of the total broadband market from 60% to 62%, while DSL's share slipped from 38% to 35%.[285] Satellite, fibre and WiFi account for the remaining 3% of broadband subscribers.

---

[285] CBS MarketWatch.com (July 2003).

Figure 25: Broadband lines (millions) in the United States

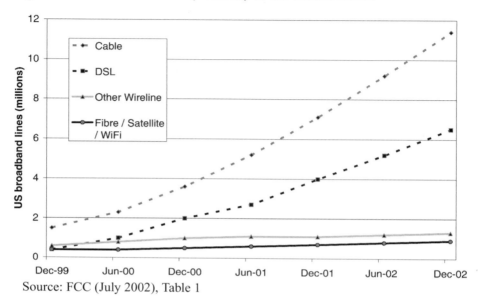

Source: FCC (July 2002), Table 1

There is plenty of evidence that cable and DSL companies see themselves as direct competitors for broadband subscribers. For example, when Verizon announced in May 2003 that it was dropping its monthly price for DSL service from 49 to 35 US dollars (29 dollars when purchased as part of package that includes long-distance and local service), cable stocks tumbled, demonstrating that investors believe that the price of DSL service affects the profitability of cable firms.[286] In recent presentations and reports to investors, both cable and DSL providers have cited each other as key competitive threats.[287]

Regulatory intervention is part of the reason that cable has maintained its lead over DSL in subscriber acquisition. The loss of subscribers to competitive local exchange carriers (CLECs) as a result of generous access terms mandated by the FCC and local regulators (see Annex II) has discouraged ILECs from extending their DSL networks to compete with the extensive footprints of the cable companies. For example, Verizon, the second largest DSL provider, could only offer DSL service on 60% of its lines at end-2002.[288] SBC, the leading DSL provider, stated in its 2002 Annual Report that:

> "burdensome FCC and state commission regulations regarding our DSL network have added significantly to our costs and delayed our ability

---

[286]Business 2.0 (May 2003).

[287]See for example: Comcast Cable Communications (2001), page 7; and SBC Communications (2003a).

[288]Verizon (2003a); Forbes.com (May 2003).

to earn a profit on DSL service. Our cable modem competitors are not subject to these regulations. This adverse regulatory environment was the primary reason we decided to slow the build-out of our broadband network. We expect to spend significantly less on capital expenditures due to this scale-back."[289]

The case for asymmetric regulation of broadband access looks particularly weak in the United States, given that cable companies, such as Comcast, Cox, and Time Warner, dominate the list of leading U.S. broadband suppliers (see Table 15). Moreover, following the bursting of the telecoms bubble in 2000-01, the business models of many CLECs have been exposed as unviable. The extent of bankruptcies amongst CLECs may appear surprising given the assertion by ILECs that they were being forced to offer access to their networks below cost. The explanation for this appears to be that cheap access attracted very high levels of entry and that many entrants (in an attempt to differentiate themselves) spent too heavily on customer acquisition, in the process driving up such costs for the whole market.[290] While CLEC spending presumably played a significant role in stimulating consumer demand through 2000, their competitive impact and likely contribution to overall market growth since 2001 has been much diminished. Meanwhile, the unsustainable rise in customer acquisition costs will have displaced potential funding of more sustainable facilities investment.

Outlook

The recent Triennial Review decision by the FCC relieved incumbent DSL providers of certain unbundling requirements, and will likely encourage increased investment in DSL infrastructure by incumbent local exchange carriers. This may enable DSL to regain market share at the expense of cable. For example, Idate forecasts that DSL will have 27-36 million subscribers by 2003, about 40% of the market.

With DSL less encumbered by access regulation, ILECS may be more willing to challenge cable operators with price cuts and new services. Verizon's May 2003 price cut may be a first step in this direction. Meanwhile, SBC has announced plans to bundle Echostar's satellite video services with its telephony and internet packages, in a direct challenge to cable company triple play strategies. According to CBS MarketWatch, many analysts expect bundled products – voice, data and video on one bill – to take off in 2004, led by middle-ranked cable companies Cablevision and Cox.[291]

Meanwhile, both cable and DSL services face a potential new competitive challenge from wireless broadband services. There has been particularly heavy

---

[289]SBC Communications (2003b).

[290]Hazlett (2003).

[291]CBS MarketWatch.com (July 2003).

Table 15: Top ten U.S. broadband subscribers, end-Q1 2003

Provider	Platform	Total subs	1Q Net Adds	% Growth
Comcast	Cable	4,037,300	417,000	12%
Time Warner	Cable	2,776,000	267,000	11%
SBC	DSL	2,469,000	270,000	12%
Verizon	DSL	1,830,000	160,000	10%
Cox	Cable	1,562,383	154,433	11%
Charter	Cable	1,272,300	134,200	12%
BellSouth	DSL	1,122,000	101,000	10%
Cablevision	Cable	852,800	82,700	11%
Qwest	DSL	551,00	16,000	3%
Covad	DSL over LLU	417,000	36,000	9%

Source: CBS MarketWatch.com (July 2003)

investment in WiFi hotspots, led by T-Mobile, which charges 29.95 US dollars for unlimited data access at its 2,700 U.S. hotspots located primarily in Starbucks (as of July 2003) and over its cellular network. This has forced a competitive reaction from other fixed and mobile operators.[292] For example, Verizon Wireless has reached an agreement with Wayport Inc. to provide broadband speed WiFi service to its customers at hotspots across the United States.[293] In May 2003, Verizon announced plans to provide extensive WiFi coverage in Manhattan by wiring 1,000 phone booths with WiFi antennas.[294] SBC intends to provide 20,000 WiFi hotspots in 6,000 locations across its service area, also in partnership with Wayport.[295]

---

[292]CBS MarketWatch.com (July 2003).

[293]Verizon (2003d).

[294]Investor's Business Daily (July 2003).

[295]Verizon (2003c).

Annex II Entrant case studies

A Bredbandsbolaget in Sweden

Bredbandsbolaget ('The Broadband Company', also known as B2) was founded in 1998 with a focus on delivering exceptionally high-speed internet access to residential and business customers. It uses fibre (ethernet) LAN technology to deliver a symmetric service of up to 10 Mbps to the home. By comparison, the next fastest residential service, from Telia, provides 2 Mbps asymmetric access. Although it only accounted for 11% of Swedish broadband users at end-2002, behind Telia with 40%[296], B2 has been a key driver of price and product competition in the market.

B2 installs ethernet networks in businesses and multi-dwelling units (MDUs), with capacity to deliver 10 Mbps per home (although in some cases the 10 Mbps may be shared between several users). Capacity can be raised as high as 100 Mbps. Installation fees are negotiable with residents associations and businesses, and may feature minimum guarantees about take-up. These sites are linked together with optical fibre with a capacity of around 1 Gbps, and then connected to municipal networks which also use fibre optics, so as to create a national network.

B2's initial roll-out was very rapid. Nearly 80% of its local access network (as of end-2002) was rolled out before end-2000. However, according to a report by Idate, it has encountered two major problems during roll-out[297]:

- ☐ Despite heavy government backing, many municipalities have not yet rolled out optical networks and many of the existing networks (70% according to B2) are unsuitable for use.
- ☐ In-building wiring has proved much more complex and expensive than originally estimated.

B2's initial business model focused solely on broadband internet provision. The very high speeds have enabled it promote innovative user activities. Notably, it actively encourages its users to operate their own servers and to create and offer audio and video content. For additional fees, its SOHO service allows clients to develop e-commerce and fee-based operations. A stated objective of the firm is to increase the availability of Swedish-speaking content on the internet through the activities of B2's users.[298]

---

[296] Informa (2003) – Telia figure excludes broadband subscribers to cable operator Com Hem which Telia sold in early 2003.

[297] Idate (2002), page 149.

[298] The Broadband Home Report (2000).

The internet-only focus created concerns that B2's business model was too narrow. Notably, its business strategy has differed markedly from Europe's other major FTTH operator, FastWeb, which has pursued a 'triple-play' strategy of voice, television and internet from the beginning, as well as experimenting with videocommunication services (see section 5.1.5). Although B2 has been talking about introducing telephony and television services since at least 2000[299], these were only widely introduced in 2003:

☐ In January 2003, it launched a voice over IP telephony service. This service is tied to ports in residential homes, so does not have the portability of an internet-based VoIP offering. B2's telephony strategy is apparently to undercut all offers and charges from Telia.[300] Subscribers do not have to take B2's internet offering.

☐ In February 2003, it introduced 'Broadband Cinema', a video-on-demand service which enables internet clients to rent films and TV programmes via their broadband socket.

☐ In March 2003, B2 became one of three certified partners for Microsoft's games console Xbox Live in Sweden.

B2 has also expanded its potential market reach by offering a DSL service of up to 10 Mbps using unbundled lines from Telia. This service is available in areas where there is access to B2's local fibre networks but there is insufficient demand to justify wiring up particular buildings.

B2's pricing strategy has been very aggressive, and has forced its larger competitors to respond with their own low-price deals. At one point, B2's monthly internet subscription was just 22 euros, although this has since risen to 35 euros. Although no longer the cheapest broadband offer in the market, it is still below Telia's 2 Mbps DSL offer and the 1 Mbps cable offers of Com Hem and UPC chello (see Table 13). B2's offer has also fuelled domestic expectations for speed and service quality from broadband, pushing cable and DSL operators to invest in improving their own high-end residential offers.

The combination of low price and high speed has proved popular with the residential market. For example, the company website boasts that as part of Swedish broadband week, its was declared Broadband Company of the Year 2002, in all categories. At end-2002, it had 88,500 customers, a penetration rate of 35% (see Figure 26). This had risen to over 100,000 by May 2003, helped by the addition of 25,000 telephony customers (of which about 10,000 are telephony only).[301]

While B2's success in attracting subscribers is clear, the extent to which it has converted this into a sustainable business model remains somewhat opaque. According to Idate, other operators have expressed doubts as to whether B2's offer

[299]The Broadband Home Report (2000).
[300]Total Telecom (May 2003).
[301]www.bredbandsbolaget.se.

Figure 26: Bredbandsbolaget – Fibre homes passed and subscribers

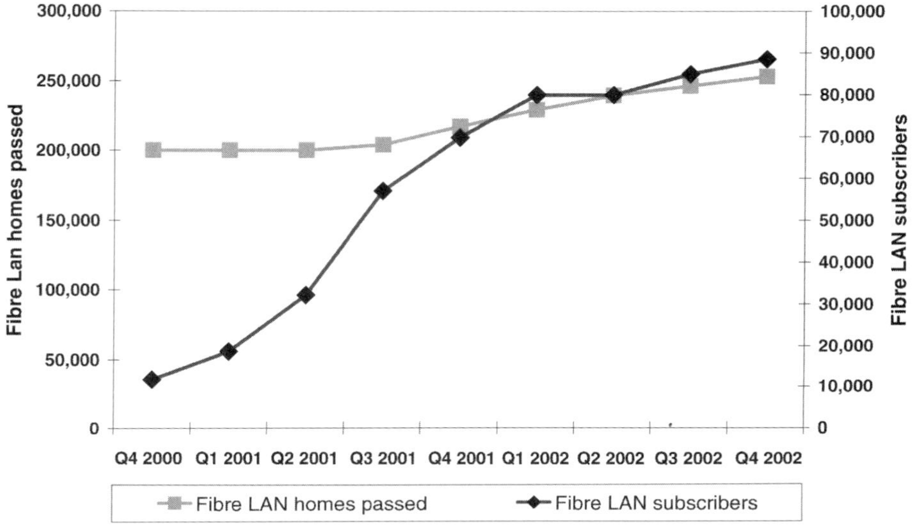

Source: Informa (2003) data

is economically viable.[302] In 2001, the company required a life-saving capital injection from its private owners (ntl, Investor, the Carlyle Group, the Continuum Group Ltd and Access Industries). It also closed its FTTH subsidiary in Belgium, Bredband Benelux, which had failed to establish a sufficient customer base. Since then, its operating position is likely to have improved, as the pace of network roll-out has slowed significantly, thus reducing capital expenditure, while price rises and subscription growth will have boosted revenues.

Looking forward, problems with utilising municipal optical networks and the focus on MDUs (owing to high installation costs) are likely to pose significant constraints on B2's future growth. However, the new DSL offer over unbundled lines should help in raising usage rates of B2's local networks. As upgrading by Telia and (especially) the cable companies is on-going, expanding the availability of broadband, it appears inevitable that B2 will lose some market share, even if it continues to increase penetration. An interesting development to watch will be the extent to which Telia and the cable operators attempt to improve their own networks in a bid to more closely compete with B2's 10 Mbps offer. Telia faces a dilemma in this regard, as wholesale access obligations potentially require it to make available any improvements in its network to third parties. The possibility of competition from third parties (who have not had to invest in their own infrastructure) freeriding on any improved offer by Telia also creates a disincentive for B2 to invest further in its network.

---

[302] Idate (2002), page 149.

B   e.Biscom (FastWeb) in Italy

e.Biscom describes itself as *"one of the main fixed broadband telecom operators in Italy."* Its strategy is to provide a complete alternative service to traditional telephone networks for consumers and businesses, augmented by innovative new services, which depend on the provision of a reliable, very high-speed broadband connection. Its Italian subsidiary FastWeb was the first European operator to offer television-on-demand.

The key to e.Biscom's ambitions is control and development of its own fibre optic networks, which permits transmission speeds up to 10 Mbps, and the use of a single IP platform to integrate all types of service, including voice, video and data. However, deployment of FTTH is expensive and demand for many of the new services that it is developing (such as video calls) is in its infancy. Therefore, the company also uses DSL connections over unbundled lines to reach customers in areas where it has not extended its own network to the home. The speeds achieved using DSL are less impressive than FTTH but have been sufficient to deploy a subset of its more advanced services, notably video-over-DSL. This flexibility is only possible because, with unbundled lines, it controls its own DSL infrastructure; bitstream or wholesale DSL access would not give it sufficient control.

The company's focus on new services has proved a commercial success in both the Italian and German markets. e.Biscom group revenues exceeded 350 million euros in the year to Q1 2003, with positive and growing EBITDA since Q4 2002, helped by strong subscriber growth and "efficient cost control".[303] Although the company has a high debt burden, this will be significantly eased by the agreement to sell its German subsidiary HanseNet to Telecom Italia, freeing up cash for FastWeb. Overall, its recent strong financial performance demonstrates both the potential viability of new entrant business models based on new infrastructure and the potential benefits of using access to unbundled lines as a complement rather than alternative to new infrastructure roll-out.

FastWeb in Italy

FastWeb provides broadband services to business and residential customers in seven Italian cities: Milan, Rome, Turin, Genoa, Naples, Bologna and Reggio Emilia. It began operations in 1999 but most of its growth has been achieved from 2002 onwards. At end-Q2 2003, it had 249,000 customers, up almost 250% from a year earlier. This rapid expansion has been facilitated both by growing consumer responsiveness to its diverse product offerings and rapid infrastructure roll-out. At end-Q1 2003, it had connected over 53,000 buildings, up from 15,000 households one year earlier.[304]

---

[303] e.Biscom (May 2003).

[304] e.Biscom, (March 2003).

FastWeb's main asset is its 10,000km optical fibre network, which passes 1.3 million households. Connections to-the-home provide speeds of up to 10 Mbps. FastWeb also used unbundled lines from Telecom Italia, which are potentially available to a further 1.2 million households. It installs its own equipment on the unbundled lines and in 2003 upgraded its residential ADSL offer to 4 Mbps, from 2 Mbps. At the time this was introduced, the fastest offer from competitors was 1.2 Mbps. Approximately 55% of its residential subscribers are connected via fibre, with the remaining 45% using DSL. FastWeb is Italy's leading provider of DSL over unbundled lines, accounting for 56% (79,400 lines) of unbundled lines at end-Q1 2003.

Deployment of new fibre is very expensive, owing to the high cost of trenching and installing individual connections to buildings and homes. FastWeb has significantly reduced costs by using Telecom Italia's Socrate network of ducts, which was built for a now defunct cable television project and passes over 1.5 million homes.[305] Nevertheless, the use of unbundled lines has been a key element in FastWeb's success story, enabling it to provide services, *"in areas where the fibre optic infrastructure has still to be rolled out."*[306] The implication of this is that FastWeb will upgrade DSL customers to its fibre network demand in a particular area reaches a critical mass, but the company does not provide an indication at what thresholds this might apply.

Amongst European broadband operators, FastWeb stands out for the range of services that it offers to subscribers and the innovative nature of many of these offerings. In addition to the standard 'double-play' of high-speed internet and telephony services, it also offers: advanced video-communication, virtual private networks (VPN), audio and video streaming, business-to-employee (B2E) wireless (WiFi) links, tele-surveillance (enabling remote access to home or office surveillance systems), video-conferencing, video-telephony, interactive TV and Video-on-Demand services. FastWeb customers enjoy access to an impressive range of content – including the latest news, sport and documentaries, as well as a large film library – supplied by two other e.Biscom subsidiaries: e.BisMedia and Rai Click (a joint venture with state-owned broadcaster RAI)

FastWeb offers a wide range of subscriptions packages and additional options to consumers (see Table 16), designed to allow subscribers to pick the services they want. Combination packages are discounted to encourage take-up of new services. For example, it charges 41 euros per month for unlimited voice or 67 euros per month for unlimited internet access, but only 85 euros for both plus its television service. As of July 2003, is was also running a special offer waving charges for its 'videocommunication' services (such as video-telephony) for six months in an attempt to encourage subscribers to try these less familiar services.

---

[305] Cisco (2002).

[306] e.Biscom, (January 2003).

Table 16: FastWeb subscription packages

Package	Monthly sub.	Main services			
		Internet	Telephone	TV	Videocom-munication
TV di FastWeb	E30	E1.9/h	Call charges	Included	Extra
Mega Internet 500†	E35	500 mins	Call charges	E10/m	Extra
Voce Senza Limiti	E41	E1.9/h	Included	E10/m	Extra
Internet Senza Limiti	E67	Included	Call charges	E10/m	Extra
Tutto Senza Limiti	E85	Included	Included	Included	Extra
Tutto FastWeb	E110	Included	Included	Included	Included

Notes: E = euros, /h = per hour, /m = per month; †First 500 minutes per month included, then E1.9/m
Source: FastWeb website 25 July 2003

Its prices are competitive with other providers of broadband access. For example, its 500 minute internet offering at 35 euros per month and its unlimited access offer straddle incumbent ISP Tin.it's standard unlimited offer at 54.95 euros per month. Both offer much higher speeds, whether provided over fibre or DSL.

Its subscription packages have proved popular. Despite its limited coverage, FastWeb had a 16% share of the Italian broadband market at end-Q1 2003. According to the e.Biscom 2002 report, its market share in the areas where it first rolled out its network now exceeds 30%.[307] Its wide product range has enabled it to achieve impressive residential ARPU of 790 euros per annum at end-Q1 2003. Although internet access and telephony are its main residential products, its video services have a growing subscriber base: at end-Q1 2003, 50% of fibre subscribers and 30% of new ADSL subscribers took this service.

FastWeb is also a commercial success story. It posted revenues of 220 million euros in 2002 and 108 million euros in Q2 2003 alone. Although it was loss making in early years, it has been EBITDA positive since Q2 2002, with its EBITDA margin steadily increasing to 16% in Q2 2003. This strong performance demonstrates the potential viability of entry strategies based on new fibre roll-out, as well as the roll that unbundled lines can play in easing the financial burden of rolling out new networks where demand is uncertain. It is important to appreciate though that the innovative service combinations offered by FastWeb are only possible because it has developed and controls its own

---

[307]e.Biscom (January 2003).

infrastructure, including DSL lines. Indeed, e.Biscom has rejected the possibility of developing new products based on Telecom Italia's wholesale DSL offering, even though this could enable it to reach a much larger audience, because it would not be able to offer the same service range at the lower speeds available.[308]

C   HanseNet in Germany

HanseNet provides telecommunications, data and internet services to business and residential customers in and around the city of Hamburg, Germany. It operates a fibre optic city network of over 1,000 kilometres, and supplies voice, data and video services to business and residential customers over DSL using unbundled lines from incumbent Deutsche Telekom. HanseNet was owned by e.Biscom, which also owns leading FTTH operator FastWeb in Italy (see previous case study). However, in July 2003, e.Biscom announced the sale of HanseNet to Telecom Italia for 250 million euros.

Since acquiring HanseNet in September 2000, e.Biscom had successfully reorientated the company's business model, which originally focused on traditional telephony services, towards providing innovative broadband network services along similar lines to FastWeb in Italy. It was rewarded with a steady rise in revenues which have delivered positive EBITDA since Q3 2002. However, shortage of cash owing to demands of developing the FastWeb network limited e.Biscom's ability to develop HanseNet's network.[309] The Telecom Italia takeover raises the possibility of fresh capital injections into HanseNet to develop its technology and network, and the extension of its successful business model to other parts of Germany.

In 2002, HanseNet introduced a new broadband services offer for residential and business customers on an integrated IP network. This offer is delivered using DSL technology over unbundled lines from incumbent Deutsche Telekom. Connections are then routed over HanseNet's local fibre network. A likely direction of development under e.Biscom would have been the gradual enhancement of HanseNet's network with fibre optic connections to the home, along a similar model to FastWeb. However, under Telecom Italia, which primarily uses DSL technology in Italy, it appears more likely that HanseNet will continue to utilise unbundled lines. According to newspaper reports, Telecom Italia has earmarked around 500-600 million euros for broadband investments abroad, with the objective of leveraging technology it has developed for the Italian market.[310]

HanseNet's main residential services are telephony and high-speed internet. The high speed of the connection has also enabled HanseNet to introduce video

---

[308] Idate (2002), page 90.
[309] Financial Times (July 2003).
[310] Financial Times (July 2003).

over DSL services, targeted both at the mainstream and niche local markets (for example, in January 2003, it extended its library to include Turkish films[311]). It offers a number of service packages linking its broadband and video products to its telephony service (for which call charges apply):

☐ *Speed-Komplett.* The basic package combines telephony and a 2 Mbps broadband connection. The monthly subscription is 61.90 euros, which is competitive with DT's main products (T-Online's 768 kbps and 1.5 Mbps services cost 63.66 and 99.95 euros per month respectively, including rental of an analogue line for basic telephony). Additional options are available to take movie access and increase connection speeds. An upgrade to 4 Mbps access costs an additional 34.90 euros per month.

☐ *Speed-Movie.* For 34.90 euros, this package combines telephony with video over DSL but excludes internet access. As with the movie option under Speed-Komplett, films can be downloaded at any time of the day for between 3-6 euros each.

Like FastWeb, HanseNet's business model involved significant upfront losses as it expanded its network and subscriber base. However, it is now posting impressive operational results. At the end of Q1 2003, it had 75,900 customers, up 45% from a year earlier, of which over 40,000 were DSL broadband subscribers. This helped drive a 25% growth in revenues Q1 2003 over Q1 2002, resulting in a positive EBITDA of 7 million euros year-on-year. Total revenues in the year to Q1 2003 were 87.7 million euros.

HanseNet's combination of services and competitive pricing has enabled it to establish its position as the leading competitor to DT in broadband in the Hamburg area. According to RegTP, DT's competitors had a 34% market share in broadband lines in the Hamburg area in 2002; compared to a national average of below 20%.[312] HanseNet accounts for a large majority of these lines; in 2003, it claimed a 30% local market share.[313] This success illustrates the potential for facility-based entrants offering innovative service packages to make significant in roads into DT's market lead, especially in urban areas.

D   ONO in Spain

Background

ONO is a cable operator with franchises in a number of Spanish regions, including southern Andalusia, Valencia, Murcia, Majorca, Cantabria and Castilla–La Mancha. Like the other major Spanish cable company, Auna, it only began rolling out its network in 1998. Consequently, from its inception, it has installed infrastructure with the objective of providing integrated telephony, cable

---

[311]Point Topic (2003a), page 421.
[312]RegTP (2003).
[313]WELT (2003).

television and broadband Internet services. In just four years, ONO and Auna have emerged as the main alternative offerings to incumbent fixed-line operator Telefónica, a status that has been recognised by the Spanish regulator (CMT), which considers them to be in position to compete in 50% of the total market.[314]

A February 2003 report by Fortis Bank on the Spanish broadband market concluded that both DSL and Cable broadband internet access technologies were viable.[315] Although it considering DSL to be at an advantage at present owing to a lower cost base, it argued that, in the near future, the greater flexibility of cable networks in terms of service offerings will play in their favour. It is already apparent that the triple-play service supplied by cable companies is proving popular with subscribers: at end-2002, 68% of telephony customers also subscribed to television and 46% also to internet.[316] Furthermore, the very high penetration rate for broadband internet amongst cable customers has led analysts to conclude that cable companies are attracting disproportionately heavy (high margin) users of telecommunications.[317]

Although Telefónica is expected to remain the market leader in broadband provision for the foreseeable future, owing to its large customer base, forecast growth for broadband access via cable is projects to significantly outpace DSL and to be amongst the highest in Europe. One reason for this is that although the cable companies are now prioritising marketing, they are continuing to extend their networks. During 2002, at the height of the telecommunications downturn, cable investment was down just 4.4% from the previous year, compared to an average decrease of 32% across the rest of the Spanish telecommunications sector.[318]

Analysis

Since its inception in 1998, ONO has grown very rapidly. By end-Q2 2003, the company had acquired nearly 540,000 subscribers and rolled out its network past over 1.9 million homes[319]. This amounted to over three-quarters of its initial planned build-out.[320] In addition, ONO has announced plans to extend its network deployment in Castilla-La Mancha, where in July 2003 it was granted a regional franchise in addition to the one it already held for the local city of Albacete.[321]

---

[314]CMT (2002).
[315]Fortis Bank (2003).
[316]CMT (2002).
[317]CMT (2002).
[318]CMT (2002).
[319]ONO (July 2003).
[320]Cableuropa (2003).
[321]ONO has promised to cover cities with a population of 40,000 or more within four years, those between 20,000-40.000 within 6 years and those from 10,000-20.000 within ten years.

The provision of *triple play* services, bundling telephony, television and broad-band internet services has been core to ONO's strategy since the beginning. Although the company faces a challenging commercial and capital market en-vironment, it is expected by analysts to consolidate its position as an important player in the Spanish telecoms and television markets.

In designing its network architecture, ONO has been heavily influenced by strategy of ntl, the leading UK operator, where much of its senior management came from. The final connection to the home uses the Siamese cable system, combining coaxial cable for television and internet service, and twisted pair copper wire for telephony. This system is much more cost effective for deliver-ing telephony than coaxial cable alone, owing to the lower cost of the terminal equipment required. Siamese cable is used only to reach a tap which serves around 6-8 homes, from which separate copper pair and coaxial cables connect to concentric layers of fibre-optic rings via nodes. The deployment of fibre optic cable close to the home allows the potential for very high data transmission speeds. Although capacity is shared amongst consumers accessing the same node, this can be increased by 'splitting nodes', bringing the fibre optic cable closer to individual homes.

ONO considers that the capital expenditure it has incurred to reach each home in its Spanish franchises has been significantly lower than the cost incurred by comparable companies at a similar stage of their development. It attributes the rapid and low cost network construction to:[322]

- □ the high urban population density and the significant proportion of multiple dwelling units in its franchises;
- □ the ability to build portions of the access network above ground;
- □ a dedicated permit team obtaining rights of way permits from local authorities in advance of planned network builds; and
- □ a state-of-the-art network design centre with the ability to create detailed network build plans in advance of actual construction.

In the early roll-out phase, ONO concentrated on the development of local net-works in areas with highest population density, to maximise revenue generation. Its returns from building out the 'final' third of its network may therefore be rather lower than previous.

This network architecture has enabled ONO to offer a coherent package of triple-play services to all subscribers from its inception. Customers have the potential to purchase any combination of the three main services that they require. However, there are discounts averaging around 25% relative to the combined price of individual services for subscribers that take more than one service. By the end of 2002, nearly 70% of ONO's residential customers sub-scribed to two or more of the three main services.[323]

---

[322]Cableuropa (2003).
[323]Cableuropa (2003).

ONO offers always on, high-speed Internet access via cable modem at a flat fee for various download speeds. The maximum speed of ONO's cable modem service is in 2003 was limited to 1 Mbps for residential customers, although the modems are capable of higher. Pricing is highly competitive and appears aimed at winning market share from DSL operators. ONO's two main internet access products are priced at 25.90 euros per month for 128 Kbps and 39.04 euros per month for 300 Kbps, on a stand-alone basis, reduced by 4.90 and 6.02 euros respectively if bundled to a package including other ONO services. By comparison, Telefónica (ADSL) charges an average of 40 euros per month for 256 Kbps services. Furthermore, activation charges are around four times cheaper than for DSL 256 kbps products.[324] ONO's typical business offering also at present provide savings compared to Telefónica.[325]

A combination of strong marketing and aggressive pricing has helped to rapidly grow subscriber numbers. As illustrated in Figure 27, growth in television subscribers has kept pace with homes passed. Although broadband internet was slower to take off, it has been the fastest growing service since early-2002. In its first quarter results, ONO picked out broadband internet as the most notable growth area.[326] Results for Q2 2003 show that 90% of the 174,120 internet access subscribers subscribed to broadband services. ONO has achieved an impressive customer penetration rate (subscribers as a percentage of homes passed) of 33.3% in only four years, whilst broadband internet access penetration has reached 9.6%.[327]

ONO's growing subscriber base has underpinned a strong operational performance. Revenues in 2002 topped 250 million euros, up from 140 million (2001) and 50 million euros (2000). Internet access revenues accounted for 39 million euros in 2002, up from 18 million and 2 million in 2001 and 2000 respectively.[328] Revenues were 85.6 million euros in Q2 2003, with further growth projected through 2003. ARPU exceeded 50 euros in 2002, well ahead of traditional European cable companies, but up to 10 euros less than its UK peers ntl and TeleWest, indicating further upside potential.[329] The company was EBITDA positive for the first time in 2002, and recorded EBITDAs of 16.8 million and 23.1 million euros in Q1 and Q2 2003 respectively, up from a loss of 2.5 million in Q1 2002.[330]

---

[324] Idate (2002), page 137.

[325] Cableuropa (2003).

[326] ONO (May 2003) [We note, that penetration figures presented in the results are higher than implied by data in Figure 27, which probably reflects definitional differences in the calculation of this figure].

[327] ONO (July 2003).

[328] Cableuropa (2003).

[329] UPC (April 2003).

[330] ONO (July 2003) and ONO (May 2003).

Figure 27: ONO – cable homes passed & selected subscriber numbers

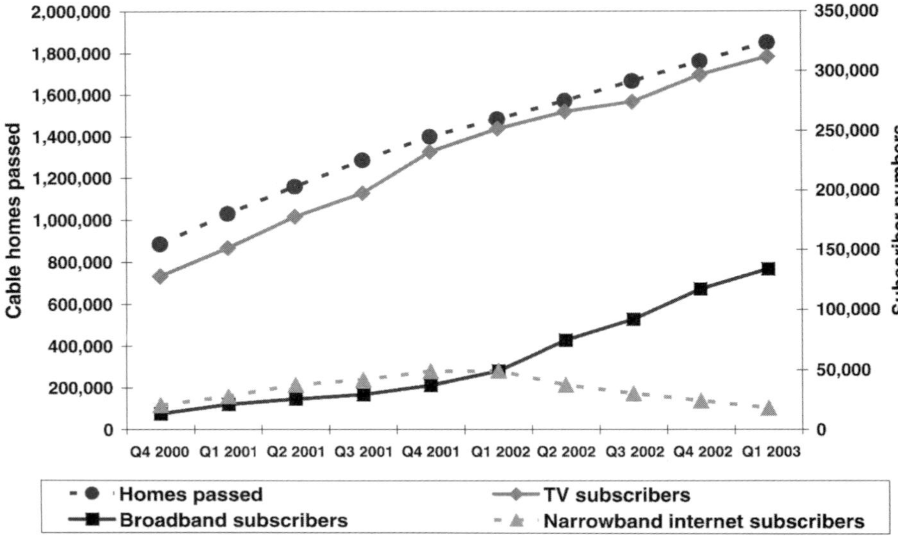

Source: Informa (2003) data

Notwithstanding this progress, the company has been troubled by poor capital market conditions since the bursting of the telecoms bubble. A May 2003 report by Standard and Poors described ONO's operating environment as "challenging", noting the *"strong competitive threat from the recent merger of the two satellite providers Canal Satélite Digital S.A. and Via Digital S.A. in the TV market – which together have 80% of the Spanish pay-TV market – and from Telefónica in telephony services, [as well as] depressed consumer demand due to the economic slowdown."*[331] As a result, there is wide expectation amongst analysts that Ono will eventually merge with the other major cable company, Auna.

The high capital expenditure related to network roll-out means that the company's ambitions are heavily dependent on external finance. In February, parent company Cableuropa announced the cancellation of 503 million euros of its bonds in a move that will strengthen the company's balance sheet. However, given that ONO is expected to incur negative cash-flow until at least 2005, this remains an area of potential weakness.

Looking forward, ONO's decision to take on the new franchise in Castilla-La Mancha is a strong sign of confidence in its own business model and raises the likelihood that a majority of Spanish people will eventually enjoy facilities-based competition in broadband. Castilla-La Mancha is a largely rural, low

---

[331] Standard & Poor's (May 2003).

income region, although it does offer the advantage that the population is largely concentrated in small towns rather than widely dispersed in hamlets. One potential threat to these expansion plans is increased competition as a result of entrants using bitstream or resale access to Telefonica's network. To the extent that these competitors can be expected to take customers away from cable, they could destroy Ono's business case for extending network infrastructure to more marginal regions. The net impact of this on social welfare in the marginal region would likely be negative, given that consumers would be unable to take advantage of the additional services provided over cable relative to DSL, and there would be no competitive pressure on Telefonica to improve its local infrastructure.

E   UPC (chello) in nine European countries

UPC is Europe's largest cable operator, with 6.6 million subscribers at end-2002. Based in the Netherlands, the company grew rapidly in the late 1990s and early 2000s through an aggressive acquisition strategy aimed at establishing a pan-European footprint. It now has interests in cable companies in 13 European countries and provides broadband internet services under the brandname chello in nine of these[332]: Austria, Belgium, France, Hungary, Netherlands, Norway, Poland, Slovakia and Sweden. UPC's financial position was badly affected by the collapse of the telecoms bubble, but it has to continued to post solid growth in both overall revenues and average revenues per user (ARPU), primary as a result of rising demand for broadband internet access.

Although UPC is a relatively new company, describing it as a 'new entrant' is somewhat misleading. Many of its businesses are long-established analogue cable operators, with mature television businesses. For example, in the Netherlands and Belgium respectively, it enjoys 90% and 85% television penetration of homes passed, and has already passed the large majority of homes in its licence regions.[333] Growth in total homes passed and television subscribers have thus been fairly static in recent years (see Figure 29), being largely limited to new housing developments. The company's focus has instead been on increasing ARPUs by selling new services (digital television, telephony and broadband internet), primarily to existing customers.

The provision of new services has required extensive investment by UPC in upgrading its traditional one-way cable networks to hybrid fibre-coax cable. The fibre provides the high-speed backbone and the coaxial cables are used to connect end users over the last mile to the backbone. In addition to allowing high-speed two-way communication, this network architecture makes it easier to increase network capacity in response to demand by extending the fibre optic cabling further into neighbourhoods so that each fibre node is shared

---

[332] The other countries are the Czech Republic, Germany, Malta and Romania.
[333] Informa (2003).

Figure 28: UPC Western European homes passed (000s/% upgraded)

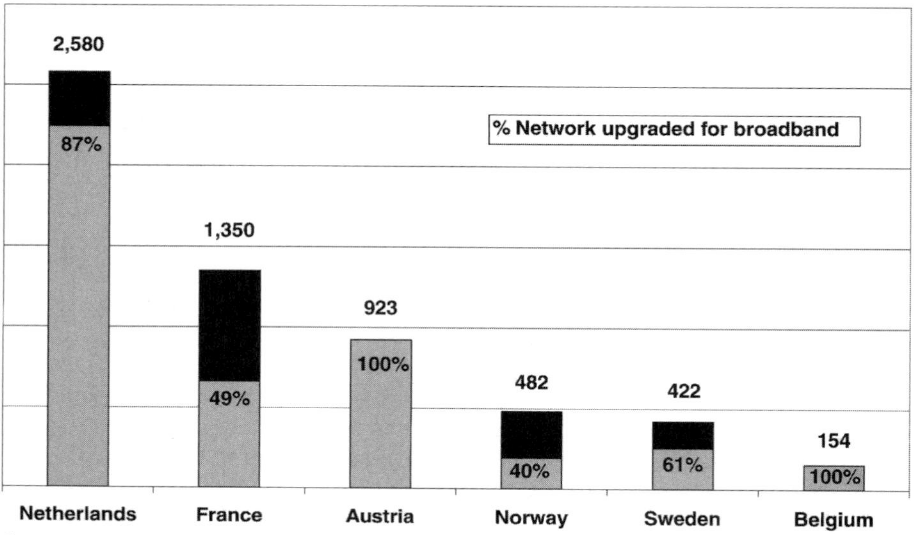

Source: New UPC Investor Presentation, 2-3 April, 2003

by fewer homes. Upgrading is about 75% complete in Western Europe, but the position varies significantly from country-to-country (see Figure 28). For example, 100% of UPC's Austrian subscribers can now receive broadband and other two-way services, but the comparative figure is only 49% in France.

UPC describes its core service offering as *"analogue triple play"*. In an April 2003 presentation to investors, it prioritised: *"a return to growth orientated strategy, bundling triple play products, internet, analogue TV and NPV positive telephony, with a measured NPV positive digital roll-out."* However, as Figure 29 illustrates, broadband internet is the key growth area in this mix. Broadband subscribers have grown steadily from 326,000 at end-2000 to 678,000 at end-Q1 2003. By contrast, the number of telephony customers has been stalled at around 450,000 since end-2001. This reflects differences in the cost of end-user terminal equipment required to carry data and voice services over fibre-coax. Cable modems for data have fallen significantly in price driven by global economies of scale, whereas comparative cost savings have not been realised for telephony over cable. This makes it difficult for UPC to compete with incumbent operators for telephony subscribers, although this may change in the future with falling prices for terminal equipment and/or technological advances with voice over IP.

For broadband services, UPC's main competitors in its local markets are the incumbent DSL operators and the ISPs using their lines. This is reflected in the competitive pricing of its chello products. In Table 7, we compared the

Figure 29: UPC cable homes passed and subscribers for eight countries

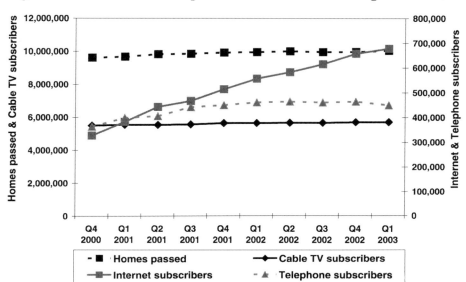

Notes: Aggregate data for UPC operations in Austria, Belgium, France, Hungary, Netherlands, Norway, Poland and Sweden
Source: Informa (2003) data; UPC website, www.upccorp.com

broadband subscription prices of European cable operators and incumbent ISPs: we observed that the subscription prices for chello are within 7% (plus or minus) of the incumbent ISP's prices for comparable ADSL services in four of the five EU countries where it operates. However, initial activation charges are generally lower than for DSL. For example, in the Netherlands, chello charges 105.33 and 175.33 euros respectively for basic and full installation (including modem hire), whereas KPN's Planet Internet ISP charges 203.95 euros to install an Ethernet modem. chello has also been expanding its range of products, differentiated primarily on available download speeds; for example, in the Netherlands, in 2003, it introduced a reduced price 300kbps 'light' offering, apparently to match the competitive threat from KPN's 256kbps product, which had undercut chello's standard 150kbps offering.

The combination of strong branding, competitive pricing and a large television customer base has helped UPC to grab a large share of local broadband markets in regions where it has upgraded its network.[334] For example, in the Netherlands, at end-2002, UPC was the country's largest broadband internet provider, ahead of KPN's national DSL, even though its footprint covers only about one-third

---

[334]Total Telecom (October 2002).

of Dutch homes.[335] In Vienna, it claims that *"about 80% of broadband Internet users are chello customers."*[336] In these areas, cable is clearly established as a viable long-term competitor to DSL.

The increase in broadband subscriptions has been the most positive aspect of UPC's financial position since 2002, supporting growth in revenues and ARPUs. At the same time, UPC has cut operating spend and slashed capital expenditure, the latter falling to 270 million euros in 2002 from a high of 1.7 billion in 2000, owing to reduced upgrade and new-build activity. UPC also appears to have reached agreement on restructuring its huge debt burden, estimated at over 8.1 billion euros in 2002[337], which should allow it to emerge from bankruptcy protection during 2003.

UPC's position as key player in broadband markets where it has already upgraded its network appears secure for the immediate future. Its chello offerings are highly competitive and appear able to withstand competition from DSL providers. However, looking forward, the company faces a number of significant challenges:

☐ Despite the emphasis on a 'triple play strategy', UPC has not yet been able to leverage fully this potential advantage over DSL operators, owing to cost and technological obstacles to introducing telephony on its network.
☐ Even after restructuring, the need to generate cash to service its remaining bank debts may constrain UPC's ability to finance further upgrades of its networks.
☐ Like its incumbent DSL competitors, UPC faces a number of regulatory challenges which threaten to undermine its incentives to invest in new build and upgrades. Most notably, in the Netherlands, the government has announced plans to open up cable networks to access. Meanwhile, in France, the Netherlands and Sweden, there are initiatives to subsidise broadband take-up which potentially favour rival platforms (fibre) at the expense of cable and DSL providers.

Given UPC's delicate financial position, the regulatory environment may well be crucial in determining the extent to which investors are willing to back future investment in the network. Ultimately, adverse decisions and/or prolonged uncertainty could weaken the company's competitiveness in the provision of new services. Furthermore, other European cable operators – many of which are much less advanced in upgrading their networks – are likely to be influenced by UPC's experience. If they perceive that regulatory obstacles are preventing UPC from adequately realising the benefits of its investments, they may refrain from the investment necessary to develop their own broadband capabilities.

---

[335] Informa (2003).
[336] UPC chello (February 2003).
[337] Idate (2002), page 40.

F U.S. CLECs

The FCC's implementation of the Telecommunications Act of 1996 provided competitive local exchange carriers (CLECs) with three ways to enter into U.S. telecommunications markets:

1. by building their own networks;
2. by leasing unbundled network elements (UNEs) from ILECS, which CLECs were free to combine as they choose; and
3. by engaging in pure resale of the incumbents' services.

The FCC set rates for unbundled network elements based on the incumbents' forward-looking long-run average incremental cost (LRAIC) – that is, the non-sunk costs that a perfectly efficient network would incur to operate a network. LRAIC rates are thus typically lower than the incumbents' actual historical costs of building and maintaining networks. Unbundled access was never thought of as an end in itself; rather, unbundling was intended to serve as a stepping stone to fully-fledged facilities-based competition.[338]

Although the resale and leasing strategies pursued by many entrants was viewed to be a success in the early stages of local loop unbundling, by 2000, business executives and analysts alike began to question the long-term viability of CLECs that relied primarily on the incumbents' network to provide service, given that regulated access was available to all comers. The CEO of one data CLEC (DLEC) observed that there was *"no profitable way into DSL unless you own the physical layer."*[339] Another analyst noted that it is *"hard to be profitable when you're running on another firm's network."*[340] Patrick Hurley, a DSL analyst at TeleChoice, observed in December 2000 that the market for DLEC services had become commoditized, and that the DLECs should focus to a greater extent on differentiating themselves from the ILECs on service terms.[341]

During 2000 and 2001, the possibility for resale arbitrage arose as the majority of state public utility commissions established their final prices for UNE-Platform (UNE-P) access, which allowed CLECs to purchase, as a package, unbundled loops, switches, and transport elements from incumbent carriers at discounted rates. Although UNE-P had previously been available at interim prices set by the FCC, the final rates set by the states were typically significantly lower, such that UNE-P rates became discounted to a far greater extent than

---

[338]See, for example: FCC (1999) – *"Goals of the 1996 Act. As noted above, our unbundling analysis takes into account whether unbundling a particular network element is consistent with the goals of the 1996 Act. We find our decision to unbundle [certain local network elements] is consistent with the 1996 Act's goals of rapid introduction of competition and the promotion of facilities-based entry."*

[339]Telephony.Online (December 2000a).

[340]Network World (November 2000).

[341]Telephony.Online (December 2000a).

rates for wholesale service.[342] According to a June 2003 FCC report on the state of local service competition in the United States, growth in facilities-based CLEC lines essentially halted in June 2001 at 6 million lines.[343] Walter McCormick, president of the U.S. Telecom Association, stated in January 2003 that manufacturers of telecommunications equipment blame UNE-P for the severe drop in capital expenditure on equipment and facilities.[344]

Nonetheless, most of the entrants that relied on unbundling have failed. This is reflected in the collapse of CLEC share prices since the peaks of 2000; for example, the market capitalisation of Allegiance Telecom fell from over US$7bn in April 2000 to just US$236mn in April 2002, while that of Focal Communications fell from over US$2bn to just US$28mn over the same period. Only a handful of the new local carriers are likely to survive, particularly the facilities-based sellers of special access in large metropolitan areas. The FCC's attempt to induce entry by creating a wholesale market in network facilities with artificially low prices has resulted in an enormous waste of resources. Indeed, much of the U.S. capital spending by CLECs appears to have been the result of a speculative bubble and is now widely acknowledged to have created excess capacity in data and voice transmission.[345]

In addition to discouraging broadband entrants from pursuing a facilities-based approach, the FCC's unbundling rules also discouraged ILECs from investing in their own facilities because they reasonably feared that the fractional revenue stream (owing to compulsory sharing) would not cover the expected costs of upgrading their networks. Line sharing now accounts for nearly all of non-ILEC DSL lines, and ILECs expect to lose over 10% of DSL customers to line sharing by 2005.[346] An upcoming study by Crandall, Jackson and Singer estimates that ILECs would wire nearly one-quarter of all non-wired central offices for DSL if the line sharing obligation were removed.[347] Limited roll-out of DSL is a key reason why cable has recently consolidated its lead over DSL in broadband provision, increasing its market share from 60% in 2000 to 62% in the first quarter of 2003.[348]

In conclusion, unbundling in the United States has been largely unsuccessful in achieving the original goal of the Telecommunications Act – namely, facilities-based competition – because it gave entrants greater incentives to exploit resale-

---

[342]Russell Frisby, president of the US Competitive Telecommunications Association (a CLEC advocacy group) explained his organization's strong support for UNE-P on the grounds that *"[r]esale has been set at a level whereby competitors are not able to enter the market profitably."* Telephony.Online (January 2003).

[343]FCC (June 2003a).

[344]Telephony.Online (January 2003).

[345]See, *e.g.* The Economist (March 2001).

[346]Crandall, Jackson & Singer (2003).

[347]Crandall, Jackson & Singer (2003).

[348]CBS MarketWatch.com (July 2003).

based arbitrage opportunities than to invest in their own networks. In Box IV, we briefly illustrate the impact of these distortions with reference to the conflicting strategies and experiences of three CLECs: Covad, Allegiance and Focal.

Box IV: Case studies of three U.S. CLECs

1. Covad

Covad's business plan was to act as a middle man by selling its services to ISPs and other telecommunications carriers, rather than provide services to end users. To accomplish this, Covad relied on the last-mile facilities of the incumbent carriers. Covad's strategy generated savings to the firm in deployment costs, but made it difficult for Covad to differentiate its product offerings from those of the incumbent local exchange carriers.

In September 2000, Morgan Stanley observed that one of Covad's greatest challenges was to effectively differentiate its services from those of competitors through the sale of additional value-added offerings.[349] Covad's heavy reliance on the ILECs has been cited by many analysts as a problem with the company's business plan. Similarly, Michael Goodman, an analyst at the Yankee Group, observed that Covad could not hope to compete with the ILECs on a pure price basis: *"Even if they price DSL at the same level as the ILECs, they're at a disadvantage because the ILEC has a better margin and its costs are lower."*[350] Covad was ultimately unsuccessful in accomplishing such product differentiation, however.

Covad was also harmed by its pursuit of rapid growth. Charles Hoffman, Covad's president and CEO, stated in an April 2002 interview that Covad's rapid growth led it to ignore critical infrastructure issues: *"There wasn't a lot of attention paid to the infrastructure [at Covad], as in; Do we have proper clients to serve revenue assurance? Do the bills we send the customers match what we think they owe us? There were a lot of basic business problems, just because it was a start-up and it grew fast."*[351]

Morgan Stanley Dean Witter cites Covad's inability to collect receivables from delinquent ISPs as a root cause of Covad's demise.[352] In all, Covad admitted that in 2000 it had over 40 million dollars in billings with *"financially distressed customers,"* which it could not fairly recognize as either revenue or accounts receivable.[353]

Covad filed for bankruptcy in August 2001, but re-emerged in early 2002.

---

[349] Morgan Stanley Dean Witter (September 2000).
[350] Telephony.Online (June 2001).
[351] Upside Today (April 2002).
[352] Morgan Stanley Dean Witter (December 2000).
[353] Covad (2001).

2. Allegiance Telecommunications

Allegiance Telecommunications is a Dallas-based CLEC that began operations in 1998 and used all three approaches (network construction, leased access to UNEs and resale) to provide services. Allegiance focused on network construction, however, and only leased one of the seven available UNEs from incumbents – the local loop.[354] Tony Parella, the executive vice president of Allegiance, stated in 2001 that he *"would never consider a strategy exclusively of resale. You're more or less a billing agent for the ILEC [if you follow such a strategy]."*[355] In 2001, Allegiance was viewed by analysts as one of the top CLECs in the United States because of its ability to generate revenue and secure sufficient investment funding.[356]

One of the keys to Allegiance's success was its tactical use of the ILECs' networks in building its own network. Allegiance leased only last mile access lines from ILECs, and it built its own equipment on either side of the last mile line.[357] As Crandall has explained, *"Allegiance has succeeded not by repackaging and reselling ILEC services; rather, Allegiance has solidified its presence in the telecommunications industry by upgrading and improving the ILEC network in order to offer customers cheaper service with superior quality."*[358]

Allegiance was forced to declare bankruptcy in May 2003. Allegiance's bankruptcy, however, was not so much the result of a failed business plan as it was the result of Allegiance's unfavourable bank covenants. Allegiance's bankruptcy was declared to be unusual because the company had increased revenues by 49 percent in 2002 and was on track to become EBITDA-positive in the summer of 2003.[359] As Phil Jacobsen of Network Conceptions put it just months prior to Allegiance's bankruptcy filing, *"[t]hey're not having a cash flow crisis. They've got tons of money on the books. They only have one problem: covenants."*[360]

3. Focal Communications

Focal Communications collected reciprocal compensation payments from established carriers for simply setting itself up as an intermediary between

---

[354] Telephony.Online (February 2001).

[355] Telephony.Online (February 2001).

[356] Washington Post (February 2001).

[357] See Ward (2001).

[358] Crandall (2001).

[359] Telephony.Online (April 2003).

[360] Telephony.Online (April 2003).

these established carriers and Internet service providers. In this manner, Focal's entry into the telecommunications market relied essentially on a taking advantage of a regulatory arbitrage opportunity. Indeed, in 1997, Focal obtained 80% of its total revenues from reciprocal compensation. When the arbitrage opportunity was revealed, regulators moved to phase it out, placing Focal in substantial financial difficulty.[361] Focal did not construct its own lines, but instead leased 100% of its access lines from incumbents. As its entire network was based on unbundled network elements, Focal could not offer either cost improvements or service improvements over the incumbent local exchange carriers.

Focal's market capitalization dropped by 80% in the first half of 2000, in large part because the financial markets became concerned about future regulatory policy on reciprocal compensation.[362] Although Focal Communications was not specifically involved in the resale of DSL capabilities, the experience is valuable because it demonstrates the danger associated with the creation by regulators of pure arbitrage opportunities – namely, that it induces inefficient entry by firms (and inefficient investment in firms) that do not contribute to meaningful competition.

---

[361] See Crandall (2001).
[362] See Crandall (2001).

Annex III   A brief introduction to market definition

For two services (call them A and B) to be competing in the same relevant market, the price of service A should significantly constrain the price of service B and vice-versa. This could come about through either:

☐ demand substitution (an increase in the price of service A could cause customers to switch to service B); or
☐ supply substitution (an increase in the price of service A could lead to the provider of service B additionally or alternatively providing service A).

Competition law has traditionally used a simple test – the hypothetical monopolist test – for assessing whether two products are in the same market or not on the basis of demand substitutability. This is the only first step in the analysis as supply-side substitution must also be considered subsequently. The U.S. Department of Justice's Horizontal Merger Guidelines, which are credited with establishing the hypothetical monopolist test[363] – define a relevant product market as: *"a product or group of products such that a hypothetical profit-maximizing firm that was the only present and future seller of those products likely would impose at least a small but significant and nontransitory increase in price."*[364]

Suppose that we start with service A and assume that it was provided entirely by just one provider. We now ask whether this hypothetical monopolist could profitably increase the price of service A by a significant and non-transitory amount (say 5 to 10%) without having any control over the price of service B. If the answer is yes, then service A is likely to be a relevant market in its own right, as its pricing is not constrained by consumers switching to alternative services (such as service B). Of course, we would still need to consider whether this hypothetical monopoly would be unsustainable in the face of supply substitution.

If, on the other hand, the answer is no, then we know that substitution to other services (say service B) is significant enough to impose a constraint on the pricing of service A even if service A were supplied by just one provider.

---

[363] See, for example, Massey (2000); the hypothetical monopolist test has been widely embraced by competition authorities around the world, including the European Commission, which explicitly adopted the test in its 1997 Notice on Market Definition.

[364] 1997 US Department of Justice and Federal Trade Commission, Horizontal Merger Guidelines. The hypothetical monopolist test is sometimes referred to as the 'SSNIP' test, to represent the fact that the test is concerned with a given firms ability to impose a 'small but significant and nontransitory increase in price'.

Therefore, the market is larger than service *A* alone; services *A* and *B* would compete to an appreciable extent were they supplied by different suppliers.

For the purposes of the example, suppose that service *B* were clearly the next closest substitute. We could now go on to ask whether a hypothetical monopoly provider of both services *A* and *B* would be able to increase profits through a significant and non-transitory price increase for both services. If so, then services *A* and *B* taken together might constitute a relevant market (subject to checking whether supply substitution is a possibility). Otherwise, there is presumably some other substitute service that we would need to add to our prototype market and then apply the test again. We might need to add a whole range of substitutes until we reach the antitrust market.

Although the hypothetical monopolist test has been widely used by competition authorities around the world, it is subject to a number of widely known limitations and its results must be interpreted with care. For example, a supplier with market power might raise price above cost until the point where it's a significant proportion of its customers would be just about to switch to an alternative product. A further hypothetical price increase might lead customers to switch to the alternative; indeed a rational monopolist should price up to the point where a further price increase would lower profits. However, in this case it would be wrong to include the alternative in the relevant market, as had we started from the competitive price level for the product (i.e. cost), a hypothetical price increase would have been profitable. This is the so-called cellophane fallacy, which suggests that where there is existing market power, markets might be defined too broadly, and so market power may not be correctly identified.

Although this is a potential concern, in practice application of the hypothetical monopolist test often leads to markets being defined too narrowly as:

☐ It is necessary to consider supply substitution, not just demand substitution when defining relevant markets. There has been much academic and practitioner comment that existing market definition methods used by competition authorities have tended to give too little weight to potential entry and supply substitution.[365]
☐ Many markets (including many telecoms markets) are characterised by competition focussed on innovation and development of new services. Current market conditions may give little indication of the potential for sudden, dislocating technical change that introduces new alternatives.[366]

---

[365] For example, Kauper (1996) observed that supply substitutability is *"a factor which over time has tended to disappear from [European] Commission decisions"*.

[366] Pleatsikas and Teece (2001).

Glossary

Technical terms	Definition
2G	Second Generation (digital) mobile technologies
2.5G	Technologies compatible with 2G mobile systems allowing high speed data transfer e.g. GPRS and EDGE
3G	Third Generation – an ITU specification for mobile communications technology which allow much higher data transfer speeds (up to 384 kbps stationary, 128 kbps in a car and 2 Mbps in fixed applications) than 2G
4G	'Fourth generation' – general term with no coherent definition used to refer to new mobile technologies that may promise data rates in excess of 3G
ADSL	Asymmetric Digital Subscriber Line – DSL technology providing much greater downstream than upstream bandwidth (see DSL)
ARPU	Average Revenue per User
ATM	Asynchronous Transfer Mode – a network technology based on transferring data in cells or packets of a fixed size, which can be used for video, audio and computer data
BFWA	Broadband Fixed Wireless Access (see FWA)
Bits	Short for Binary Digit, the smallest unit of information on a machine
Bitstream	Type of access product, where the incumbent installs its preferred ADSL equipment and configuration in its local access network, and then makes this access link available to third parties, to enable them to provide high speed services to customers.
Byte	Short for Binary Term, a unit of storage capable of holding a single character (normally, a byte is equal to 8 bits)
CLEC	Competitive local exchange carrier – (US) term for entrant fixed-line telecommunications providers
Co-axial cable	Type of wire consisting of a central wire surrounded by insulation and then a grounded shield of braided wire, primarily used by the cable television industry and for computer networks, such as Ethernet
CPS	Carrier pre-selection
DLEC	Competitive local exchange carrier (CLEC) offering data services

DOCSIS	Data Over Cable Service Interface Specification – an ITU-approved interface standard for cable modems and supporting equipment
DSL	Digital subscriber line – a technology that uses sophisticated modulation schemes to pack data onto copper wires
DSLAM	DSL access multiplexer – a mechanism located at the local telephony exchange that links many customer DSL connections to a single high-speed ATM line
EBITDA	Earnings before interest taxes depreciation and amortization
Ethernet	A local-area network (LAN) architecture
Fibre optics	Fibre optic cables consists of a bundle of glass (or plastic) threads, each of which is capable of transmitting data modulated onto light waves.
FSO	Free space optics – a technology that transmits data from point to point and multipoint using low-powered infrared lasers
FTTH	Fibre-to-the-home – installation of optical fibre from a telephone switch directly into the subscriber's home
FWA	Fixed wireless access – wireless systems in a fixed locations designed for point-to-point signal transmissions through the air over a terrestrial microwave platform rather than through copper or fibre cables
GPRS	General Packet Radio Service – a standard for mobile communications which runs at speeds up to 115 kbps
ICT	Information, Communications and Technology sector
IEEE	Institute of Electrical and Electronics Engineers, best known for developing standards for the computer and electronics industry (e.g. the IEEE 802 standards for LANs)
ILEC	Incumbent local exchange carrier – (US) term for incumbent fixed line telecommunications operators
IP	Internet Protocol – specifies the format of packets and the addressing scheme; most networks combine IP with a higher-level protocol called Transmission Control Protocol (TCP), which establishes a virtual connection between a destination and a source
ISDN	Integrated Services Digital Network – an international communications standard for sending voice, video, and data over digital telephone lines or normal telephone wires. ISDN supports data transfer rates of 64 kbps
ISP	Internet service provider
kbps	1,000 bits per second (see bits)
LAN	Local Area Network, a computer network that spans a relatively small area
Leased lines	Permanent telephone connection between two points set up by a telecommunications common carrier (e.g. a T-1 channel is

	a type of leased line that provides a maximum transmission speed of 1.544 Mbps)
Line sharing	Type of LLU, where only the high frequency portion of the local loop (used for high-speed data transmissions) is provided to third parties
LLU	Local Loop Unbundling – Provision of access to third parties of the network elements used in the local loop. Full LLU refers to a situation where a third party installs their own equipment and configures their own local access network (see also Unbundling, Line Sharing and Bitstream)
Local loop	The connection between the home and local exchange
LRAIC	Long-run average incremental cost
LRIC	Long-run incremental cost
MAN	Municipal area network, a data network designed for a town or city
Mbps	1,000 kilobits (1,000,000 bits) per second (see bits)
MDU	Multi-dwelling unit
MEA	Modern Equivalent Asset – the value of an asset with the same level of capacity and functionality as the existing asset
MMDS	Multipoint Microwave Distribution System – a fixed wireless broadband technology (see FWA)
MMS	Mobile Messaging Service
MNO	Mobile network operator
Modem	Modulator-Demodulator – a device that enables a computer to transmit data over telephone or cable lines (etc), by converting data between digital and analogue signals
NPV	Net Present Value
NRA	National Regulatory Authority
NRF	EU New Regulatory Framework for telecommunication
OLO	Other Local/Licensed Operator (see also CLEC)
PLC	Power line communications
POP	Point-of-Presence, an access point to the Internet.
PPL	Point-to-Point Laser – alternative technology for transmitting data signals
PPP	Public-Private Partnership
PSTN	Public Switched Telephone Network – traditional telephone system based on copper wires carrying analogue voice data
PTO	Public Telecommunications Operator
RCU	Remote Concentrator Unit – used for consolidating copper pair lines between the home and local exchange
SDSL	Symmetric Digital Subscriber Line – DSL technology providing identical downstream and upstream bandwidth (see DSL)
Siamese cable	Cabling system combining coaxial cable for television and internet and twisted pair copper wire for telephony – used by some cable companies for the final connection to the home

SME	Small and medium-sized enterprise sector
SOHO	Small office / Home office sector
TCP	See IP
TDD	Time Division Duplex – a 3G network mode designed to be used in unpaired spectrum bands
Triple play	Combined provision of voice, data and television/video services (usually over the same platform)
Twisted pair	Cable consisting of two copper wires twisted around each other, used in traditional telephone systems
UMTS	Universal Mobile Telecommunications System – a 3G mobile technology that will deliver data speeds up to 2 Mbps
Unbundling	Provision of access to the network elements used to deliver a particular (communications) service e.g. voice telephony and/or broadband
UNE	Unbundled network elements – parts of a network that ILECs are required to offer to their customers on an unbundled basis.
UNE-P	Unbundled Network Elements-Platform – the FCC ruling requiring ILECs to make their network facilities (UNEs) available to CLECs at rates determined by US state public utility commissions
USO	Universal service obligation
VDSL	Very high-speed DSL – Uses fibre to the curb connections to achieve much higher bandwidth over the copper local loop than standard DSL (see DSL)
VoIP	Voice over Internet Protocol – use of the Internet as the transmission medium for telephone calls
VPN	Virtual Private Network – a network that is constructed by using public wires to connect nodes
WACC	Weighted average cost of Capital
WAN	A computer network that spans a relatively large geographical area (see also LAN and MAN)
W-CDMA	Wideband CDMA – a high-speed 3G mobile wireless technology which can reach speeds of up to 2 Mbps for voice, video, data and image transmission
WiFi	Wireless Fidelity – a generic term for any type of 802.11 WLAN, promulgated by the WiFi Alliance
WLAN	Wireless Local Area Network
WLL	Wireless Local Loop (see FWA)
xDSL	Generic term for all types of DSL technologies

References

Academic publications

Aghion, P and P Howitt, 1992, *A Model of Growth Through Creative Destruction,* Econometrica 60, 323-351

Alleman, J and E Noam, 1999, *The New Investment of Real Options and its Implications for Telecommunications Economics,* eds.

Armstrong, M, 2001, *Access Pricing, Bypass and Universal Service,* American Economic Review 91 (Papers and Proceedings), 297-301

Baron, D, and R Myerson, 1982, *Regulating a monopolist with unknown costs,* Econometrica, 50: 911-930

Bauer, J, JH Kim, S Wildman, August 2003, *Broadband Uptake in OECD Countries,* Presented at the 2003 ITS Conference, Helsinki

Bittlingmayer, G and T W Hazlett, 2002, *Financial Effects of Broadband Regulation,* Manhattan Institute

Bourreau, M and P. Dogan, June 2002, *Service-based vs. facility-based competition in local access networks,*

Brigham, E F, L C Gapenski, and B R Daves, 1996, *Intermediate Financial Management*

Cave, M et al., September 2002, Papers On Access Pricing, Investment And Entry In Telecommunications, CMuR Research Papers, available at users.wbs.warwick.ac.uk/cmur/publications

Crandall, R W, 2001, An Assessment of the Competitive Local Exchange Carriers Five Years After the Passage of the Telecommunications Act, available at www.criterioneconomics.com

Crandall, R W and C L Jackson, 2001, '*The $500 Billion Opportunity: The Potential Economic Benefit of Widespread Diffusion of Broadband Internet Access*', available at www.criterioneconomics.com

Crandall, R W, J G Sidak and H J Singer, 2002a, 'The Empirical Case Against Asymmetric Regulation of Broadband Internet Access', *Berkeley Technology Law Journal*

Crandall, R W & J Alleman (Editors), 2002b, Broadband: Should We Regulate High-Speed Internet Access?, AEI Brookings Joint Center for Regulatory Studies, 2002

Crandall, R W, C L Jackson and H J Singer, 2003 (forthcoming), 'The Effect of Deregulating Broadband on Investment, Jobs, and the U.S. Economy', *Criterion Working Paper*

Crandall, R W, A T Ingraham and H J Singer, 2004, '*Do Unbundling Policies Discourage CLEC Facilities-based Investment?*', *Topics in Economic Analysis & Policy*, 6, available at http://www.bepress.com/bejeap/topics

Distaso, Lupi & Manenti (September 2004), 'Platform Competition and Broadband Uptake: Theory and Empirical Evidence form the European Union', presented at the 2004 *EARIE and ITS Conferences*

Dixit, A K and J E Stiglitz, 1977, Monopolistic competition and optimum product diversity, *The American Economic Review*, 67:3, 297-308

Dixit, A K and R S Pindyck, 1994, Investment under Uncertainty, *Princeton University Press*

Goolsbee, A, 2001, 'Subsidies, the Value of Broadband, and the Importance of Fixed Costs', in *Broadband: Should we Regulate High-Speed Internet Access?*, Crandall, R W and J H Alleman, eds. 2002, 278-294, Brooking Institution Press

Hausman, J A, 2003, '*Cellular, 3G, Broadband, and WiFi*', Shann Memorial Lecture at the University of Western Australia

Hausman, J A, 2001, 'Competition and Regulation for Internet-related Services: Results of Asymmetric Regulation', *MIT mimeo*

Hausman, J A, 2000, 'Regulated Costs and Prices in Telecommunications', in Madden, G and S J Savage, *The International Handbook of Telecommunications Economics*

Hausman, J A, 1997, 'Valuing the effect of regulation on new services in telecommunications', *Brookings Papers on Economic Activity, Microeconomics*

Hausman, J A and J G Sidak, 1999, 'A Consumer-Welfare Approach to the Mandatory Unbundling of Telecommunications Networks', *Yale Law Journal*, 109, 417

Hausman, J A, J G Sidak and H J Singer, 2001, 'Cable Modems and DSL: Broadband Internet Access for Residential Customers', *American Economic Association Papers & Proceedings,* 91

Hazlett, T W, 2003, *The irony of regulated competition in telecommunications,* Science and Technology Law Review, available at www.stlr.org

Horvath, R and D Maldoom, 2002, *Fixed-mobile substitution: a simultaneous equation model with qualitative and limited dependent variables,* DotEcon Discussion Paper, 02/02, available at www.dotecon.com

Kauper, T E, *The Problem of Market Definition Under EC Competition Law,* in B. Hawk, in International Antitrust Law & Policy 249 (Barry E. Hawk, ed., Sweet and Maxwell 1996)

Laffont, J-J and J Tirole, 2000, Competition in Telecommunications, MIT Press

Laffont, J-J and J Tirole, 1993, *A Theory of Incentives in Procurement and Regulation,* MIT Press

Madden, G and S J Savage, 2000, *The International Handbook of Telecommunications Economics Volume II*, Edward Elgar

Odlyzko, A, September 2003, *The Many Paradoxes of Broadband,* First Monday, Vol 8, no. 9, available at http://firstmonday.org

Pleatsikas, C and D Teece, 2001, *The analysis of market power and market definition in the context of rapid innovation,* International Journal of Industrial Organisation, 19 (2001) 665-693

Posner, R A, 2001, *Antitrust Law,* University of Chicago Press

Rappoport, P, D Kridel, L Taylor and K Duffy-Demo, 2001, 'Residential Demand for Access to the Internet', *University of Arizona Working Paper*

Rappoport, P, D Kridel and L Taylor, 1999, *An Econometric Study of the Demand for Access to the Internet*, in Loomis, D G and L Taylor, 1999, '*The Future of the Telecommunications Industry: Forecasting and Demand Analysis*', eds., Kluwer Academic Publishers

Razavi, B, R A Brealey and S C Myers, 1996, *Principles of Corporate Finance*

Sidak, J G & H J Singer, 2003, *Interim Pricing of Local Loop Unbundling in Ireland: Epilogue,* 4 Journal of Network Industries 119

Sidak J G & J A Hausman, 2005 (forthcoming), *The Failure of Good Intentions: Is Regulation or Competition the Future of American Telecommunications?*, forthcoming Cambridge University Press

Sidak J G & J A Hausman, 2005 (forthcoming), *Did Mandatory Unbundling Achieve Its Purpose? Empirical Evidence from Five Countries?*, Journal of Competition Law & Economics

Trellis, G J, S Stremersch and E Yin, 2003, *The International Takeoff of New Products: The Role of Economics, Culture and Country Innovativeness,* Marketing Science, 22:2, Spring

Varian, H R, 1999, *Estimating the Demand for Bandwidth*', Berkeley: University of California, Berkeley mimeo

Vickers, J, 1995, *Concepts of Competition,* Oxford Economic Papers, vol. 47-1, 1-23

Vickers, J, and G Yarrow, 1988, *Privatization An Economic Analysis,* The MIT Press, Cambridge, Massachusetts

Ward, S, 19 March 2001, *An Interview with Neil Druker,* Barron's, 30-32

Regulator and government material

Analysys, September 2003, *Summary of Research in Broadband Conducted by Analysys Consulting Ltd for the Scottish Executive,* available at: www.scotland.gov.uk/library5/society/broadbandresearch.pdf

Analysys, DotEcon and Hogan & Hartson, May 2004, *Study on Conditions and Options in Introducing Secondary Trading of Radio Spectrum in the European Commission, report for the Radio Spectrum Policy Unit of the*

Information Society Directorate-General of the European Commission, available at http://europa.eu.int and www.dotecon.com

ART, March 2003, Internet, a Review of the French Market, available at www.art-telecom.fr

CMT, 2002, *Annual Report 2002,* available at www.cmt.es

ComReg, June 2003a, Quarterly Key Data, available at www.comreg.ie

ComReg, June 2003b, Quarterly Market Commentary, available at www.comreg.ie

ComReg, June 2003c, Broadband Market in Ireland – Presentation to Joint Oireachtas Committee on Communications, Marine and Natural Resources ICT sub-Committee

DCMNR, June 2003, Dermot Ahern launches broadband MSE procurement process, Press release, available at http://www.dcmnr.ie/

European Commission, September 2003, *Broadband Access in the EU,* COCOM03-40 and Annex, Communications Committee Working Document

European Commission, February 2003a, *Electronic Communications: the Road to the Knowledge Economy,* Communication from The Commission to The Council, The European Parliament, The Economic and Social Committee and The Committee of the Regions

European Commission, February 2003b:

> RECOMMENDATION 2003/311/EC, 11 February 2003, *On relevant product and service markets within the electronic communications sector susceptible to ex ante regulation in accordance with Directive 2002/21/EC of the European Parliament and of the Council on a common regulatory framework for electronic communication networks and services,* published in the Official Journal of the European Communities, L114 / 45-49
>
> EXPANATORY MEMORANDUM, to the recommendation on relevant markets (2003/311/EC)

European Commission, June 2002a, *eEurope 2005: An information society for all,* Communication from The Commission to The Council, The European Parliament, The Economic and Social Committee and The Committee of the Regions

European Commission, June 2002b, Eurobarometer 125

European Commission, June 2002c, 8th Report on the Implementation of the Telecommunications Regulatory Package

European Commission, June 2003, 9th Report on the Implementation of the Telecommunications Regulatory Package

European Commission, June 2004, 10th Report on the Implementation of the Telecommunications Regulatory Package

European Parliament and the Council of the European Union, published in the Official Journal of the European Communities:

DIRECTIVE 2002/19/EC, 7 March 2002, *On access to, and interconnection of, electronic communications networks and associated facilities (Access Directive),* L108 / 7-20

DIRECTIVE 2002/21/EC, 7 Match 2002, *On a common regulatory framework for electronic communications networks and services (Framework Directive),* L108 / 20-49

DIRECTIVE 2002/22/EC, 7 March 2002, *On universal service and users' rights relating to electronic communications networks and services (Universal Service Directive),* L108 / 51-77

REGULATION (EC) No 2887/2000, 18 December 2000, *on unbundled access to the local loop,* L336 / 4-8

Eurostat, Yearbook 2004

FCC, June 30, 2004, *High-Speed Services for Internet Access, available at http://www.fcc.gov*

FCC, June 8, 2004, *Federal Communications Commission Releases Data on High-Speed Services for Internet Access*

FCC, October 2003, *Broadband Internet Access in OECD Countries: A Comparative Analysis,* A staff report of the Office of Strategic Planning and Policy Analysis and International Bureau

FCC, June 2003a, *Customer Lines Reported by New Entrants Totalled 25 Million at End of 2002 Represents 13% of Total Access Lines,* FCC News, available at http://www.fcc.gov

FCC, June 2003b, 31 December 2003, *High-Speed Services for Internet Access: Status as of December 31 2002*

FCC, 23 April 2003, *FCC Begins Inquiry Regarding Broadband over Power Line,* Press Release

FCC, February 2003a, *Order on Remand,* Attachment to Triennial Review Press Release

FCC, February 2003b, *Review of the Section 251 Unbundling Obligations of Incumbent Local Exchange Carriers,* Separate Statement of Chairman Michael K. Powell (Dissenting in Part), CC Dkt. 01-338

FCC, July 2002, *High Speed Services For Internet Access: Status as of December 31 2001,* Industry Analysis & Technology Division, available at http://www.fcc.gov/wcb/iatd/comp.html

FCC, March 2002, *Inquiry Concerning High-Speed Access to the Internet Over Cable and Other Facilities, Declaratory Ruling and Notice of Proposed Rulemaking,* CS Dkt. No. 02-52

FCC, February 2002, *Inquiry Concerning the Deployment of Advanced Telecommunications Capability to All Americans, Third Report,* 17 F.C.C. Rcd.

FCC, November 1999, *Implementation of the Local Competition Provisions of the Telecommunications Act of 1996,* Third Report and Order, available at www.fcc.gov

FCC, 1995, *Motion of AT&T Corp. to be Reclassified as a Non-Dominant Carrier,* 11 F.C.C. Rcd. 3271

Industry Canada, July 2003, *Allan Rock, Andy Mitchell and Rey Pagtakhan Announce $1.7 Million in Funding for Broadband Business Plan Development,* Press Conference, available at www.ic.gc.ca

Italian Government, Ministry of Communications and Ministry for Innovation and Technologies, *Task Force on Broadband Communications,* 2001 (English translation 2002); available at www.innovazione.gov.it/eng/intervento/banda_larga/task_force/

IT Korea, 2002, *II Korea's IT Policy,* Korean Ministry of Information and Communication, available at www.mic.go.kr

Korea National Computerization Agency & Korea Ministry of Information and Communication, July 2003, *White Paper: Internet Korea 2003*

Massey, P, October 2000, *Market Definition and Market Power in Competition Analysis: Some Practical Issues,* Ireland Competition Authority, Discussion Paper No. 11, at 13

Nalebuff, B, February 2003, *Bundling, Tying, and Portfolio Effects, Part 1 – Conceptual Issues,* (UK) DTI Economics Paper No.1

Nalebuff, B and D Majerus, February 2003, *Bundling, Tying, and Portfolio Effects, Part 2 – Case Studies,* (UK) DTI Economics Paper No.1

ODTR, 2002, *Future Delivery of Broadband in Ireland,* Consultation paper

OECD, May 2003, *Regulatory reform in telecommunications: Germany,* Working Party on Telecommunication and Information Services Policies

OECD, December 2002, *Broadband access for business,* Working Party on Telecommunication and Information Services Policies

OECD, 2001, *The development of broadband access in OECD countries,* Working Party on Telecommunication and Information Services Policies

Office of Technology Policy, U.S. Dept. of Commerce, 2002, *Understanding Broadband Demand: Review of Critical Issues*

Oftel, August 2003, *Broadband – a consumer guide,* available at www.oftel.gov.uk

Oftel, June 2003, *International benchmarking study of Internet access (dial-up and broadband),* available at www.oftel.gov.uk

Oftel, May 2003a, *Annual report 2002,* available at www.oftel.gov.uk

Oftel, May 2003b, *Two million sign up for broadband,* press release

Oftel, April 2002, *Oftel's Management Plan 2002/3,* available at www.oftel. gov.uk

Oftel, January 2001, *International benchmarking of DSL and cable modem services,* available at www.oftel.gov.uk

Oftel, 1996, *Promoting Competition in Services over Telecommunication Networks,* available at www.oftel.gov.uk

PIU, 1999, e-commerce@its.best.uk, UK Cabinet Office Report

Industry surveys, news reports and corporate material

Advanced Television, May 2002, *Sweden subsidises broadband,* available at www.advanced-television.com

Baskerville, 2002, Broadband Status Report, Executive Briefing, available at www.dslforum.org

Baskerville, July 20, 2004, Mobile Communications, No.381

Boston Globe, May 2003, Verizon Customers See Internet Cost Dip, article by Peter J. Howe

Business 2.0, May 2003, *Verizon's Bold Move,* article by Eric Hellweg, available at www.business2.com

Cableuropa, 2003, *Annual Report 2002,* published in the Securities and Exchange Commission Form

Cambridge Strategic Management Group, 5 April, 2002, *Assessing the Impact of Regulation on Deployment of Fiber to the Home, A Comparative Business Case Analysis,* submitted as attachment to Comments of Corning Inc. in CC Docket Nos. 01-338, 96-98, 98-147 (filed 5 April, 2002)

CBS MarketWatch.com, July 2003, *Is the Tide Turning Away from Cable?,* article by Bambi Francisco, available at www.cbs.marketwatch.com

Cellular Online, June 2003, available at http://cellular.co.za/news_2003

Cisco Service Provider Solutions, 2002, *A Full Video Internet!,* available at www.cisco.com

CNET News.com, July 2003a, *Cometa Hot Spots To Get Cold Shoulder?,* article by Shim, R and E Hansen available at http://news.com.com/2100-1039-1027529.html

CNET News.com, July 2003b, Endless Summer of DSL Discounts, article by Jim Hu, available at http://news.com.com/2100-1034_3-1023465.html

CNET News.com, April 2003, The Storm Over Broadband Bundling, article by Randolph J. May, available at http://news.com.com/2010-1071-997226.html?tag=nl

Cochrane, P, 28 May 2003, *Peter Cochrane's Uncommon Sense: The right technology for the right job,* available at www.Silicon.com

Comcast Cable Communications, 2001, *2000 SEC Form 10-K*

Committee on Broadband Last Mile Technology, Computer Science and Telecommunications Board, Division on Engineering and Physical Sciences & National Research Council, 2002, *Broadband: Bringing Home the Bits,* National Academy Press

Commonwealth Telephone Enterprises, 1999, *1998 Annual Report,* available at http://www.ct-enterprises.com/investorrelations/pdf/cte_ar.pdf

ComputerWeekly.com, June 2003, 3G – 4G to the rescue?, available at www.computerweekly.com

ComputerWeekly.com, January 2003, *Liberty Broadband is Latest Victim of Price Trends,* available at www.computerweekly.com/Article 118597.htm

Covad Communications Group Inc., 24 May 2001, *2000 SEC Form 10-K 80,* available at www.covad.com

Cullen International, September 2002, *Broadband stimulation in France, Sweden and Ireland,* commissioned by Corning

CyberAtlas, December 2000, *Cable or DSL? Consumers See Little Difference,* article by Michael Pastore, available at www.cyberatlas.internet.com

Datamonitor, March 2003, *European Consumer Broadband Markets: Not Just a Fat Pipe Dream,* available at www.datamonitor.com

Deutsche Bank Research, February 2003, *Germany's broadband networks – Innovation on hold,* available at www.db.com

DotEcon, February 2001, *Network Charge Controls and Infrastructure Investments,* Submission to Oftel Price Control Review, available at http://www.dotecon.com/publications/index.htm

Dow Jones Business News, 10 July 2003, *NTT DoCoMo Expects To Hit Fiscal Year Goal Of 1.46 Million 3G Users,* available at http://biz.yahoo.com

DrKW Research, September 2003, *European Wireline, ADSL – Light at the End of the Tunnel*

e.Biscom, July 2003, *Agreement between e.Biscom and telecom on the sale of HanseNet,* e.Biscom press statement, available at www.ebiscom.it

e.Biscom, May 2003, e.Biscom Q1 2003 results presentation, available at www.ebiscom.it

e.Biscom, March 2003, First quarter 2003 report, available at www.ebiscom.it

e.Biscom, August 2003, e.Biscom Q2 2003 results presentation, available at www.ebiscom.it

e.Biscom, January 2003, *2002 Annual Report,* available at www.ebiscom.it

ECTA, various dates 2002-04, *DSL Scorecards* and accompanying *News Releases,* available at www.ectaportal.com

Enders Analysis, 2002, '*Korean Broadband, Wireless & TV: Different? Or the Same, Only More So?*'

Enders Analysis, 2003, '*UK Broadband and Internet Trends*'

ETNO office notes, 11 June 2003, *7th meeting of the Communications Committee*

Europemedia, June 2003, *Continued progress in UK broadband market – regulator,* available at http://www.europemedia.net

FinanceAsia.com, April 2002, Korea's MOIC discusses its role in Korea's Internet Revolution, available at www.financeasia.com

Financial Times, July 2003, *Telecom Italia to buy HanseNet,* available at www.ft.com

Forbes.com, May 2003, Verizon Jolts High-Speed Service, article by Scott Woolley, available at www.forbes.com

Forrester, June 2003a, *Europe's broadband focus shifts to profit,* available at www.forrester.com

Forrester, June 2003b,*Forrester Thinks Public WLAN Hotspots Will Be The Next Dot-Com Crash,* Forrester Research press release, available at www.forrester.com

Fortis Bank, February 2003, El cable acelera, Telefónica llega antes

Frankfurter Rundschau, June 2003, *In der Kabelbranche tritt das schnelle Internet gegen digitale Fernsehprogramme an*

Hanaro Telecom, May 2003, *Hanaro Telecom Announces 2003 First Quarter Results,* Press Release

Hanaro Telecom, January 2002, *Hanaro Telecom Kicks Off Wireless LAN Service,* Press Release

Hanaro Telecom, January 2001, MIC to Open KT Last-mile Network Next Week, Press Release

Idate, 2002, *European Broadband Markets,* available at www.idate.org

IDC, 2003, *European Broadband Access Services Market Analysis: 2002-2007,* Market analysis

Informa, 2003, World Broadband Database

Internetnews.com, May 2003, Bundling for the Broadband Edge, article by Erin Joyce , available at www.internetnews.com

INTUG (International Telecommunications User Group), 2001, *Local loop unbundling*

Investor's Business Daily, July 2003, *Verizon Wireless Sees Room for It and Wi-Fi,* article by Reinhardt Krause

ITU, September 2003, *Promoting Broadband,* ITU Internet Reports

ITU, 2003, *Promoting broadband: Background paper,* Workshop on promoting broadband

ITU-T, 1997, Recommendation I.113, *Vocabulary of terms for broadband aspects of ISDN*

Korea Telecom, 2003, 2002 Annual Report, 38

Los Angeles Times, March 2001, *100,000 Subscribers of NorthPoint DSL Face Disconnection,* article by Elizabeth Douglas

McKinsey & Co. and J P Morgan H&Q, April 2001, *Broadband 2001: A Comprehensive Analysis of Demand, Supply, Economics, and Industry Economics in the U.S. Broadband Market*

MIC, 2003a, Internet White Paper 41

MIC, 2003b, Internet White Paper 42

Morgan Stanley Dean Witter, December 2000, Covad Communications Corp., Investext Report

Network World, November 2000, Caution Flags Flying as CLEC Woes Mount, article by Michael Martin, available at www.nwfusion.com/news/2000/1120clec.html

Netzwettbewerb Durch Regulierung, 2001, *Vierzehntes Hauptgutachten der Monopolkommission gemäß §44 Abs 2000-2001*

newswireless.net, April 2003, *London's Soho to get blanket 802.11 cover for voice, data,* article by Tony Smith, available at www.newswireless.net

NTT DoCoMo, 2002, *A Decade of NTT DoCoMo: 1992-2002,* at 169 Dai Nippon Printing Co.

ONO, July 2003, *Second quarter results 2003,* available at www.ono.es

ONO, May 2003, *First quarter results 2003,* available at www.ono.es

Paul Budde Communications, June 2003, *Netherlands – Broadband Networks and Services*

Point Topic, April 2003a, *DSL Worldwide Retail Directory,* available at www.point-topic.co.uk

Point Topic, April 2003b, *Drivers of broadband,* available at www.point-topic.co.uk

Powell, M, 2001, *Digital Broadband Migration Part II,* FCC Press Conference, available at http://ftp.fcc.gov/Speeches/Powell/2001/spmkp109.txt

RegTP, February 2003, *2002 Annual Report,* available at www.regtp.de

SBC Communications, 2003a, *2002 Annual Report,* 23

SBC Communications, 2003b, 2002 SEC Form 10-K

Standard & Poor's, May 2003, European High-Yield Telecommunications, Industry report card, available at www.standardandpoors.com

Strategy Analytics, January 2003, *Residential Broadband Internet Subscribers - Global Market Forecast,* available at www.strategyanalytics.com

Strategy Analytics, 2002, *Residential Broadband Internet Subscribers – Global Market Forecast,* Viewpoint

Taoiseach, March 2002, *New Connections: A Strategy to Realise the Potential of the Information Society,* available at http://www.taoiseach.gov.ie/upload/publications/1153.pdf

Telephony.Online, May 2003, *Bundling Up,* article by Glenn Bischoff, available at www.telephonyonline.com

Telephony.Online, April 2003, *Allegiance Threatened by Bankruptcy,* article by Ed Gubbins, available at www.telephonyonline.com

Telephony.Online, January 2003, *USTA President calls UNE-P a 'Failed Experiment',* article by Glenn Bischoff, available at www.telephonyonline.com

Telephony.Online, June 2001, *Charles McMinn,* article by Chris Sewell, available at www.telephonyonline.comhttp://www.telephonyonline.com/

Telephony.Online, February 2001, *A Question of Strategy,* article by Carolyn Hirschman, available at www.telephonyonline.com

Telephony, December 2000a, *Who's Saving Whom?,* article by Liane H. LaBarba, available at www.telephonyonline.com

Telephony, December 2000b, *Headed For a Fall?,* article by Vincent Ryan, available at www.telephonyonline.com

teltarif.de, May 2002, *Kabelbetreiber ish geht das Geld aus,* available at http://www.teltarif.de/arch/2002/kw19/s7871.html

The Broadband Home Report, June 2000, *"Bredband in Sweden" – Pioneering the LAN model,* available at http://www.broadbandhomecentral.com

The Economist, June 2003, *Is the "Wi-Fi" wireless internet boom about to turn into a bust?,* available at www.economist.com

The Economist, May 2003, *Move over 3G, here comes 4G,* available at www.economist.com

The Economist, March 2001, *Drowning in glass: the fibre-optic glut: can you have too much of a good thing? The history of technology says not, but that was before the fibre-optic bubble,* available at www.economist.com

The Inquirer, May 2003, *Paris Close to Widespread Wi-Fi Coverage,* available at www.theinquirer.net

T-Mobile Press Release, 8 May 2003, *T-Mobile Bundles Wireless Voice and Data With "Wi-Fi" Hotspot Service,* available at www.t-mobile.com/company/pressroom/pressrelease72.asp

Total Telecom, June 2003a, WLAN equipment shipments up 120% in 2002 – Gartner, DeHavilland Information Services for Total Telecom, available at www.totaltele.com

Total Telecom, June 2003b, *Number of WLAN-enabled notebook users expected to reach 58m in Europe by 2008 – ABI,* DeHavilland Information Services for Total Telecom, available at www.totaltele.com

Total Telecom, June 2003c, *Netherlands deploys largest European hotspot,* DeHavilland Information Services for Total Telecom, available at www.totaltele.com

Total Telecom, June 2003d, *Mobile penetration rate now 78.74%,* DeHavilland Information Services for Total Telecom, available at www.totaltele.com

Total Telecom, May 2003, *The broadband opportunity for VoIP,* available at www.totaltele.com

Total Telecom, March 2003, *Riverstone announces ethernet deal with Telia,* available at www.totaltele.com

Total Telecom, October 2002, *Euro cable operators must prepare for different futures,* available at www.totaltele.com

UPC, *Annual Report,* 2002, available at www.upccorp.com

UPC chello, February 2003, *UPC welcomes 700,000th chello Internet customer in Vienna,* Press Release, available at www.upccorp.com

UPC, *New UPC Investor Presentation,* 2-3 April, 2003, available at www.upccorp.com

Upside Today, *Inside: Covad,* April 23, 2002, article by Jerry Borrell

Verizon, 2003a, *2002 Annual Report*

Verizon, 2003b, *Verizon Answers Call from Small and Medium-Sized Businesses,* Verizon News Release,

Verizon, 2003c, *SBC Reveal Big Plans for Wi-Fi*

Verizon, 2003d, *Verizon Wireless Extends Its High-Speed Internet Access With Hundreds of Wi-Fi Hot Spots,* Press Release

Washington Post, February 2001, *Riding up to the Challenge: 4 Upstart Telecom Companies are picking up where the Bells Left Off,* article by Yuki Noguchi

Washington Post, November 2000, *Verizon Terminates Deal to Buy Stake in NorthPoint,* article by Peter S. Goodman

www.webopedia.com

WELT, July 2003, *Italiener greifen nach Hamburger Hansenet,* available at http://www.welt.de/data/2003/07/30/142613.html

Yankee Group, September 2003, *Europe's Cable Companies Must Innovate to Survive in the Third Age*

Yankee Group, 2002, *Residential Broadband: Cable Modem Remains King*

Yankee Group, March 2001, *Residential Broadband: Cable Modems and DSL Reach Critical Mass*

ZD Net UK, 2 October 2003, *Free Spectrum Boosts Irish Broadband*

Index